COVERING GROUND

COVERING GROUND:
essays for now

DONALD PHELPS

CROTON PRESS, LTD.
NEW YORK
1969

Many of these essays first appeared in *The Nation,*
The Second Coming, National Review, Kulchur,
Moviegoer, Noose, The Promethean, Wivenhoe Park
Review, Rally, The World, and *For Now* magazine.

First Edition, 1969
© Copyright 1969 Donald Phelps
Library of Congress Catalog Card Number: 77-77371
Manufactured in the United States of America

Croton Press Books are distributed by Small Publishers' Company, 276 Park Avenue South, New York
City

Contents

Note

    As the title suggests, these essays were written to confront various specific situations, as those situations presented themselves, or were discovered. I have, therefore, refrained from the Monday morning quarterbacking of updating references, revising opinions, etc. Only three corrections of fact have been made; and two references to the format of FOR NOW magazine, where those would have been simply confusing. Otherwise, I hope it will be obvious that many an enthusiasm, judgment, *obiter dicta* would have been much different had the essays been written from this much different plateau of events. They were not, hence they are not.

    As for the idiosyncratic punctuation — the often spastic disposal of hyphens, commas, parentheses — which lends occasional sentences a breathy, tongue-tied sort of rhythm — I wish to explain that that is exactly how I talk.

D.P.

The Human Landscape
of Donald Phelps

For the last few years there's been one critic (or Critic) whom I've grown to trust, to learn from; and I've come to feel that his presence is of the greatest importance to the vitality of the creative experience, as it exists at this most dangerous juncture—surrounded by an oblivion of noise and meaningless gesture. His name is Donald Phelps, and this volume of his selected essays makes available for the first time a significant body of his work.

In this short introduction, I will just record a few personal responses to Mr. Phelps' work, and then leave you to the real matter at hand: the careful reading of a complex and brilliant critic.

*

His landscape is one which is constantly expanding. In this landscape, Mr. Phelps moves with careful force, sometimes stepping on the toes of those who want to set up NO TRESPASSING signs, and as he moves he is "bearing witness to the world". In his work, anything and anyone is fair game; his essays reveal a range of expression from sharp and complex explorations, to cutting and whimsical humor:

"You get angry at the risk of your social standing: it is more advisable to show your resentment toward someone whose hearing is organically impaired; since he will feel guilty anyway, about not hearing, and will probably, at best, display only token resentment. Your audience, if any, will be polite toward you, if not openly sympathetic; being firm in their belief that a little rough treatment is good for the physically handicapped." (from THAT IS . . .)

This cutting insight is but one example of Mr. Phelps' abilities. There are essays on social manners, essays on writers and artists, on comic strips, on public and private personalities; recommendations for politicians, statesmen, jurists; and there are longer, more extended essays on life and communication. This is only a small account of the total scope and concern of this critic. It is not my intention, here, to explain or discuss the various aspects of his work. I am clearly someone who is totally biased in favor of Mr. Phelps, both as a critic and as a prose-fiction writer; and because of my bias, what I would finally say would tend to be an inferior repetition of Mr. Phelps' own work. There's just no point to that kind of self-indulgence on my part. My recommendation is that you pick up this volume (long awaited by those who have followed his work) *and read it.*

What you have here is a starting point, and it brings together a good cross section of what Mr. Phelps has been up to for the last ten years or so. Most of the essays included here appeared first in his own magazine, FOR NOW (in my opinion, the best little magazine now being published on the East coast) and in other magazines such as *Kulchur* and *Second Coming.* But, the important thing is not where they were published, but that they were written, and that no matter where they were published, their impact and thrust cannot be ignored for long; though certain groups and individuals would feel more secure if they were.

There is no predicting how the individual reader will respond to the work in this volume; and this is as it should be. The greatest failure of what has been called "the best contemporary criticism" (academic or non-academic), with but a few exceptions, is its lack of anything really approaching confrontation and contact, with subject or audience. The critics usually have nothing to say. They (and often their subjects) fail to do more than offer the pose of penetration. They concern themselves with the surface of meaning. They are masters of tone (a subject which Mr. Phelps has dealt with in his long essay on Depressed Art, hopefully to appear soon in a separate volume). And when you come right down to it, surface tone and pose of penetration just do not offer very much. Mr. Phelps penetrates, and is not afraid to give, in detail, the location where he is standing. There runs through Mr. Phelps' work a sharp sense of responsibility, both in what he is saying and in how he says it. He is not afraid to cover a lot of ground in the territory of his personal and cultural experience. His responsiveness to America and "the American Grain", as well as the world beyond his locale, would have touched the heart of William Carlos Williams. Grounding himself in the details and specifics of his own identity, Mr. Phelps ranges out toward the establishment and confrontation of universals; and, in my opinion, there is no living, or at least no active critic, who does it as well.

Mr. Phelps' prose style is not always easy. It is not a prose which can be read at the surface. It is linked closely to the process of the struggle to explore and develop the territory that his mind and senses cover. It is a prose style which is constantly developing toward cleaner and sharper articulation; rich and always worth the effort of the reader totally to immerse himself in its richness.

There are no hierarchies or conditions as to what are "the proper concerns" of a critic. The proper concerns of *a man* are anything and everything that he contacts; and all these things are fit subjects and should be open to tough, hard criticism. I have spent evenings with Donald Phelps, talking, reading things to each other, talking, and drinking; and there have been times when we have gotten into serious and critical talk about the qualities of different Irish whiskies (or other booze); as serious as the talk about a particular artist or writer, or the issues involved in some political or social crisis or problem. And, it seems to me that this is the test of a great critic (and/or artist): that he can bring his mind to bear on anything that presents itself to him and deal with it with the same trenchant insight and, at times, wit (in the true, the medieval, sense of that word).

It would be a mistake, however, to assume that Mr. Phelps is just another "pop critic". The fact that a good part of his work concerns itself with what has come to be called "pop culture" is not to say that he deals with it like the purveyors of the "pop mentality". When you read enough of it, I think and hope, the driving force and thrust of his work will become clear to you. You will make contact with his struggle to bring together, as fully as possible, a detailed account of the process of moving through a diverse and everchanging human landscape. It is, in Mr. Phelps's unique vision, a landscape in which he is able to see the relationship between the art of a comic genius like Ernie Kovacs, the history of film, the political and moral failings of America, the writing and art of the best and worst artists and writers (past and present), and the general concerns of human values and justice. It sounds like a lot, and it is. Even the weak moments, the moments when I, for one, disagree or feel that he has fallen short, seem to support my feeling that this is a criticism — an art — that is organic; a criticism that grows and explores, never asking or needing unanimous approval or adherence.

The landscape grows, and over the years Mr. Phelps has added more to the total record of his movement through it. He adds, also, to our resource of information and insight into our individual and collective condition. This volume introduces only a small part of the record. It is a beginning and I hope it will be followed by the publication of more and more of his work. It is this work that has brought many of his contemporaries to the awareness that Donald Phelps is emerging as one of the most important critics of his times.

Harry Lewis

Loss
of
Space

The most interesting writers in America today, seem to me those who have become physicists and geographers: those, like Gil Sorrentino, Fielding Dawson, Ed Dorn or Robert Creeley, who celebrate, lament or merely take note of, the loss of space. I should say, more accurately, the displacement of space — that space which was the artist's imagination — by the space which is distance; which has been invoked by science and communications media; which extends itself by filling itself: i.e., with mathematics; with news; above all, with language.

The sense of distance which prevailed among artists in earlier centuries, and the earlier eras of this one, was of *indeterminate* distance; which empowered the artist to imagine an orderly and commandable world; one which he could knead into that lump of approximates which is metaphor. In this role, metaphor was a more than legitimate device for rendering the artist's truth about the world, of whose order the metaphor offered an easy-to-handle scale model.

When, however, the artist began to measure distances, when that Ptolemaic poison first entered his blood, metaphor ceded to the web of energies which is process: the fixed points disappearing; every stage of distance specific, yet giving place to the next.

The major casualty of the last two decades' changes in American writing, has been that "depth" which considerable theory, at least, has held indispensable to art. The notion of depth pre-supposes the art-work as a mineshaft, plunged through the artist and on into the earth. The world must pass through the shaft — i.e., the static ego of the artist — before he can accredit it as intelligible, and return it to his audience.

The common aim of artists like Dorn and Sorrentino seems to me, a latitudinal journalism; by the tenets of which, the artist's obligation is, *not* rendering the world intelligible according to his immediate lights; but, covering ground: bearing witness to the world. This does not mean, the pat sort of news journalism: the old intelligibility notion, boiled down.

Nor am I referring to that surrender of art, to the density of the world: an unfortunate by-product of today's situation. The artists I cite testify not only to the world, but to the imagination as well; the imagination, however, not as a private, spontaneously gestated preserve, but as an elemental force, commingling with the world. The movement of that writer who is Sorrentino, or Dawson, or Dorn, is the movement of an implacable centipede across a table-top; the movement dictated by a world in which so much is seen, and so little recognized, by so large a community, that the writer enjoys a kind of freedom not duplicated heretofore; a freedom, moreover, to be maintained only by the most stringent affirmation of candor, vigilance and chastity; through the fusion of such qualities, to lay one's own track across the formidably copious, yet self-filling, space of today's world. As to originality, much of the writing I mention, apart from its debts to Frenchmen like Butor, Robbe-Grillet, Camus (nor may we disregard Jorge Luis Borges — perhaps, in his way, the most resonant influence of all) may recall, for many, strains of 1920's "proletarian realism." I am not being cute when I say that, to me, the most important difference between today's writers and those of the twenties, is that today's writers are writing today. And they are helping to restore to fiction, a function honored by art long before the twenties; the function of telling the truth; that particular truth for which only the writer knows the language.

II

Gil Sorrentino's novel, *The Sky Changes*, codifies the preoccupation — and the medium — which loss of space represents to those American writers. Codifies, not only by its sheer excellence; but by its acrid reversal of the American open-road romance. For the cuckold husband, his wife, and the driver — the wife's latest in a procession of lovers — *only* the sky changes. The husband's hope — which, through the novel's zigzag advances, grows more feverish, more superstitiously eager, and even more shadowed by the novel's foregone conclusion — is, that change of setting, during a cross-country trip from Brooklyn to Mexico, will affect a change of self. This, the catalytic fantasy, is the traditional obsession of highway romance; which sees the landscape as woman to the traveller; who begets on it strong and beautiful children of self-discovery.

Sorrentino works a crucial variation on this ancient fantasy: an odyssey of spiritual onanism, movingly and brilliantly executed. Sorrentino is a poet, as well as a literary critic and author; and the best of his poet's concentration, the angular succinctness and self-sufficiency, are to be found, I think, in *The Sky Changes*; a succession of setpieces, with a special inflection for that term, for the sets remain empty. Tennessee, Kentucky, New Orleans; they are receptacles for the ever-weaker dribblings of the husband's self-punitive impotence. A moderately gifted man in decline, the husband's dead ego is a more suasive force than his imagination. He has become, in the near-prostration of his consciousness, a man of settings; and, in considerable degree, the counters of the various landscapes — the policemen, the decrepit southern court-houses, the mesas, are the only immediately real aspects of his journey. Such are the various married couples whom the couple visits en route: old friends, each home a reliquary harboring an emblem, or fossil, or putrid shred of the gutted marriage.

Sorrentino's foremost success throughout the book is the interlacing of the marriage and the journey. The relationship is never allegorical; its surfaces speak too obviously for themselves, not for sub-surfaces of meaning. The themes are united by the husband's yearning for distance: distance from the coffin of his mother, whose life insurance furnished the journey; distance from the suspicion, later awareness, of his wife's relationship with the driver. In terms of the journey itself, the longing for distance expresses itself in the man's attachment to spectacles and tableaus: a series of staged events, in which he casts himself, his wife, and his two children. From one standpoint, *The Sky Changes* offers a panorama of American Spectator Sports, seen as a series of shabby disasters: the waxwork of the James Brothers in Missouri; the visit to the Grand Canyon (and, afterward, the stone mementoes smuggled past the tollgate); the drinking-party, sparked by third-rate local whiskey. And every episode — Sorrentino's poet-sense again! — is a microcosm of the novel's situation, with its own center of intensity: a miniature form.

Sorrentino's outstanding distinction — and the distinction of the other writers I have mentioned — is, that he longs deeply for the space which has been devoured; the kind of distance which has been deposed by that mathematics which acts upon his, and the others' writings. The secret of each man's originality is — as always — *not* rootlessness, but the painful wresting of self from one's roots; often using the roots to lever one's self-extrication.

Sorrentino's career of the last ten years, represents a progress against — sometimes, by way of — the fluencies of an alert, narrow-lensed intelligence, as quick to observe and infer as to convey its observations; and a high-stepping moral dogmatism, which, moreover, constantly seeks to strengthen itself with the borrowed strengths of extraneous authorities: i.e., those academic categories with which, in the middle years of *Kulchur* magazine, for example, so much of Sorrentino's criticism seems impacted: even some of the best, like his long appreciation of Hubert Selby.

I do not mention the contradictions in order to deplore them. Indeed, at best, Gil Sorrentino's moral stringency betokens a passionately romantic conservatism: the sort of conservatism he described in his best critical writing to date, the appreciation of Jack Spicer: that which conserves what is good, what is cleanly, what is morally irreducible. And, being passionate, his rigors are vital; even when they borrow the trappings of this or that authority-figure; but the more so in his recent work, where even his intolerance is essentially generous; so that his offhand annihilations of Frost, Snodgrass and Lowell, provide the impetus, the necessary blast-off for his just and more-than-discerning praise of Spicer, and others.

Sorrentino's romanticism shows repeatedly in groundswells beneath the whizzing flatness of *The Sky Changes*. A few times, sentimentality seems impinging upon us. At such moments, we realize that Sorrentino has found, in the travel-narrative of *The Sky Changes*, a sort of convention which is all-but-ideal for the degree of freedom he has so far achieved. The very means by which the husband seeks distance from the reality of himself — the constantly-replaced slides of Americana — provide the means of Sorrentino keeping his own distance from the work; provide a safety-lock, as it were, whereby he delivers himself and his art from one another. Such transposed romanticism — by which I do not deprecate it — is Sorrentino's desire for an art-work which can outlive the identity of its author, his personal intentions and solicitings — which threaten to steam its surface while it is yet new.

By token of his however-forced reconciliation of the opposites within himself as artist, *The Sky Changes* represents Gil Sorrentino's fullest success thus far: a distinguished contribution to the writing I have tried briefly to describe: a novel of marriage a hundred times as worth reading as, say, Richard Yates' *Revolutionary Road*; and (the more shame to Hill and Wang, for having traduced their initial courage!) perhaps one-hundredth as well publicized.

If Sparrows
Could Sing,
Could New Yorkers
Hear Them?

On certain days, the outstanding characteristic of New York seems to be its echoes. This is not a prelude to Jimmy Cannonish reminiscences; but a way of noting the strange deafness which regularly infects so many New Yorkers. Strange, because it occurs in people whose hearing, obviously, is organically sound: the person to whom you've just had to repeat a comment six times, will hear perfectly another remark, in the same situation, same voice level, same diction. On certain days, then, every office, store, and restaurant seems to have become either an echo corridor, or a pet shop filled with people trying to teach myna birds and parakeets to speak. The distance isn't the only reason, although it can help: if you're standing anywhere from four to ten feet away from a co-worker or acquaintance, you should prepare to deliver your opening remarks in a hod-carrier's bellow. And even that won't be enough: whatever the original volume, it will have to be stepped up at least 15 decibels the next six times, with the possible effect of communicating your conversant's disease to the bystanders. Indeed, New Yorkers have become so accustomed to this condition, that very often their shouts are not instructions or requests, but little monologues: jokes, private opinions, songs. After these irrelevancies have notched the sound barrier, they go ahead with their message.

You get angry at the risk of your social standing: it is more advisable to show your resentment toward someone whose hearing *is* organically impaired; since he will feel guilty anyway, about not hearing, and will probably, at best, display only token resentment. Your audience, if any, will be polite toward you, if not openly sympathetic; being firm in their belief that a little rough treatment is good for the physically handicapped.

The sufferer from New York deafness, on the other hand, is a little ward of democracy: he enjoys all the privileges of the physically handicapped, with none of the social embarrassments. He is firm in his assurance that he is doing his neighbor a favor by pretending to listen to any remark that he has to make — that's what free speech is all about, isn't it? — without the additional imposition of trying to understand. It seems to be a popular belief that intelligibility floats in the air, like a sort of phlogisten, with nothing about it of complexity or shading or challenge; and that words, at best, are merely magnets for this substance; so that a man's speech is supposed to work instantly, like a mechanical instrument; and if it doesn't work in your presence, he has no more business getting annoyed with you, than if his car's engine were to break down while you were riding with him.

This condition is, at times, over-compensated; as witness those strange little knots of explainers and interpreters, whom New York occasionally spores. As a long-time movie-goer, I have had special occasion to encounter these people, and savour them. I have been told, for example, that my favorite cockney comedy of last year, *Sparrows Can't Sing,* has been withdrawn, so as to provide it with sub-titles; whose purpose would be to translate the cockney dialogue, which a supposed large number of New Yorkers has found unintelligible. I can only say,

as a non-cockney and non-visitor to London, that I found
a minimum of the dialogue unintelligible; that I strongly
suspect many cockneys don't find each other easy to understand (a lot of speech has a tinkling inanity, like
Preston Sturges' dialogue, or the patter songs of G. and
S.); and, finally, I doubt whether that many New Yorkers
understand the dialogue in that many of their native
films. The point seems to be, that they can condone
unintelligibility on native ground; but not a foreigners'
unintelligibility, which carries a strong smell of illicit
profit. (At least, they haven't dubbed *Sparrows Can't
Sing*.)

Another example of explaining occurred recently in
a movie theater where I went to watch the Japanese
film, *High and Low*. Unlike *Sparrows Can't Sing*,
this was copiously supplied with sub-titles. Apparently,
however, these were scarcely enough for a middle-aged
man sitting in back of me with a lady companion. Every
sub-title that appeared on the screen, this man would
read, word for word, with a voice resonant enough, and
enunciation crisp enough, to delight a Foreign Legion
top sergeant. After about ten seconds of this oratorio,
I moved down about five rows. I couldn't hear the words
so clearly anymore, but I could still *hear* them; now,
however, due to some peculiarity of the accoustics, the
sibilants were outstanding: I kept hearing sp, sp, sp, like
a nest of conspirators in traffic. Finally, I moved to
within about four feet of the screen, where I found relief. The players were a little more grainy-looking, but
their dialogue was their own Japanese; and the task of
interpreting it restored in full to the distributors.

I'm *sure* that the woman wasn't blind; if she were,
I suspect she would have been alone: blind people tend
to visit movies as much for escape from their social
dependence, as for the more conventional sorts of escape.

Then, too, wouldn't he have described at least part of the action, scenes, etc.?

No; I hold for the explanation that the man was a chronic explainer: a condition originally benevolent, but aggravated to elephantiasis-like proportions by New York deafness.

There are at least two explanations for this condition, which, I hope, will not be discounted because of their elementariness. They can be expressed as slogans: 1) *Words are weapons.* Which is to say, that New Yorkers, long acclimated to hearing unpleasant noises of all kinds, have learned, almost as a reflex, to distrust language as merely another unpleasantness; more so, because it is a distraction from the familiar distractions to which they have become used. In fact, the ordinary auditory conditions of New York are a little like those of a battle-ground. A loud voice is just another alert-siren; while a soft voice may be alarming, either because (maybe as a by-product of gangster movies?) a soft voice betokens warning, or menace; or because it betokens a confidence, therefore additional, and usually unpleasant, responsibility. So, the New Yorker asking you to repeat what you just said, is the equivalent of a TV cop asking the suspect to turn his pockets inside out and place his hands palms-down on the table.

This is the first slogan, and the second is like unto it: 2) *Words are food.* New Yorkers have become used to language being diced, hashed, scallopined, and pre-chewed for them by newspaper headlines, newspaper stories and advertising material of every variety. The saturation of space to which this has led makes it difficult for the average New Yorker to retain any instinct for the flavor of language which is being used at all sensuously, or eccentrically or distinctively. Even if he doesn't actually read all that material, its presence infects the language used around him, the frequency of language, the dimensions of language. Language today can, in one sense, communicate more ideas more quickly; but the contracting of time and space has resulted in the flattening-out of both language and ideas. And even the more intelligent New Yorkers have suffered from the ministrations of English instructors who confuse their classes with correspondence courses in journalism; thereby, teaching the student to watch his language as though it were his sugar content. Get your reader's (listener's) attention in the first sentence; use short, simple sentences; "Adjectives we must not love, but nouns and verbs a plenty of." The observance of which will place you in the company of Guy de Maupassant; Hemingway (the patron saint of all journalism instructors, everywhere); Damon Runyon; Ring Lardner; William Allen White and George Orwell (if not of Herman Melville, Charles Dickens, Charles Lamb, George Jean Nathan, or James Agee). No wonder that they are accustomed to regard language as they are accustomed to regard the food they eat; as somehow onerous and time-destroying, although necessary to be tolerated.

Lest I confirm myself as anti-progressive, here are two provisos for dealing with this affliction.

1) Use familiar language. This does not necessarily exclude foreign accents, if these are familiar to New York. Nor does it apply entirely to vocabulary. New Yorkers are a people as rhythmic, in their way, as the Balinese, and inflection-conscious as the Chinese. A sentence of many clauses, or a peculiarly transposed clause, is tantamount to enclosing yourself in a soundproof telephone booth. Even if you observe these rules, your conversant still may not perfectly understand you; but he will accept you as part of his psychic metabolism.

2) Pantomime is all-important. I don't mean explana-

tory gestures, although these may be helpful, if not complicated or esoteric. By "pantomime," I chiefly mean fitness of facial expression and tone of voice, to the content of your speech. Courtesy no longer means something pallid and simple, like courtliness or modesty; but something as rigorous and intricately demanding as the Donskoi Ballet. When asking a druggist for change so you can use the telephone booth, your eyes should be fixed on him, your gesture economic and forceful, and your presence bulging with that ritualized candour which speech instructors identify as "projection." On the other hand, if you voice your request in what you think is an adequate tone, but with lack of coloration or gesture, and your eyes flitting here and there, your conversant will react to you with a silent, bemused interest, as though to a song; then, after ten seconds, ask you to repeat everything you've just said. Your intensity of dedication must carry the day. Indeed, if you're strenuous enough, the idea may occur to him that you are about to drop from apoplexy, on his premises! —in which case, to quote a certain television advertisement, the gates of hearing will open.

Nets
and
Neighbors

Douglas Woolf's "Bank Day"—the first of his stories which I remember reading, and which still impresses me as a codification of his singular virtues—begins with a crippled army veteran awakening early one morning "with his head, and his impatience, buried beneath the cover, waiting for the alarm (which did not know that it was set) to sound." He rouses his pregnant wife ("Martha was grunting quietly. Thank God I love you, he thought, kissing her somewhere as he passed by.") Together, they piece out a succession of ceremonies—letting the cat out of the bathroom, putting on the radio, fixing breakfast —which, as described by Woolf, take on the luminous solidity of Hemingway's fishing description in "Big Two-Hearted River"; plus a steel-etching austerity and edge which only gradually—in occasional discreet flourishes of phrase, then in the aggregate rhythm of phrases, lines and paragraphs—discloses its credentials as poetry. And only gradually—like the settling into focus of an etching's pattern—do we learn the purpose of the early reveille: it is the husband's turn to visit the blood-bank, donating his blood for the money which will sustain them.

Many stories, some of the best included, will unbend, stand on their hind legs for a reasonable space, and even canter a little. "Bank Day"—like most of the handful of Woolf's short stories—coils upon itself increasingly as it progresses: if the reader is moved by it, he finds himself within the conch-like furl of the poetic image which is

"Bank Day"—or, "Fly Man," "Fair-Weather-Wise"; the image, and the world of which the image is coalescence.

The element of this world, of course, is language, the very precision and carefully-tempered serenity of which testify to its liberation by Woolf. In this element, solid-seeming and evasive as spilt mercury, realism, surrealism, lyricism and burlesque bear equally valid witness to the motifs and preoccupations of Douglas Woolf's universe. Illusory appearances do not so much yield to reality, as set the tone for reality: the reality of poetic metaphor, in which illusion and "fact" are melded. Woolf's stories and novels are filled with misleading or mystifying appearances, which are not explained—his art at its best in no wise involves explanation of reality—but rather amplified. The forest rangers in *Fade Out* appear at first as soldiers in an unexplained skirmish. The daughters of the pacifist hermit in *Wall to Wall* appear at first quaintly inexplicable as the figures in a primitive pottery design. And in what may be Woolf's most extraordinary story—"Fair-Weather-Wise"—a father's Saturday afternoon walk with his little girl is overlain, by the presence of airplanes from a nearby field, with the ashen tone of a Rosselini war film.

The universe of this fiction comprises southwestern America: Arizona, New Mexico, a wedge of Los Angeles. It is substantially the same territory evoked by William Eastlake's first three novels; and, although he scarcely shares Eastlake's primary-colored sense of myth, or his deeper-throated rhetoric, Woolf shares in great degree Eastlake's sensitivity to the inter-filtering of current American landscape and popular folklore, not excluding night-club monologues (the mortifying situations of which, as recounted by Woody Allen or Alan King, appear to have suggested some of Woolf's best short stories) and, more weightily, a basic theme: the nets of interdependence toward which people repeatedly gravitate; the interdependence of marriage, of community, of love; the ways in which people need to replenish such interdependence, even at the quick of solitary fortitude; and the ways in which, past a certain point (usually unobserved by those most agonizingly involved) such interdependence becomes purely lethal. The visual pattern often suggested to me by Woolf's stories is a spinney of Pollock-like lines, intersecting, separating and converging again.

Eastlake, who well recognizes the agonies of interdependence, usually manages for the most part to celebrate its heroisms. Woolf pays closer and darker attention to the inequities of interdependence, especially that of family. "Fly Man" is almost a magic-lantern reversal of "Bank Day" 's situation: the exchange of roles between husband and wife, appealingly gallant in the latter story, becomes, in "Fly Man," discomfortingly perverse and, at last, sinister. Here, again, the husband is a crippled veteran; but this time, his disablement is emotional and mental. An apparently harmless psychotic, he has assumed, with evident zest, his wife's domestic chores while she earns a successful living in various defense plants. The story encompasses their preparations to leave their West Coast home for a more lucrative site, in Minnesota and its great centerpiece (in what is surely some of Woolf's most overtly controlled and, beneath the Vermeer-like mosaic of detail, somberly powerful writing) describes the husband's ritual of dismantling the various fly-traps which he has assembled throughout the house. Beneath the seemingly gentle comedy of his compulsive puttering, Woolf conveys to us, like a contrapuntal grating, the undertones of prospective disaster. The wife has obviously become increasingly pained and repelled by her husband's no-longer dismissable madness; while the husband, throughout his evermore-rococo going-away ceremony, in which the fly-snares become as giddily elaborate as the more ominous cartoons of Saul Steinberg—makes us aware of the glacial rage and self-contempt which underlie his finicky executions. As the story concludes, they are setting off in their heavily-laden automobile (". . . climbing into the car, into the back, he could smell the sweet insecticide"); as the man, with a gesture become menacing in context, slaps at an invisible fly.

A few of Woolf's stories of the last three or four years have turned toward a kind of fantasy more formalized than that of "Fly Man" or "Bank Day"; somewhat partaking of science-fiction. Appliances and apparatus have always played, in his stories, a role as ubiquitous and versatile as the Navajos of Eastlake's novels: the automobiles in *Wall to Wall;* the pestilential airplanes in "Fair-Weather-Wise"; the camera and projector and dental equipment of *The Hypocritic Days.* In "Cougher" and "Rest Stop" and his one-act play, *The Love Letter,* Woolf is advancing a few steps further than in the formerly mentioned stories the theme of interdependence: this time, in terms of the processes which involve, sometimes pulverizingly, men with machines and mechanized systems, as well as with each other; so that human relationships and communications become regimented. Woolf, however, is no social critic in either the good or the bad senses of that term; and his "science-fiction" is no more related to George Orwell or Cyril Kornbluth than any of his fiction is related to that of John O'Hara, say, or Philip Roth. The stories I mention are basically simply new perspectives of people's sometimes insensately terrible demands on each other; and the desire both to remain a human being and to meet at least some of those demands; those in keeping with one's humanity.

"Cougher" and *The Love Letter* both deal with worlds in which the sacrifice of one's privacy has become a standard of life. In "Cougher," the ill who visit clinics are tattooed with their case histories—as much as their skins will accommodate—and, when no space is left, are disposed of. This story, not only because of its slight debt to "In the Penal Colony," seems to me one of the few I have read which can sustain the maltreated name of Kafka. *The Love Letter*—somewhat marred by the confinement of its stage form (the extensive stage directions suggest Woolf clinging by one hand to a more congenial medium) and by a patly sententious resolution—evokes a community of homeless people who are furnished packing boxes to live in at the post office—provided they write and receive enough letters to justify their residence. "Rest Stop" expands, not too elaborately, on a question which Woody Allen or Lennie Bruce might have asked, and answered: tooling cross-country, at the full of the population explosion, what happens to the inevitable stop beside the road?

Throughout his short fiction which I have read, Douglas Woolf's ostensible purpose is *not* to explain, but to clarify, contemporary American reality as he sees it. This, as I have already suggested, sets him apart from such as Philip Roth who, in lecture and essay, has been cross with the world for not cooperating with him so that he can produce the new American fiction (fortunately, Roth himself, in *his* fiction, has occasionally relied on his author's right hand, rather than his lecturer's left; and, in *Letting Go,* for example, produced some fiction of distinctive, if uneven, stature). The error of such a view is that it assumes a competition between the writer and reality; as though the paradoxes of life were obstinate land-contours, which needed only a newer, shinier caterpillar tractor: a new fictional formula to plough up the truth. Woolf, in all I have read by him, never commits the gaffe of trying to out-absurd or out-complex the world which he knows. He writes as both a recipient and witness of it; bringing to bear on isolated perceptions as much of clarity and an often desperation-tempered serenity, as he can. He rests his achievements on what will seem to some the shockingly old-fashioned assumption that not the world, but his art, rests in his hands. Knowing that what he can see at any given moment will almost certainly be limited, he nonetheless stands by his eyes. In just this, I feel, rests his formalism; which is not (thus far in his career) confining; but which is the subtle permeation of his art, knitting together complexities rather than resolving them, of his poet's discipline and the mind it represents: a formalism very nearly classical.

The limitations of Woolf's achievements—as well as different, sometimes richer emphases for the themes I have mentioned—are to be found in his three novels, in which he tries to elaborate and more directly widen the vision of the stories.

In his first novel, *The Hypocritic Days,* published in Majorca some ten years ago by Robert Creeley, the ugly side of emotional dependence and its demands is seen at its darkest. Here, Woolf is writing about parasitism and mutual castration of parents—in particular, fathers—and their children. The book features some of Woolf's most explicit commentary on these relationships, and some of his sharpest-edged *mise -en- scéne,* as well as an impressionistic brittleness into which the bones of the story finally collapse.

Emasculation and voyeurism emblematize the book's opening and closing scenes. It begins with Charles Ashton, the protagonist, having his teeth treated; while the dentist, his fiancée's father, draws malicious comparison between his own baldness and Charles's prospective loss of teeth. Charles returns home to his own father, a vapid ex-jockey who combines the roles of mother and, in a curious way, younger brother. Over the supper table, the young man and his diminutive father toast each other in black cherry soda, like two children playing house: a vignette which, pathetic and subtly disturbing, entails some of the best writing in the book. Leaving his father, Charles, in a comic variation of the ceremonial motif—but also bearing overtones of the major theme—climbs a flag-pole on behalf of an elderly neighbor, only to find, after descending, that he has raised the flag upside-down, in symbol of distress.

The remainder of this short book involves Charles with his friend, the wicked patriarch of his age group, Lloyd Lippincott: a paralytic who, as spokesman for his generation, proposes to avenge himself on his parents through his incapacity. Lloyd holds weekly "orgies"—elaborate necking-parties for which his father, a flaccid, alcoholic screen-writer, supplies prints of romantic Hollywood films. In the novel's terminal scene, as Charles works the projector, the horrified guests discover that Lloyd's father—with how much conscious malice we don't know—has substituted a stag movie which mocks the impotence of the young people, and precipitates havoc. As carefully delineated as Woolf's best writing, the scene carries additional impact because, as in most of Woolf's fiction, sex is given only subordinate emphasis. The connecting strain is the search by people for emotional fulfillment through others; but often so ineptly, or hostilely, that they instead impose their weaknesses on others. This confusion of motives, and the impotence which attends it, consitute the hypocrisy of Woolf's title.

The book, to me, is at last a failure because the intensely realized set-pieces I have described amount to no more than their sum: not a short story—certainly, without the compactness of Woolf's stories—and without a novel's mutation and advancement. Although Woolf evidently means for his social landscape—Los Angeles, adjoining Hollywood—to counterpoint and enlarge the personal story, the background never seemed to me more than cursory and gratuitous. Above all, Charles himself never does much more than react; and, at that, react not in any particular voice of his own, but in a voice which could as easily be an extension of Woolf's narrative voice in the stories: appraising, commenting, deflecting the grosser impact of this or that scene. In a real sense, Woolf seems not to have the right crudeness for a novelist: he is still pre-eminently concerned with rallying and controlling experience through the language of metaphor.

Although it eventually unwinds too far for its texture, Woolf's second novel, *Fade Out,* is superior to *The Hypocritic Days* in humor, poignancy and purposefulness of form. (I feel with this book that Woolf *needed* to write a novel, and that this need helped organize and direct his perceptions.) Essentially, the book's theme is the parent-child collision of *The Hypocritic Days,* as seen from the older generation's viewpoint. Mr. Twombly, a retired bank clerk living with his daughter and salesman son-in-law and *their* daughter in New York City, finds himself in the position of an indulged but annoying child (again, the Woolfean shuffling of roles) whose granddaughter keeps an eye on him to make sure that he is wearing his new, painful false teeth. Moreover, his presence acts as an abrasive to the anxieties and antipathies of his family: tremulous daughter, high-pressuring and high-pressured son-in-law, and granddaughter, fat and be-pimpled, whose chafing awareness of her puberty makes her resent both the responsibility which her grandfather's presence imposes, and his attempts at friendliness. Indeed, Mr. Twombly's only intimates are his pet turtle (which symbolizes his own patient insularity) and Behemoth Brown, an aging ex-pug whose family situation parallels Twombly's (Woolf devotes a handful of amusing, touching and awesome words to a description of this big fellow rising from his armchair). At last, Mr. Twombly is accused of molesting two little girls of the neighborhood (it is typical of Woolf that, while showing the old man's affection for the children as indisputably innocent, he makes no attempt to suppress its glimmer of eroticism); and, although the charge is quickly disproved, it supplies the family with sufficient excuse to dispatch him to the old people's home. Making his escape, he embarks, with Behemoth, in search of a new home and some sort of stature.

At this crucial passage, curiously enough, the novel, as well as its characters, begins to fade out, regaining only intermittently the vitality of its first half. In this first half, Woolf has orchestrated, with much more dexterity and sense of shape than in his first novel, the episodes in which Twombly tries to make good on the job his son-in-law has obtained for him (selling greeting cards), or knocks about uptown New York with Behemoth, or rubs his family the wrong way. Unlike Charles Ashton's somewhat moony encounters, Twombly's adventures convey the vitality of his pride and his desire for undemeaning love. Moreover, Woolf's sensitivity to the situation, and his warmth for Mr. Twombly's simple, resonant virtues, enable him to show Mr. Twombly as a *figure* rather than as a character, in a series of episodes which, with their tone of serio-comic *scherzo* (modulated occasionally by the bassoons of satire) resemble sections of Eastlake's *Portait of an Artist With Twenty-Six Horses.* One of the funniest scenes—which, however, keeps its eye cocked at the main theme—features a tele-

vision unit in Central Park, trying to induce some reaction to its blonde starlet among the fat, comatose
snapping-turtles which have been conscripted as the vil-
lains of a science-fiction drama. Twombly and Behemoth
are present only as spectators; yet, the sequence, with its
burlesque commentary on the way the old men are being
"handled" by their in-laws, keeps them very much in the
foreground as presences.

The opposite seems to be true of most of the cross-
country excursion. Once they reach the southwest, with
its pueblos and ghost towns, the story regains much of
Woolf's *esprit,* deepened by the eloquence of his landscape images, and the beautiful concluding episode, in
which Twombly meets his mirror-image: a man who has
inadvertently caused his children's death. There are one
or two good scenes along the way; although I felt that
with the appearances of the man who wants to start a
juvenile delinquency lobby, and the manic author, Woolf
was too intent on ramming home what seemed rather
spongy jokes, to extract from them much of his characteristic humor or poetry. On the whole, this entire section depends on Twombly and Behemoth as its unifying
elements; and here, deprived of the domestic situations
which had vivified them (without taxing Woolf's capacity
for characterization) Twombly and Behemoth fade out,
leaving scarcely even spectators: only Woolf's eye, Woolf's
voice, are present; and those, of course, are never really
absent. Moreover, of the trip itself, it seems both simplest
and fairest to say that not enough happens: it is at once
too rushed and too attenuated. I kept feeling it as
obligatory; the last feeling one should have about a
voyage of such import.

His last novel to date, *Wall to Wall,* is his most consistently successful: more superior to *Fade Out* than
Fade Out is to *The Hypocritic Days;* the most substantial

sign, as yet, not only that the novel fulfills a definite expressive need for Woolf, but that he can make of the form something new: albeit as tense, piercing and mandarinish as his short fiction. The story is much more a fable than either of the preceding novels, although no less a protean commentary on present-day America. It is a fable of imprisonment: like nearly symmetrical pillars, each of the opening and concluding episodes features a mental hospital: the sanitarium on the west coast, at which Claude Squires works as part-time aide; and the eastern sanitarium where, at the end of his journey, he visits his deranged mother. The intervening episodes and images reprise, with varying subtlety, this theme of confinement. Commissioned by his father, a sleek salesman of used cars, to deliver an automobile in the middlewest, Claude meets a succession of people—his frigid married sister; a wetback laborer making his latest sally to enter the United States, a pacifist hermit living with his daughters in an abandoned mine; his customer, the elegant lady who never leaves her armchair—all of whom are facing imprisonment, fighting it, or more-or-less cheerfully subscribing to it. Because of the frankly allegorical theme, Woolf is not embarrassed, as he seemed to be toward the conclusion of *Fade Out,* by his difficulty at sustaining character. Indeed, Claude gives Woolf's intelligence freer play than either Ashton or Twombly, because Claude's reality, as chief figure in an allegorical fable, resides in his functioning as an intelligence, as a source of perceptions and reactions. Part of the essential failure of the bus trip in *Fade Out* was, that Woolf skirted the emotional significance—surely integral to his story—of Twombly and Behemoth confronting the volatile changingness of their lives. Claude, on a mission half-cynical (errand-boy for his father) and half introspective (seeking the emotional associations of his mother and past acquaintances) can move in and out of his experiences while, like the best picaresque heroes, shaping them through his mere entrance. His relationship to the automobile, which helps connect the book, is realized with a wonderful fullness of humor, lyricism and eroticism both burlesque and sensuously true. The tone is of an irony more sad and ruminative than *The Hypocritic Days,* and more consistently weighty than much of *Fade Out.* Woolf seems to respond, here, to the felt pressures of a real journey, a sense of *physical,* as distinguished from solely metaphorical, countryside which augments the mordancy of his episode about the pacifist mine-dweller. Here, despite his apparent liking for the man himself, and (grudging) admiration for his ideals, Woolf does not stint at showing his subterranean Utopia for the comic horror which it would almost certainly be in life: the dreadful, pallid vegetables, the daughters, born attractive, who have been deformed by their hideaway existence. Here, the caricature draws from Woolf's intimation of the reality; instead of being a nervous imposition on reality.

More important even than enlargement, Woolf's poetic and satiric talents, no less original and rewarding for their narrowness, find in *Wall to Wall* a recharge of seriousness. It refreshes our hopes—even beyond the small, fine core of his best work—for new extensions of his career as novelist—perhaps, even as dramatist—as he recasts his own map of America.

Force
and
Violence

The recent Supreme Court decision regarding interrogation of suspects by police, has overshadowed—a peculiarly apposite word—the importance of Mayor Lindsay's civilian review board. Still, why not? Mayor Lindsay has certain attributes in common with Justice Warren, as, indeed, with President Johnson—most notably, that all three gentlemen have my spiritual well-being much at heart. Let's proceed.

The Court has, of course, ruled that all persons held for interrogation by police, must be informed, first, that anything they say may be used against them; second, that they are entitled to a lawyer. Fine. This part of the decision strikes my un-jurisprudent mind as unexceptionable. If, as has been claimed in some quarters, any arrests and convictions have been, or will be, menaced by the ruling, I can only say that such arrests and convictions will probably deserve to be invalidated. I note, by the way, that I have referred to convictions and arrests having *been* menaced—no, the Warren Court has put me in the wrong there by an addendum to its ruling, making that ruling non-retroactive. The curious and rather typical sense of legal expediency which this reflects, may warrant some further comment later along —or may not.

As I have said, however, the above stipulations merely spell out what the Constitution has declared. I see nothing revolutionary about them, or, indeed, about any of

Justice Warren's quoted judgment: not revolutionary, at least, in the sense of "original." It's Justice Warren, after all. And I should most certainly approve the provision of legal counsel for anyone who wants it and cannot afford a lawyer, or has had no experience with lawyers.

But the seams start popping with Justice Warren's specifications that the suspect be advised of his right to *remain silent;* and that "if the individual indicates in any manner, at any time prior to or during questioning, that he wishes to remain silent, the interrogation must cease." To many admirers of the decision, I'm sure, these specifications will seem to follow from the right of counsel and the right not to incriminate one's self. So, I'm sure, do they follow in Justice Warren's mind; for Justice Warren's would appear to be the kind of plodding imagination which, having no talent for the specific, prides itself, quite erroneously, on its talent for abstraction. In my opinion, the Justice's elaborations are untrue to what I interpret as the purpose of the right-to-counsel and anti-self-incrimination clauses. The whole purport of these would seem to be, that the suspected person retains his right of moral choice: that, in other words, *he has as much right to protect himself as the investigating officer has to obtain validly all pertinent information.* An exceedingly explicit ruling, but also exceedingly humble. For it recognizes that the right to ascertain the truth *must* accommodate recognition of the individual's privacy; and the uncertainties of conscience.

Justice Warren's dicta present not the slightest awareness that uncertainty ought to exist, of any kind. What, for example, in this context, does the right to remain silent mean? Not that there is no duty to co-operate in a peaceful investigation. Not that there will be no penalties for silence; for all sorts of social penalties have attached, and will attach to a witness or suspect remaining silent on crucial information. What right has any investigating officer to present such a generalization, which extends far beyond the precinct-room boundaries, unless he accompanies it with a careful statement of the suspect's responsibilities?

But the Warren Court's decision is replete with certainty about such matters, even as the (conscientious/intelligent/humane) detective's or policeman's view is replete with uncertainty. For, to begin with, the job of law enforcement officer—and this applies to the worst as well as the best—is brutally paradoxical: requiring an ordinary foot patrolman to be as alert as a sentry and as judicious as a judge, while confronting dangers that judges have rarely, at least in recent decades, had to face; to make split-second decisions about his own and other men's lives, which carry, into the bargain, the burden of his relations with the community which he is supposed to protect. Above all, the policeman repeatedly and constantly faces the central job of communication: communication with neighbors, and communication with outsiders; communication with the inarticulate, and communication with the all-too-articulate; and with the brutalized; and with the shattered; and with the displaced; and with the mad.

It is on this most sensitive tissue of communication, that the bulk of the Warren decision sets its hippo foot. The significance of the stipulations—especially the one concerning the suspect's "right" to halt interrogation—is, that the cruelest paradoxes of the policeman's job—those I have mentioned—do not exist. For these stipulations say nothing about the suspect's right to give information; they say nothing about his right to change his mind, to put aside his suspicions (which, indeed, might have been amply justified) about the arresting officer. That which is loosened, let it not be tied. The suspect and the arresting officer might be two entities in Limbo.

The dicta would seem to have been predicated on a muddled interpretation of "force." What, indeed, should force, illegitimate force, mean in such a situation? The third-degree, certainly; but, beyond that? Should it mean the kind of force applied by lawyers in their cross-examination of witnesses? The kind applied by psychiatrists during intensive examination? The kind applied by teachers, when, through questioning or lecturing, they try to elicit some intellectual rebound from the students? Illegitimate force surely means the bad psychological force of bribery ("You can beat the chair, or get a shorter sentence, if you tell us," etc.) and intimidation. But does the Warren decision guarantee that a shrewd cop, who has observed the formalities, will not continue to use those devices? What the court has done, I should say, has been, to identify *all* force as illegitimate force. They have thereby overruled the all-important force of authority (which, granted, is a dirty word in many lexicons).

This is of cardinal importance because force and violence are crucial concepts to life in the United States. The more pity that they are frequently treated as identical; since each plays an important, a valuable, role on occasion, in our government as in our daily life; whereas to confuse them is to foster chaos. Force, I should interpret as mainly conservative, mainly the product of the Establishment. We regard force as massive, overwhelming, unavoidable: i.e., the forces of nature. We regard it as that which *can* be conserved (who talks of "conserving" violence!) and as a natural faculty, a natural outgrowth, of strength.

Violence, on the other hand, is the faculty of radicalism. It does not conserve, nor can it be conserved; rather, it sunders and scatters: *violates*. Although violence may be prolonged, of course, *acts* of violence characteristically operate on short fuses. Violence is the special property and function of the underdog, or the man who regards himself as underdog; and, while force may pre-suppose no anger—only the desire to get something accomplished, make the wheels turn, etc., violence, it seems to me, almost invariably pre-supposes, if not anger, then some passion germane to it.

It is easy to see, I presume, why disaster may lie with identifying, or confusing, force and violence, as the Warren decision seems to have done. The end result is almost invariably to put the advantage with the Establishment, which can safely ignore the confusion, since the Establishment commands both force *and* violence. The Establishment in this case, is the Courts; which should be amply grateful to the Supreme Court for taking the heat off of them, and their processes; which, I should wager, are responsible for more false sentences than most of the county sheriffs in the United States taken together.

The relationship of police to the courts, in a sprawling nation like ours, and a loosely woven city like New York especially, could probably not be much clarified by any Supreme Court decision. But the effect of this particular decision, it seems to me, is to deny the precarious and volatile relationship of the police to the courts; again, by pretending that it is very simple. Thereby, the court has endangered the still more precarious and volatile relationship of arresting officer to suspect: the obligation —no matter how often abused, or slighted—to *clarify*. This is the duty of any investigating officer, as it is the duty of a legal process. And, flouted by one department, it surely will not—can not—be respected by the other.

For the whole bent of the Warren decision seems to me negative: the stopping up of loop-holes with cheap putty. How can anyone *not* see the connection between the sort of mind which produced this decision (and, afterward, as much as admitted the ramshackleness of its endeavors by declaring that the law was *not* retro-active! Who ever heard of a just ruling, which the judge could not afford to make retroactive?) and the mind which produced the flatulent rhetoric, the blowsy sophistry, of the decision against Ralph Ginzburg? Who, granted, is a trashy, self-vaunting pitchman, but surely no peril to any society that deserves to exist. As for the Warren Report—well, I haven't finished reading *Inquiry*.

Worst of all, the court has decreed that the worst police in America—the crooks, the brutes, the sluggards —are to set the standard of behavior for every police-man. Surely, this is the burden of the ruling. I recall it was William Buckley (in an address to the police, about two years ago) who pointed out that even the police deserve to be presumed innocent until proven guilty. That is the worst of the Supreme Court ruling; that, and not the number of suspects who may escape trial. Such molecular affairs will have to be confronted as they always have been, in the molecular course of that police routine which the Supreme Court may comfortably ignore. But the guilty have laid down the law.

Satire
With
Its Fingers
Crossed

Jules Feiffer's charming, finesse-ridden cartoons—just out in a second volume, *Passionella* (McGraw-Hill, $1.75) —could hardly want a heftier cheering section than those popular culture seers (John Crosby, Richard Watts Jr., Steve Allen) to whom Satire is the Secret Word for Tonight, even when they aren't sure of the precise definition. According to the way "satire" has been played up in any number of TV forums, newspaper interviews (Al Capp and James Thurber are favorites) and daily think-pieces, all that is required to oust the Republican Administration, institute civil rights in every state, re-habilitate the New York subways, *and* reform popular culture overnight, is a first-class satirist of the caliber of Swift, Goya, Aristophanes, Molière, Hogarth, Rabelais, Juvenal, Arthur Kirssen, Cervantes, Finley Peter Dunne and Mark Twain. And that—according to recent articles on Jonathan Winters, Bob and Ray, and Jules Feiffer— is just what these critics are getting at the rate of around 12 a month, in the slow season.

Only within the last 10 years or so has the satirist been nominated by so large a majority for his new role: chaperone for those critics who like to hold hands with "high art" while playing kneesies under the table with "low." Of course, the satirist has long been the favorite hero-villain of many intellectuals and pseudo-intellec-tuals: he embodies their longing to act (when necessary) aggressively or even violently, while keeping intact both their moral integrity and (usually) their immunity from legal retaliation.

However, only with the emergence of Popular Culture as a Popular Subject could these critics cash in on satire's fugitive similarities to popular art: the give-and-take communication with the audience at large; the cat-burglar's vagrant dependence which both display toward established art forms as a ready-made kind of expression; above all, the habitual veering toward self-destruction of both satirist and popular artist—the one, by risking self-exposure in his attack on human failings; the other, by poising his personality against the routinized production of comic strip or night-club act.

Despite such similarities, "satire" is probably the most misused term in pop-culture criticism since the dowsers of yesteryear hunted for "poetry" in every Marx Brothers comedy and Torchy Blaine thriller. The most unlikely selections of the past year include Al Capp (slapstick exhibitionism), Bob and Ray (nonchalant throwaway comedy) and "Maverick" (tepid Joe College funning). It's hardly any surprise, among such nominations, to find that Madison Avenue whizbang, *Gent* magazine, incorporating a Satire Department for its readers' slower-breathing moments.

I suspect that the identification of the affable grand-standers mentioned above with the recalcitrantly nasty talents of Swift and Juvenal stems from an earlier, but hardly less ridiculous, distortion: the view—still cherished by so many literary critics—of every satirist as the rough, tough, yet molasses-hearted claims-adjustments man for the human race, ready to "serve mankind" or "make a better world" at the drop of a political pamphlet. There's nothing like the role of good-natured entertainer—or social reformer—to help us identify with the satirist, and, incidentally, sidestep the anxiety that he may be talking about us.

Such an attitude, of course, also sidesteps the fact that satire is essentially moored to the artist's individuality, and depends quite as much as any other form of "serious" art on its creator's feeling of apartness from the audience at large. At best, the satirist—Voltaire, Swift and Aristophanes are three good examples—can gain much impact from playing his inner resistance to this audience against his outward bids for its favor; but the satire of the above three drew its scratchy persuasiveness far less from any desire on their part to "improve conditions" than from the self-centered, arrogant and completely unsportsmanlike intensity with which they showed their fellow-man his unmeasured capacities for folly and viciousness. Certainly, like any artist who takes himself and his work seriously, they hoped that it would have its effect; but never in terms of "public relations" of any kind.

I found little of this sustained intensity in Feiffer's *Passionella*. The book contains four picture stories: A podgy chimney-sweep shifts her contours and fortunes to the notes of a Leroy Anderson melody; a four-year-old is drafted into the Army, where his protests are met with injunctions to "be a man" from officers, psychiatrist and chaplain; a neurotic man-in-the-moon prepares to defend his planet and his frustrations from the approaching earth-scientists; the bomb-to-end-all-bombs-and-everything-else-on-earth is finally perfected by the scientists.

Feiffer presents his picture stories with the suave decorum of an all-night disc jockey reading personal messages to middlebrow liberals. His most ingratiating and original talents are a sharp sense of absurd fantasy, which deprecates both itself and the reality that sets it off (as in the "George in the Moon" story), and an architecturally precise sense of timing and placing. This latter is at its best in the cliché-laden title story, where Feiffer keeps his failing gags and situations tearing about with the collisionless smoothness of the characters in a Samuel French bedroom comedy. Even in an almost identical succession of drawings (as are most of his weekly comic-strips), Feiffer can inject a shimmy into the saraband rhythm of conventional book-illustration, stretching or bending characters' heads with each change of mood, or rakishly tilting his letters. In fact, whatever your thoughts about him as white knight of the intellectuals, Feiffer often makes it fantastically difficult not to laugh whenever he wants you to.

However, Feiffer's tireless catering to the "Ins" really does him no more good as a comic-stripper than as a satirist. The eventual effect of any comic-strip's standardized routine is a standardized reaction in the audience: a self-satisfied confidence in the strip's continuing style, ingenuity and rate of production; and in the audience's relationship to it and to the artist. Feiffer's major innovation here consists of juicing the confidence with a dash of pseudo-intellectual self-esteem by an approach identical with that of family-situation shows on television: Cute-disdainful caricatures of Bronx matrons, lonely children and professional beatniks are set up to draw queasy laughs from the people who buddy with them on the street or in apartments every day. This archness is used to skewer the bite-size morsels of William Steig, Robert Osborne and the UPA cartoons which mainly comprise Feiffer's gags and drawing style. All this is too palatable a serving for the stomach acid which usually sours the recognition-laughs of real satire. Even Feiffer's most telling things—the occasional swipes at President Eisenhower, New York *Post* Editor James Wechsler or the government's security chiefs—have the specialty-act air of a Catskills resort waiter singing tenor on Saturday night.

As even Jules Feiffer's rather special case indicates, satire has little commerce with the popular arts. The obsessions to which the satirist usually devotes his career are secondary to the fluent excitement of the best comic strips or movies (always excepting the occasional work of a Dovchenko or von Stroheim). And, in fact, the traditional approach of satire may be inappropriate to an American public which is too conversant with violence and ugliness in its daily life to worry about the potential violence and ugliness within its after-dark soul.

The
Muck
School

   I think there is no denying that at this stage of American life the discreet, twisted-lemon-peel comedy of Shelley Berman and Elaine and Mike—perhaps even the genuine, infinitely more robust models of Voltaire and Beaumarchais—are about as relevant to a broad swath of America as the Morris dance. Far more significant to many American audiences is a strain of gritty, un-housebroken, garbage-happy burlesque typified by *Mad* Magazine; by the mis-named "sick comic," Lennie Bruce; and that raucous bullyrag of Evelyn Waugh's phantasmal eccentrics: John Horne Burns' very bad but enormously memorable novel, *Lucifer With a Book*. The greater number of critics and journalists who make it their business to reach various conclusions about pop culture haven't, I think, come face to face with this trend as yet: being content, as usual, to follow popular art from about ten blocks behind, like a TV G-Man team tailing a litter-bug.
   Now, I'm not embarking on a crusade: I am not proposing that such ingratiating and civilized clowns as Elaine and Mike take a walk for themselves off the Yakashimaya Building. I would say, though, that their biggest handicap is their trying to make all American life fit for public consumption, whereas in fact, a good chunk of it is hardly suitable for private contemplation. Ask Ernie Kovacs, Lennie Bruce, or the staff of *Mad*. Their humor—which might be called the Muck School of

American Comedy—probably owes its existence to an inert layer of disgust and passive resentment which lies like a pool of candle-wax in nearly every city-dweller's soul. This feeling is about as useful and creative as the contents of the occasional alleys between bar and novelty store along Sixth Avenue; and, I'd be willing to bet, inaccessible to any treatment in any conventional kind of serious art. Violence—the custom-tailored, flossy sort of violence common to current movies and television shows —is only a small part of it. Only the lower kinds of popular art—those which do not pretend to re-create or elevate emotions, but only to match them and extend them— are capable of realizing these feelings, which usually resist accurate representation on all but the most subjective levels of art. The perfect conditions for Muck Comedy can be detected, I think, if you take a not-too-brisk walk along Sixth Avenue in the lower forties at any hour of the day; or if you visit, at any time between 9 and 12 A.M., one of the Movie Row caverns around Times Square; watch the frequent reactions of the audience to any film prolific in scenes of sadism, rough-house, sexual fumadiddles or simple larceny; and gage these reactions against the reactions which Archer Winsten or Bosley Crowther has informed you are mandatory to watching such films. The only American pop-culture critic of recent years I know of who regarded these audiences with anything but the usual social critic's *risus sardonicus* of enlightened condescension was Jim Agee. Unfortunately, he over-idealized them (in his remarks on "Curse of the Cat People," and "Cornered") as the Great Heart of America; whereas the Times Square audiences are as resistant to sentimentalization, quick-trigger analysis or—often as not—conventional ideas of decency and fair play—as are contemporary teen-agers, who include a whopping stratum of "Mad" readers. This isn't surprising, in a group for whom "Ya dirty slob!" will ever be a favorite humorous outcry.

Actually, both these frequently overlapping groups share a kind of sour truce with the towering bulk of squalor and ugliness and latent violence which can be detected in the early TV shows of Ernie Kovacs—many of which could have been stocked from the get-yourself-a-pipe-shaped-like-a-toilet-bowl novelty stores of Midtown Manhattan; or in the orgiastic spewing of Jack Davis's *Mad* cartoons, which combine the finicky discernment of a C.P.A. with the emotional patterns of an axe murderer. This underlying attitude combines an unconditional desire to absorb or at least evade any ugliness or violence, with a willingness to use it as a weapon at the earliest opportunity. The majority of American critics whom I have read seem to prefer the notion that the great American mass audience is all atwit for art to come along and enlighten it. I certainly can't blame them for rejecting a good part of Muck Comedy, if their taste so dictates; but I can blame them for overlooking—on the apparent supposition that things are never as bad as you know they are—the truth that American mass audiences can, and have, molded their own kind of popular art and will react to it on their own terms, which might easily be surprising, and even distressing, to a good many critics, movie producers, youth board workers and clergymen.

This is probably the main reason why Muck Comedy can hardly be connected with any comic trend before it, and why it will probably, for a good while yet, resist embalming by the experts of Esquire magazine and television interview shows. It hardly owes anything to the graceful brainstorming of the Marx Brothers. Even when they were coasting, they had a delicacy and near-sweetness which are strange to Jack Davis and Lennie Bruce;

and, far more important, they represented an era in which destructiveness and messiness could still be regarded as optional to the individual; when violence could still be managed with the help of wit and audacity; and when certain extremes of violence were still difficult enough to imagine for audiences to consign them to a realm of harmless nonsense. I certainly don't claim that the Marx Brothers comedies could find no audience today: they always have and will for some time; but I think that their sort of comic nihilism is out-dated beyond recall. Nihilism of a much more massive sort is so little debatable today that I think the only choice of attitudes toward it lies between violent resentment and a participation which needs no cue from any team of comics. Violence and destruction are so far from "optional" by now that probably the nearest comic art can approach it is through the average *Mad* cartoon: a churning cascade of ordure, wrecked machinery, unwholesomely pretty girls and mangled carcasses, interwoven with manic sensuousness.

I hardly think that Muck Comedy bears much stronger a resemblance to Surrealism, which—apart from its genuine merits—is too formal, literary and brittle for many American audiences, and otherwise reflects the penchant of certain European intellectuals for making little laboratory cultures of reality. Surrealism—at least, as represented by two of its leading exponents, Jean Cocteau and Salvador Dali—embodies a kind of wistful hope that the disintegration of existing institutions and forms can take place safely within an artistic vacuum; according to which assumption they can be recreated in more fantastic, charming and exciting forms.

The essential contrast between Surrealism and Muck Comedy is probably clearest in the occasional use of Surrealism by one of Muck's earliest and most popular promoters, Ernie Kovacs. About four months ago, I happened to see on television, as part of a comedy spectacular, Kovacs' own treatment of the Swan Lake Ballet, which he had re-cast, with gorillas—armed with bunches of bananas—playing the swan princes. This undoubtedly sounds like a choice addition to the culture-mugging campaign which is led by those people who outfit classical paintings with presumably uproarious captions. All I can say to those who missed the Kovacs show is, please accept my word for it that it was lovely; that the Tchaikovsky ballet, having been led down the garden path, was not subjected to any manhandling; and that the effect was of a haunting and disarming strangeness which recalled to me the best moments of Cocteau's *Beauty and the Beast*.

Apart from these lyrical interludes—which sometimes went rancid with coyness or self-felicitation—Kovacs' major specialty was demonstrating to his public the immeasurable crumbiness of so-called professional television. Kovacs—whose jutting cigar only needed an American flag hanging from it to complete the image of business-like confidence—would sashay about the studio, a smile of rakish self-importance rubber-stamped on his face, while there proceeded on all sides the combined activities of scavenger hunt and wrecking crew. One of his more quiet interludes was his rendition— outfitted in a ratty kimono—of a "genuine" Chinese folk-song entitled "Snow is Falling on Fujiyama," which he sang to the accompaniment of soft, white clouds of old mattress ticking and camphor flakes, lavished on him from above. One of his triumphs consisted of a commercial celebrating the allure of a kids' food product called Choco-Spin whereby the sponsors hoped to reform child diet. Choco-Spin consisted of spinach leaves immersed in melted chocolate; and, had it ever been undertaken seriously, Kovacs' ad might well have succeeded beyond easy belief. While a voice intoned the Choco-Spin story ("Your alimentary canal means something to the folks here at the Choco-Spin Factory!") a pair of hands were shown dipping and fondling the demoralized spinach leaves with the discreet voluptuousness of a professional haberdasher, or the lead in a stag movie. The result was a crude but perceptive realization of a childhood image for which Dr. Carl Jung might have sat in as technical advisor. As a matter of fact, many of Kovacs' rowdier sequences were counterpointed with a strain of child-like fantasy. One, which might almost have been a re-write of A. A. Milne, was a cliff-hanger serial using dolls as the actors, and a toy train when the heroine was tied to the railroad tracks. These childhood images usually carried an unemphasized directness which offset the possible sugariness of a big-time comic recalling his lost innocence.

Lennie Bruce's comedy also makes much use of boyishness; but Bruce's child is considerably older and a different type: the kid who delights himself at the twenty-five cent movie matinees, where he passes time between intermissions by yelling obscenities at the screen, guffawing or belching vociferously. Unlike Mort Sahl's intricate plaiting of wit, off-handedness and topicality, Bruce's loose-rigged skits feature a veering abandon whereby the comic often doesn't appear to know himself where he is going or even whether it will be funny, but hopes that his audience will enjoy the roller-coaster ride. His favorite burlesques translate some form of huckstering, like commercialized religion, into the sour-dry terms of Broadway hustling. Oral Roberts interrupts a sales conference with a request to the Pope: "Get me one of those Dago sports cars, will you?"

Bruce has been called—occasionally, by Bruce—a "sick

comic"; but in general this category includes only his worst stuff, like the skit based on a bomb disaster. This type of comedy is far more smug and queasy-mouthed than the best of Bruce's humor, which consists of playing a game of Russian roulette with absurdity, realism and his audience's feelings. Sick comedy in keeping with its name, utilizes the invalid's sense of superiority and smug cruelty; and any such fixed position, obviously, spells disaster for a comic whose forte is carefree spit-balling. Even in his best stuff, the reliance on Broadway attitudes and cute Yiddishisms sometimes undoes Bruce: you can't handle Broadway commercialism without some of the greasiness rubbing off, and he occasionally seems more glib and more arrogant than he can afford to. But his best routines make good use of an uncowed brashness which seems continually on the lookout for the chance absurdity of "respectable" institutions.

Probably the high mogul of Muck Comedy is *Mad* Magazine, most of whose brain-loose abandon seems to proceed from an inexorable resentment against decency, good taste, good art, restraint, and anything settled in contemporary humor or life. *Mad* is not only one of the most popular of American popular art works, but in a way archetypical, because its main theme and source of comedy is the conspicuous waste which is the staple of both American low art and most of American street-level life. A typical *Mad* panel is a tapestry of uncontrollably screaming figures, demolished kitchenware, pools and rivulets of indescribable fluid and those disasters which usually rate the choicest photo-space in the *New York Enquirer*. These cartoons mobilize the documentary naturalism of nineteenth-century drawing with a squirming, glossy senuousness which is reflected in the machinery, the blood and the coiffures and backsides of the beautiful girls who punctuate each episode. The main problem of the typical *Mad* sequence seems to be whether a genuinely funny gag or parody can shoulder its way through a deluge of gluttonous messiness and hyperbolic violence. Both the humor and the sheer awfulness of *Mad*—which are inseparable—depend on the intimate response of the New Yorker to the wastefulness with which he comes in direct or indirect contact every day: the scraps of discarded food which adorn the streets — New York's insignia ought to be a half-eaten pizza lying on the sidewalk—the junkiness of "aristocratic" fountain pens or nail-clippers which show the pampered obstinacy of aristocrats; the surfaces of billboards, brick walls, sidewalks, with their badges of mucus, erosion or obscene inscription. These sights have a kind of casual horror which is well beyond the bereaved sadness of which poverty is capable, because the everyday horror of New York is too blatant and self-conscious for the half-knowledge of tragedy. Probably the most original achievement of *Mad* and the whole vein of comedy which it stands for, was to realize so completely a dimension of American city life which—except, perhaps, in 1890's burlesque—has only been acknowledged indirectly or queasily, in popular humor. Probably its most obvious departure from earlier comedy—and this is true to a lesser extent of several recent comic trends—is that it sees the awfulness of modern life as something that isn't worth attempting to control, or submit to reason, but can only be wallowed in, for whatever laughs can be scavenged from the garbage-heap. The things in *Mad* that can be unquestionably called bad on its own terms consist of its nerve giving way: fizzled out gags, or lapses into simpering college-humor, like its burlesques of classical paintings or good middlebrow poems—parodies, like the one on "Wreck of the Hesperus," which usually strike a level of middle-browism far below that of the original.

Mad's current best—by which I mean, that which the greatest number of persons can read without a bottle of dramamine by their side—is probably embodied in Don Martin, whose unique degree and kind of madness deserve, and have received, a separate department in the magazine. Martin seems to be extendedly celebrating the removal of his fore-brain. His characters are of similar mind: each of them has cheerfully cashed in his eligibility for the human race, and gone off on a career of impersonating dead fish, corrupted jack-in-the-boxes or AWOL spools of toilet-paper. Each of Martin's episodes is a study in how expendable the ordinary human form can be. One of his best recent strips deals with a man who has sprung his neck (no, I can't put it more clearly) and visits a pair of dangerously mad chiropractors. The doctors, delighted with his condition, use him successively as a swivel-chair, then as a screw-driver; and finally—to the accompaniment of a gay little tune in which the patient joins—as a musical top.

I hope that this account of Muck Comedy has, above all, made clear what I think it is; without committing me as a fully-paid subscriber or as professional exterminator. Far more relevant than critical approval or disapproval is that Muck Comedy typifies a whole layer of American life to which much current criticism has paid scrupulous inattention except through the clumsy game of "Blind Man's Buff" with which some intellectuals think it politic to approach mass culture. For me, there is something not obviously, but certainly, wrong with any approach which requires a term like mass culture to cattle-pen a whole area of current living; and perhaps the Muck School of American Humor furnishes its own comment on this situation.

Notes
on a
Pernicious
Virtue

> ". . . only a crawling, growling polypod,
> sprinkling forth, a variety of voices, broken
> down into a variety of words . . ."
>
> Andrey Biely

> "For I believe that they are all the same
> man at heart and that a good one; and they
> can be brought together sooner or later . . .
>   "My system . . . might be called Mono-
> man or Manunity."
>
> Samuel Pollit

* * *

I have tolerated people who espouse tolerance for rather a long time, I suppose. The turning-point—getting-wise point, if you prefer—must have come at about the time when—in an article on a very tenuously related subject—I praised what I called the good Jewish intellectual liveliness and good Jewish visceral energy, of a certain venerated drama critic; whereupon I was treated to a cataract of reproachful pieties, from an acquaintance (and fellow-admirer of the man I was discussing). He maintained that (a) the traits I endorsed were to be found among other nations and (b) that we are born individuals. An old friend and a humanist: his argument's locutions didn't quite add up to the little word "racist"; but then, one of us had to observe the Judaeo-Christian civilities. Something, however, must have been happening to me even then: while I hadn't quite the stomach, or the patience, to pursue the argument, I at least rejected sulking and chafing, for some reasonably pointed questions. The most pertinent of these can be gathered under two headings: Did I say what he thought I said? and, Did he mean what *he* said?

To begin with: Did I mean that *all* Jews, *everywhere*, possess certain inherent traits, which reside in their Jewish glands and muscles, are distilled throughout their Jewish blood, their Jewish nerve endings?

Obviously not, for several reasons; the most relevant one being, that if I believed such an assumption, the emphasis, and phrasing, of my remark must have been completely different. I would then be referring to (as I saw it) a universal truth; so, would not allude so directly to this or that "good Jewish" characteristic (does one speak of "handsome Negro darkness?" I should be more oblique, not more candid. Exponents of tolerance may have trouble grasping this point; since (for reasons I'll try to expand a little later) they are devotees and arch-manipulators of clichés: those perennial candidates for truth, which can stage numerous public appearances, since the vagueness of their position usually forestalls their becoming unbearable.

If I concede that other peoples possess the traits for which I complimented the Jews, does *that* invalidate my observation? No; since I have conceded that the remark does not apply to Jews universally: having disclaimed false certainty, I can make free with uncertainty. I know that other peoples possess those traits; but I do not know in what proportions among various groups (any more than does my friend; nor, I wager, a sizeable number of statistics-flaunting anthropologists). Nor am I at all sure that every national, ethnic and religious community possesses even the criteria for those qualities. For example, do the Maoris possess the standards for "intellectual live-

liness?" I would doubt that intellect as western civilization defines it, matters one whit to the Maoris or to many
other primitive nations; although surely, like all human
beings, they entertain standards of *intelligence:* which
they may define as wit, or skill, or spirit, or whatever.
Does "visceral energy" obtain in every national group
imaginable? Again, I don't think so: calling to mind the
impoverished gypsy tribes of Spain (depicted by Bunuel
in *Terre Sans Pain*); or, perhaps, the Carmelites and similar ascetic groups. Appetite, yes; health, yes, even among
the moribund and leprous. If I were willing to reduce my
phrase to these elementary human terms, there would be
no more to say. But I am referring, not to elementary
human traits, but to human-created complexes of traits;
namely, the characteristics of *style.*

The exponents of tolerance list among their impedimenta of sweet reasonableness, the demand that you
break down your terms. I would insist, in reply, that
some terms cannot be broken down (into the tongue of
tolerance, which, naturally, sings its maker's praises).

To my next question: Since I was not referring to universal Jews, to whom was I referring? Or, what was my
object? I answer, that I was referring to a single individual, the distinguished man whom I thought to
praise; my object being, to focus his individuality through
the lens of his cultural—*not* "racial"—heritage: the tradition of craftsmanship, the dialectical apparatus, the reconciliation of spiritual and temporal values, which has
distinguished Jewish intellectual tradition at least since
Hillel and Maimonides. Even if "all" other peoples possessed such traditions (and what am illuminating commentary on tolerance, that its exponents should impose
such demands on their fellows!) does one deny praise to
the Jews? Even a million Michelangeloes (not beyond
belief) would not entitle us to withhold praise of the one
we know.

Is it even possible to conceive of *individuals,* except as in relief, against the cumulae of "generals": cultures, tribes, nations? If it is impossible to say that character traits are inherent in races, is it not monstrous to propose that "individuality" is inherent in *all* nations, everywhere? Thus placing on each single man, the burdens of his culture. By Norman Corwin's standards, this may be feasible; not by mine. *Is it not more nearly right to see individuality as an electricity, sparked by the collisions, or simply rubbings, of the man against the culture?*

The concept of tolerance to which I refer, however, opposes such a notion of individuality; and, indeed, as I shall try to show, individuality itself. For I believe, and wish to demonstrate, that tolerance has lost that original meaning which, even today, bequeaths to the word a Chanel #5 of sanctity. The increase of communications —and of people—and the corresponding multiplication of reasons, of alternatives to which any man can feel he has access: such extended pluralism may account, in part—in great part—for the corruption of tolerance; which no longer advises us to judge with attention to the situation which we are judging; but, rather, tells us, usually with glib misreading of the New Testament, not to judge at all; to suspend judgment permanently; and, along with it, our common sense, and the more fundamental part of our self-respect. Yet, so obviously negative an attitude must operate from a purpose, a marshalling drive. This, I shall presently attempt to amplify.

One target of the tolerists is the Italian journalist, Barzini; whose book, *The Italians,* attempted to rally the consciences of individual Italians, by apostrophizing the Italian nation *as an individual:* as a collective type. Many readers might have seen Barzini's work as a chivalrous, if angry, gesture on behalf of the individual; but not "Judge" Michael Mussmano (whose title I enclose in quotes, not to cast doubt on its authenticity, but to barricade it symbolically from the buffooneries of its owner.) All a-bloop with his patented righteous hysterics, Juge Mussmano accused Barzini of stereotyping, and fostering anti-Italian hostility; and, borne ahead by his outraged idealism, even produced, as counterattack, a book about LaGuardia, Caruso, and a roster of Italian-American celebrities: a work which, so far as I know, can only be found now in those public libraries whose fun-loving custodians have bestowed it in the "Sociology" section

Another *bete noir* of tolerance is LeRoi Jones, who—in much of his personal journalism of the 1950's, and especially in his occasional pieces for *Kulchur*—was scaldingly acerbic about writers, like James Baldwin, who made commodity of their "individual" sensibilities.

LeRoi's most recent critics (their number much increased since 1961) have, I think, scanted the most important contribution (despite the tarnish of his frequent opportunism and extravagance) of his latest performances. He has contributed to America a genuine Negro theatre: the product not exclusively or even predominantly of his ill-starred Black Arts Theatre; but of his often remarkable personal essays in *Kulchur* of the fifties and early sixties; and of his poetry, in *Preface to a Twenty Volume Suicide Note* and *The Dead Lecturers;* in which he dons a variety of costumes—vaudeville hoofer, Alpine climber, cowboy—and identifies himself with pop-heroes of the thirties like Nick Charles; Duke Mantee; and Dr. Fu Manchu; always with the disarming balance of mockery and wistfulness toward his sporty disguises; always with the ultimate object of illuminating himself, in the glossy highlights of the adopted personalities.

His most recent costume, of course, has been the purple cape and leopard-skin headdress of Black Muslimism. Thus identifying himself with a widely-publicized body of Negro militancy, he has also, I think, gone gravely if not disastrously wrong: i.e., by submitting himself to the machinery of publicity which previously ingested his old opponent, Baldwin. Indeed: in doing so, LeRoi has demonstrated, however obliquely, that his awareness of individuality's importance is no less intense than Baldwin's; because the old, good traits of his *Kulchur* essays and poems—the short-fused wit, the mock-leisurely poise; the common-sensical shrewdness, flashing through the moss of specious romanticism—surface again and again, like a glimpsed familiar face, in the harrowing tedium of a strange mob. Just these, the medallions of his grace, are LeRoi Jones' real gifts to the Negro people—focussed, for those seeking them, by the filter of his recent demagoguery and grandstanding. The tolerance people never sought such evidence of personal grace; but rather, clove, whooping with delicious horror, to the tailgate of LeRoi Jones's Black Maria.

LeRoi Jones reminds the rest of us that even the much-abhorred stereotype—even the most flagrant, at that—can serve as costume for individuality: that is, not merely dress, or armour, but a means of focussing the role. In LeRoi's case, it would appear to suggest also—this preference for dressing-up—a solicitude for his individuality, an instinct for tactical concealment—which is really not so different, at times, from the self-defensiveness which he scorns in Baldwin and Abrahams. But he has sought his *own* costumes.

Individuality is not a location, but a means of changing location, or of being changed by it. When we apply types or categories or even stereotypes to the sighting of individuality, we ought to do so, not as though drawing a map, but as though charting a course on a ship. When such categories are badly used, we do not smother individuality: we blind and stifle ourselves; acknowledging that our compass is shattered. But this possibility does not say that individuality cannot, and should not, be evaluated, by those who can do it.

Does tolerance recognize individuality? I think not, in terms of the reasons indicated above. Tolerance can conceive of individuality *only* in terms of location, of terrain. No: it can't even truly *conceive* of individuality; for it refuses to recognize the only terms—immeasurability, inequality, style—which define the individual. Tolerance boasts that it "allows for" individuality. Exactly: you cannot "allow for" individuality, you cannot make a vacancy for individuality. To do so, is to build an altar "to the unknown god". From the viewpoint of tolerance, individuality stands in dire need of niches and caves: cowering, brittle, infinitely vulnerable. But those vacancies were not designed for the terrific energy of individuality. They serve as refuge for the squeamish spirit of the tolerant man: which pulls in its horns when the individual shows itself.

*   *   *

Of what is tolerance composed?

(1) *Greed.* Specifically, the greed for the unfamiliar. Like all greeds, that of tolerance is born of the desire, not for its apparent object, but for desire itself: self-perpetuating desire; desire which can be trusted to supply its own energy (but never does); desire which, in due course, will consume its owner. Such is the open mind, on which tolerance vaunts itself; but which had better be called, the Open Maw. The personification of the Open Mind is Bernanos' leech-protagonist, Monsieur Ouine; with his mania for cleanliness, so tumescent that, in dead of night, he hears the cracking and pattering of the sods he has scraped and chipped away. The open mind of tolerance aspires to love that which it consumes; but it cannot truly consume the unfamiliar, the new, the individual. For tolerance, every instance of newness has the same value, or non-value: rather than consume, it shrivels.

The man who genuinely seeks "the good" in every

ideology/attitude/man would exemplify a discipline, as well as an ardor, scarcely excelled by the most stringent Dominicans. For, against the onslaught of each new good, he would have to re-orient his own sets, recast his weapons, and, above all, prepare to be disarmed each time. The tolerant man requires no such vigilance, no such accessibility: he cares only for the *existence* of the new, not for its identity; for the juice lingering from what he has compulsively spat out.

(2) *Fear*. Specifically, the fear of being wrong. That is, the fear of boundaries; which the tolerant man dreads, as reflections of his own boundaries, which he abhors even to face. The most genuinely flexible men I have read, or known—Igor Stravinsky, Shaw, Professor Morris Roberts, Richard Howard, Gil Sorrentino—are also, by no coincidence at all, the most positive in their antipathies, prejudices, judgments. Tolerance would say: If they only weren't so dogmatic! But that very dogmatism, for the man of any intellect, is the *means* of flexibility. It is not an outpost, but a vehicle; and his seeming stiffness is only the stance of the captain on the bridge. They are "wrong headed" only in their eagerness to do battle with wrongness, with the unmanly fear of wrongness. Tolerance, by contrast, is immobile; because tolerance, like a senile stock-holder clipping his coupons while the company business goes on without him, settles for shares and snippets and tokens of the outlying world. Instead of colliding with ideas, it softens them, or tries to, with the saliva, "interesting." "Interesting" renders the most outlandish chunks malleable and harmless; although, in contrast with wasp venom, it only paralyzes the user.

* * *

Tolerance dreads certainty, with a teen-age virgin's dread of imaginary rapists; and it uses certainty in a parallel way, to quicken itself. "You're not *certain!* You *can't* be certain!" It brandishes a spinster forefinger under any speculative nose. But speculation loves certainty, and courts it with an often sheik-like ardor. Speculation, unlike tolerance, knows that scientific certainty is the exclusive property of scientists (a truth admittedly hard to keep in mind, so often has it been contraverted by ministers and writers who ought to rely on its own terms; which, unlike those of tolerance, are not cribbed and diluted from scientific terminology). Such terms affirm boundaries, rather than deny them; starting with the boundaries of a man's own body. But the terms of faith recognize that the boundaries are those of a vehicle, whose tracks can lead anywhere, as far as—and, fairly often, intersecting with—the tracks of science. Such is the meaning of *commitment, position.*

I hope that, as an editor, I would never print the works of LeRoi Jones, or Revilo P. Oliver, or M. P. Shiel, or other outstanding reactionaries and bigots, because I found them "interesting," by the definition outlined above. On the other hand, I would go down on my knees to print these men's jeremiads and hortations, if their own reckless tracks—tracks! no matter how undulating or wilderness-bound—offered directions for my thinking, for my character.

How, then, should intolerance be defined? (In terms of the opprobrium which is, often unjustly, assigned the word) The intolerance to reject, I think, is that which limits life unwarrantedly: which peels off strips of life, from fear of swallowing the tuber whole. It is *not* what we so often call intolerance: that hostility to tolerance which engages the whole being, which enlists one's entire sense of life and of one's self; so that, in fact, the steam pressure of one's commitment is so overwhelming, one can only discharge it—which is to say, express it—through the spigot of a seemingly narrow belief, or attitude: which, however, is not narrow in the sense of stopping or confining; but only in the sense of providing intense access to one's sense of reality, and dedication to it. The difficulty comes when you think the valve is still functioning, whereas it has actually ceased, has clogged and the issue of emotion caked, leaving only a fetid trickle: i.e., bigotry.

Bigotry and tolerance both aim to cripple the body of a man's faith, which is to say, the body of man: bigotry through paralytic constriction, tolerance through paretic softening.

*　　*　　*

I suggest that the current popular liberal notion of tolerance as a cardinal virtue, is, in fact, a self-protective reaction against violence, which now appears to be following a curve of inflation parallel to that of money. Violence has even acquired its own system of checks and credit cards—words, speeches, even chance phrases—which are convertible at a moment's notice into the most extraordinarily disproportionate quantities of violence. Tolerance makes the classic error of identifying violence—which is short-lived and essentially uncontrollable—with force— which is massive and eminently controllable; and thus, hysterically, sees the violence of rape and castration in the force of ideas and commitments; thus, tries to circumvent such violences by divesting ideas of their force, by ingesting all of them; which is, in fact, attempted suicide, self-inundation, through the exercise of monstrous greed. Not that good suicide, by which the doer tries, as it were, to drag life with him into death, one corner snagged between his teeth.

Leroi Jones,
Discovered
Alone

Although at least two of LeRoi Jones' plays *Dutch-man* and *The Slave*—are easily to be seen, or read, by New Yorkers, his essays have yet to be made handily available through reprinting. Most of these personal journalisms and reviews of books, poems and jazz recordings (also, one uproarious movie critique: his piece on Otto Preminger's *Porgy And Bess;* well worth hunting down, in whatever literary Casbah Hentoff and Williams' *Jazz Review* now occupies) can be found in various issues of *Kulchur,* most of which, happily, can still be bought in Village bookstores such as the Eighth Street Bookshop. Mr. Jones tells me that publishers, always chary of small forms like essays and short stories (an elephantine reflex?) have held out against anthologizing his essays—a sorry decision, in view of the essays' pelting impact, their dexterity and compactness, as of sea anemones, their eloquence and their crankiness, superior in certain respects to the distinctions of Mr. Jones' plays. Read collectively, in the magazines where they first appeared, they offer a fluid LeRoi Jones anthology, with the side-gravy of reading Mr. Jones in his original element: the company of writers such as Gil Sorrentino and Joel Oppenheimer and Edward Dorn, with whom he has always worked and conversed; and the further context of that reality with which —jauntily or irritably—he has been equally conversant.

Conversant and, in a particular way, obligated—very much as the Japanese couple in *Woman in the Dunes* is conversant with, and obligated to, the element which imprisons them. Reality to LeRoi Jones is adversary and partner; and, in the view which is clear to me from his writing, his vocation gives him no dominion over reality, no right—as it did in the view of so many nineteenth-century writers—to remake reality; anymore than it gives him the right, as James Baldwin suggests it gives James Baldwin, to separate his individuality, like a Holy of Holies, from the profaning jostle of the world.

Yet, his own concern with individuality centers and accelerates the series of LeRoi Jones' essays and reviews. Its imprint, like the reverse side of a letter, is seen on his complaints and diatribes against the clichés of role-playing and the mechanisms of false individuality; above all, the mystiques of phony or self-infatuated estheticism. Here, in his review of the "avant garde" volume *An Anthology of Chance Operations* (see *Kulchur*, #13, Spring, 1964) or his polemic against Baldwin and the South African journalist, Peter Abrahams (*Brief Reflections on Two Hot Shots, Kulchur*, #12, Winter, 1963) Mr. Jones seems to be responding from a fleet current of witty commonsense, translucent and unpontifical, in which his discernments of foolery and duplicity appear like intuitive flashes. Here, as in the best of his poetry, the writing is briskly empirical and pragmatic; the style off-handedly elegant behind the lasso-like colloquial rhythms; the observations disguised as aphoristic wise-cracks, whose flipness is as misleading as their casualness:

"Jackson MacLow is dull because he thinks you're going to learn something from him. I knew an old man once in Newark who could whistle with peas in his mouth. Nobody ever called him hip."

"How can a painting tell you people are vulgar (unless the painter has put a microphone in it, out of which comes the voice of Stanley Gould . . .) and if it did that it *should* be picketed, having traduced every viewer who has ever seen Donald O'Connor without being convinced it was art."

"You cannot tell me what I mean by Socialism. Only I can tell you. But I can tell you what Mr. Abrahams means, and what Mr. Baldwin means, and they will not even open their mouths, to say anything, but that they are well dressed, educated and have feelings that are easily hurt."

Speaking of microphones, would not these comments, with their sealed-up fun and nasty accuracy, sound appropriate from behind a night-club monologuist's microphone?—provided the night-club monologuist were a poet. Such passages, for me, side-swipe the quirky, sour-sweet, provocative essays of Paul Goodman (I think not only of the rather too-much-bruited socio-political essays, but the too-little-praised literary reviews, as well as the excellent film reviews which *Moviegoer* has reprinted from *Partisan Review*). Both writers regard their poetic roles as visas through all manner of social terrain; both care, in this regard, not about establishing their official credentials as social critics; but rather about the *laisser passer* afforded them by *language* (plus, of course, such personal knowledge as they carry in their knapsacks). Both, I suspect, owe much to French journalism, and both—together with several contemporaries—claim an ever-increasing debt from American journalism for their enlivening and intensifying of its uses.

The important difference of the two writers lies, I think, in their *personae*. Goodman has always (i.e., since the outset of his critical career) adopted the pseudo-naive voice of an outsider, a wise kibitzer who is detached from social establishments but very much involved in their functioning. This paradoxical stance of involved detachment enables Goodman at his best to engage in seeming hyperbole and romanticism (he prefers Utopianism) without lessening the value of his analyses and finger-pointing. LeRoi Jones hasn't any such high-comic detachment, such formulating instinct, as Goodman. As a Negro, he finds himself, not at the peripherae, but at the center of the events he contends with, even in his literary role. Where Goodman plots and diagrams, Jones singles out instances and details, nail-heads of the truths which he accepts and expects his readers to accept.

His eclecticism, I think, is closely attached to this involvement. More than a shifting of techniques and voices, it involves a nervously pragmatic attentiveness, and a sense of style as response to an endless succession of challenges and pressures. Above all, it means in LeRoi Jones' case, I believe, a goading awareness of writing's perishability before the world one knows about; but, added to such awareness, one's determination to make writing not capital, but perhaps a foraging tool, and weapon.

Insofar as such eclecticism doesn't mean a mere trying-on of various costumes, it is mainly to the good, I think, in the essays. But it is also, on occasion, a component of LeRoi Jones' worst writing. I think of his romanticism, which has shown up, rather disastrously, in some of the more recent political pieces: the one in 1959-60 on Castro's Cuba; some of occasional writing on civil rights and Negro militarism. When I say "romanticism," I mean rather a yearning for romanticism; for that sort of grandiose vision, overarching those meanly practical considerations which LeRoi Jones has shown himself capable of seeing so clearly. When Mr. Jones gets away any considerable distance from the specific object, whether book or event (his descriptions of the Castro supporters' rallies shimmer with vivacious life) he seems to leave the plains country of his best polemical journalism, and enter a strange, gaseous bayou terrain, strewn with rubbishy phrases about cutting throats, or the stupidity or perfidy of *all* white liberals—rubbish which has been left behind by such litter-bugs as Jimmy Baldwin and John Oliver Killens. This is excruciatingly true of his letter to the *New York Review of Books,* in which he proposed to refute Philip Roth's critique of *Dutchman.* I can only feel relief that this letter is not at hand for quotation; particularly since Roth, replying, exceeded himself for wit and composure.

II

None of this applies, however, to such occasionals as LeRoi Jones' review of *Porgy and Bess;* and it applies in only limited fashion to his *Brief Reflections on Two Hot Shots,* one of his most important recent articles. Mr. Jones' irritation at two eminent Negro journalists (James Baldwin in particular; poor Abrahams seems mainly to have been, in police parlance, picked up riding in the same car; especially since, although Jones quotes from Abrahams throughout, and Baldwin almost not at all, it is Baldwin's presence which bulks largest) is based on their self-estimate as individuals. The opening quote which he cites is Abrahams' comment about his indecision as to whether to spend a revolutionary weekend as guest of Kamyatta, or a colonialist-journalistic weekend in a hotel furnished by the British government: ". . . It dawned on me that I had become, for the moment, the battlefield of that horrible animal, the racial struggle. I made up my mind, resenting both sides. . . ." Mr. Jones' prompt response is, that: "[Abrahams' statement] curdles the blood when you realize that it is coming from a black man, and not the innocent white liberal made fierce by homosexuality." He notes of Abrahams that he is "sickening beyond belief," "out-baldwining James," and adds, "Why should anyone think of these men as individuals?"

If the entirety of the three-and-one-half page essay featured mere elaboration of these statements, and their tone, I don't mind saying that I would probably regard it as his worst: the arm-flailing, hear-ye-ing embodiment of all those demagogic faults I have mentioned. Yet, what follows not only counterbalances but to a considerable extent vindicates, by clarifying, the overbearing militarism of these quoted passages. For, in the remainder, LeRoi Jones goes on to elucidate his own feelings about individuality:

"If one has nothing TO SAY but, 'I can feel,' or 'I am intelligent,' there is really no need saying it. These things in themselves are very boring. So many people are intelligent, and, you bet, sensitive. Unless a man will tell you something, pass on some piece of information, about the world, and by so doing, show you that part of the world he moves in, there is little value in what he is saying. It is like a high diver perfecting all his moves in the house."

Here, the cockiness of tone is plainly only a point-up of the reflective, even patient basic tone, with its more generous humor. And, more:

"Individuality is only gained by first realizing that it is not important in its most superficial states. The quality of an idea (or life) makes it singular: what it is about. It must be specific and useful, and function in the world; be, even, an interpretation of that world, that permits a man to use himself. The singular man uses, first, himself. That is why he is singular. Because few do."

The touchstone of these passages' honesty is, I think, their emphasis on the tone of the *craftsman*: the tone of an instructor rather than of a high-priest or a parade-ground generalissimo. Such craftsmanship, I submit, is the powerful norm of LeRoi Jones' morality, as of what is best in his writing. And here, his sense of the writer's vocation helps focus those truths which, on other occasions in similar essays, have been distended by rhetoric.

But, more: the sort of epigram-as-coda which LeRoi Jones himself seldom achieves:

"If Abrahams and Baldwin try to forget about this struggle, and be individuals, some gruff realist brings them back, usually with one not even carefully chosen word or phrase. That is a very shaky individuality to my mind. Where I am most singular, in the taking hold of material presented me each second by the world, there is not the least chance that one word is going to throw me back, and into some chattery panic. But knowing what is the world's and what is your own, is to me a very priceless and basic knowledge."

This, then, is not a claim that a Negro must needs be a certain kind of individual, a high-pistoning engine of social upheaval. He says, rather, that personality, in Negroes as in all men, is not a hidden diamond mine nor secret gland, to be tended and prayed over and propitiated. Nor has he any patience with the thought that such things as ethnic heritage and social circumstance are only a sort of masquerade costume, with which writers like Baldwin can, as Zorros, titillate their white public, all the time assuring them that the disguise is their making. I dislike much of Baldwin's writing, and I don't think that I am crying "peace, peace" when I suggest that neither Baldwin's nor the unfortunate Abrahams' presence, stage front, is necessary for us to appreciate the forcefulness and rightness of Mr. Jones' major premise, or to recognize those — not only those two writers, indeed! — who jump to his sharp whistle.

His position, I find, is really not so very different, in all important respects, from Ralph Ellison's in the extraordinary essay, "The World and the Jug": that the relationship of individual Negroes to their situation, like that of all men entitled to call themselves individuals, is the relationship of fishermen to the tides with which they struggle, barter, occasionally almost merge, throughout their lives. That LeRoi Jones presents this as — in the best possible sense — an esthetic confrontation, the problem of an artist, only re-inforces the validity of his statements, at their best, as statements by a Negro for Negroes. And, at their best — at *his* best — his comments are those of a realist, whose running contest with the world is his vindication and joy.

Dashiell Hammett's
Magnum Opus

Dashiell Hammett's originality is summarized in a banal phrase: he believed in his world, that it was the only world. He participated in this world, yet was not entirely of it: surveying, recording, maintaining clarity. In terms of these functions only, the Continental Op stories remain as Hammett's most successful writing. The Op, although allegedly directly influenced by Hammett's Pinkerton experiences, is Hammett's least autobiographical hero, and his least romantic. Hammett's other protagonists — Ned Beaumont, Sam Spade, Nick Charles — all represent increasingly romanticized prisms of Hammett's character, with Beaumont easily the most accurate and appealing. In comparison, the Op is an exercise in self-suppression — even his outward traits — fat, forty — are, obviously deliberately, completely at variance with Hammett's when he began the series.

The Op was a perfect functionary, and, as such, his role in his universe was both passive *and* controlling. By contrast, Spade and Charles dominate their worlds by charm and bullying and maneuvering; but their worlds also seem carpentered for them, the supporting characters too apparently their foils (although Spade's crypto-criminous ruthlessness is convincing for a while).

Unfortunately Lillian Hellman, in her notes on Hammett introducing the recent anthology *The Big Knockover*, only adds to the gallery of Hammett's self-romanticizations her own, whereby Hammett emerges as a charming, occasionally benevolent but rather steely autocrat, who commanded instinctive respect from writers who had never met him before, walked out on someone who bluffed about his knowledge of existentialism, and, in general, behaved like one of those worthy, stiff-spined old ladies in Miss Hellman's plays. Although Hammett seems to have solicited no such *magnificat* from Miss Hellman, the increasing tone of his writing, from *The Maltese Falcon* through the unfinished *Tulip*, suggests that he did little to discourage the *paterfamilias* image.

Beside those devilish and mellow cavaliers, Spade and Charles, Ned Beaumont and the Op are rather passive men, vitalized mainly by their dedication to their jobs, and, intertwined with that dedication, their devotion to personal ties — particularly their filial attachment to their bosses: Beaumont to the political boss, Paul Madig (in one of the best American political novels ever written) and the Op to the Old Man, head of the Continental Agency. Beaumont is gallant and forebearing, but also the most vulnerable of Hammett's heroes: a lunger, as Hammett had become, and a physical pushover. There runs through his adventures, as through many of the Op's (particularly the masterpieces, *Red Harvest* and the two-part *Big Knockover*) a threnody of anxiety, of imminent assault by the world. Such anxiety, I think, was of a piece with that need for insularity and order which made Hammett a sometime devotee of mathematics and music. In *The Glass Key* and the Op stories, he apprehended both the desire for order and its futility in a world from which the principle of order has vanished. From the apprehension, he evolved an art which constantly points to the territory beyond art. His genuine role was not that of the manipulator Spade, but the surveyor Op — the Eye, recording and focussing. He seems there to have realized that he had no other control over the world; and, through such realization, the Op becomes the natural center of his universe, the Eye of the Hurricane, and the natural extension of a crass, extravagant, incessantly tumbling landscape.

Hammett's very special sort of romanticism was the counter-force to his awareness of the world. It was the romanticism, evidently, of a man lacking the capacity to *build* his own truth. His were the instincts of a formulizer and tabulator, but by no means a passionless one. The mechanism he devised through his prose was, quite obviously I think, an act of desperation. He was, by Miss Hellman's report, a compulsive reader who might have been much more highly, not to say more accurately, honored in the 18th or early 19th centuries. A romantic, in other words, of sufficiently omnivorous curiosity and sufficiently constricted, though luminously graphic imagination, to seek whatever mechanisms might be available for locating rather than constructing his truth. The mechanism which he evolved, marvellously, was a plot comprising a series of episodes — apparently separate, yet overlapping, like the squares of a Mondrian painting — which, in their very neatness, highlighted the chaos from which they sprang. Nor did the "solution" — usually, the climax to a succession of minor solutions — restore or impose order. Only truth was restored, reality justified.

Hammett's very dread of reality and awareness of its insistence combine, I think, to involve the reader in his world as unconditionally as in that of any imaginative writer since Defoe. He never insists on this reality, never solicits the reader to engage in it. He is totally opposed, in this, to the trend represented by writers like John D. MacDonald (the recent MacDonald, in particular) who seem intent on peering at reality through an official eye — not the private eye of Hammett — which they demonstate through little journalistic essays on Florida, the pollution problem, modern art, the unions, interspersed throughout the story; with the usual result that their own inventions disintegrate completely. Hammett is no journalist but, simply, his own witness.

The creative imagination in Hammett's work usually takes the form of lying. A poet is a blackmailer; a murderous lawyer invents a "new life" for his bludgeoned client; a writer becomes a multiple killer and fiendish persecutor. All of these creatures are parasites; all of them exercise over their associates, and the heroes, the same alluring bedevilment. They represent the formidable counterforce to reality which, I think most clearly, Hammett sensed within himself as an alternate form of self-destruction. In his unfinished story, *Tulip*, Hammett, in his own person, meets this counterforce, embodied in a loquacious, boozy, tirelessly scheming army buddy who continually urges Hammett to collaborate with him in a book about their James Jonesish past. He represents the truth which is no longer true — the insidious aspect of creativity which Hammett, with his rational puritanism, must have felt as the most virulent mask of the Adversary.

The cleavages which Hammett felt within himself were most frequently dramatized in terms of a classic opposition: the war between generations. Reviewing Hammett's four novels, we find the murder of a son by his father; of a mother by her daughter; the rivalry of mother and daughter for an older man; and a girl's excessively intense devotion to her murdered brother. In at least two Hammett stories which come immediately to mind, older men (a) turn over to the police and (b) kill after deliberate provocation, young men whom they have regarded as sons. Hammett himself, we are made aware by Miss Hellman's account, embodied both the benevolent (though occasionally strict) father, in his relations with her and with other younger writers, and the rebellious son, in his relations with his superiors at the Pinkerton Agency and his earlier jobs, and with the government, which he defied during the congressional investigations, and with the Communist Party, of which he is said to have been bluntly critical. Even were Miss Hellman's report only fractionally true, Hammett's fiction is incontrovertible. The Continental Op personifies the good daddy in his relationship with his clients (especially in *The Dain Curse*) and, if not rebellious, the sometimes recalcitrant son in his relationship to his boss, The Old Man — the most coldly severe and, at the same time most impressive, father in Hammett. Sam Spade is the bad daddy, with his (calculated) rages, his aura of unsavoury sexuality and his ruggedly satanic aspect. The very recurrence of this theme in Hammett's work, objectifying his creative stresses, insures the genuine originality of his work. And those stresses, never overcome, were reconciled forcibly by Hammett's morality of work, in which the work of writing became one with the work of detection: an act of seeing clearly and saying plainly.

The
Runners

The heroes of Allan Dwan's best films, I would suggest, are fugitives: people figuratively, or more often actually, on the run. Their terrain (in films like *Tennessee's Partner, Montana Belle, Slightly Scarlet, Silver Lode, The Restless Breed*) is a broken field of guilt and suspicion and misunderstanding; which, in tally, suggests Hitchcock. But, unlike Hitchcock, Dwan's interest is in his heroes' resourcefulness, their athletic suppleness, even — especially — their innocence and grace. Unlike Hitchcock, he shows no interest in pummeling or immobilizing them; quite the opposite. Dwan is a former football player with Rockne, a former director of Douglas Fairbanks (*Robin Hood, A Modern Musketeer*). The skimmings and skirtings and manipulations of his characters assume — the more space they're given — the double fascination, grace and contest, of a great sporting event.

His concern with movement offers a strong reason, I suspect, why Dwan, in the thirties and early forties, so often seems to have been a clearing-house for some of Hollywood's most formidable brassware. The Ritz Brothers, Shirley Temple — But seeing the Ritzes' *Three Musketeers*, or Shirley's *Heidi* — or a worthier piece of pottery, *Friendly Enemies* (1941) featuring the two Charlies, Winninger and Ruggles, as German Americans floundering among divided loyalties — Dwan surprises me repeatedly by his equalness to the task. My first recollection of *Heidi* is neither Shirley herself, nor even Jean Hersholt's Alm Uncle (with those oddly Santa Claus-like whiskers on the rough old hermit); but the delightful wooden shoe ballet which Shirley sings and executes, about halfway through the film; its buoyant, arc-ing figures and controlled picture-book backdrop, so far from Johanna Spyri's warm reality, but close to authentic, quite physical fantasy.

But for me, who have seen very little of Dwan's silent work (though its obvious legacies help make his work today lively and original), the pivot of his best films lies with a few brilliant, compact, quite overlooked comedies filmed by him in the middle forties: *Brewster's Millions, Up in Mabel's Room, Getting Gertie's Garter, Rendez-vous With Annie.* Three of these — the first three — were free adaptations of decades-old Broadway farces; the second and third were what once were called "bed-room farces". In all of them, however, Dwan reduced the conventions of second-rate stage humor to pure speed: these comedies are fantasies of speed and maneuver, all prurience (except what serves to clock the players) boiled away: seamless, translucent, and not so much funny as exhilirating; the laughter is that of excitement and relief, paired as at a hockey game or horse race. The actors look longer, less heavy, more reed-like than ever before: Dennis O'Keefe, Marie MacDonald, Ruth Hussey, Jerome Cowan. Again, his heroes are eluders and evaders of archetypal kind: entangled by lies and misunderstandings, adding to their number, O'Keefe and Cowan and Eddie Albert keep their films alive by their quick, sinuous navigations; and an incriminating garter or lingerie, an inconvenient million dollars, becomes a marker in an intensely followed paper-chase.

I'm not talking about themes; Dwan's preoccupations are not themes in the sense that they are structured or amplified, or intended to emerge through the films; they are, simply, *preoccupations,* and they are simply there. Nor would consistency of theme matter in the slightest if Dwan were a mediocre artist (many of whom have exhibited thematic consistency). But he is an artist of intense dedication, recurrent freshness (especially in those films made when he was well into his seventies) and acute beauty — and the beauty of finely-executed, well-gauged motion, which he loves in his characters and displays in his visual style. Thus does the content of his films at last become their theme: that the sheer ability to stay on one's feet can be at last self-redemptive and lovely.

Dwan's best films seem to me triumphs of brisk, clear intelligence which can extract the essentials of narrative and character from a shaggy screenplay; an economy which fuses expediency and elegance (so that a high-budgeter like *Suez* and a cheapie like *Silver Lode* show the same urbane fluidity;) and a quiet intensity of storytelling which follows even clichés which their screenwriters have stopped believing in, to their natural conclusions. Thus the vaguenesses of an underwritten script can afford Dwan genuine perceptions about the shiftiness of innocence and worldiness, or evil — qualities which are constantly changing hats in his films. Even in a tacky little Dorothy Lamour reject like *Pearl of the South Pacific*, I got a pleasant start watching Virginia Mayo's hilarious camp of a sea-going doxie impersonating a lady missionary — next to *White Heat*, the best casting I've seen of this second-string Susan Hayward. And in the same picture, the usually-unctuous Basil Ruysdael has been coaxed into giving a cold arrogance to the role of the islanders' benevolent white leader.

A signal specimen of Dwan's talents, though not one of my favorites, is *The Restless Breed*, in which — from a skimpy script and production, and such usual deadweights as Scott Brady and Rhys Williams—Dwan at times elicited a subtly disquieting reversal of *High Noon* — type western values. Here, the entire suspense comes from Dwan's visualization of Brady's zigzag course between opposing moralities. Determined to trap and murder the smuggler who killed his sheriff-father, Brady is argued at by sheriff (a relatively subdued Jay C. Flippen) and minister (Williams, who stands here and there, turning his Toby Jug ogle to the camera to convey piety) who represent morality; and the minister's ward, an all-but-mute Ann Bancroft, who doesn't want him to get killed. Well, after a number of centuries, this remains a promising plot-situation — but only when good writing uses it. Dwan, however, turns the film into a web of sinuous, evasive motion. Brady is kept in the foreground — getting drunk, bullying hangers-on at the bar, snuggling with Miss Bancroft — and, in a stunningly executed sequence, dispatching three or four of the boss heavy's aids in a brilliant synchronization of ambush tactics. Even Brady's beefy petulance is turned to the advantage of the hero's late-adolescent ambiguity. The result frequently suggests an extended pantomime of a man struggling to free himself from obsession.

But my favorite Dwans are complicated jobs like *Passion* and *The Most Dangerous Man Alive* and *Tennessee's Partner*: with their coruscations of plot, their picaresque chains of incident, through which Dwan traces a skein of narrative logic. The dual effect of these films is, an overall winding smoothness of the film's movement, counterpointed, scene by scene and frame by frame, with angular, jabbing action and crisply diagrammed imagery. Dwan has carried from his silent period the silent film-makers' preoccupation with making every shot, every camera set-up do its maximum share, the film taking responsibility for its own world. Thus, in *Passion* every phase of the operetta-like plot — a young *ranchero* hunting down the land-grabbers who have murdered his family, enmiring himself in deception and slaughter — is translucently clear, leaving abundant room for those moral questions which seldom take priority in such melodrama — least of all in the "adult" varieties. The often stale-looking features of Cornel Wilde and Yvonne De-Carlo here seem removed from the contexts of their past films; directed so hard and so fast that no room is left for such associations. In his one science-fiction film, *The Most Dangerous Man Alive*, Dwan produced a masterpiece of rootless bitterness — very parallel to *The Restless Breed* — from the performances of Ron Randell and Debra Paget (excellent as a gangster's dumb, sluttish ex-girl friend) and a typically unpromising story about a dead hoodlum, resurrected — and turned into a potential walking holocaust — by nuclear radiation. The climactic scene of Randell perishing on a mountain top — a fusion of *High Sierra* and Euripidean tragedy — commanded a more genuine awe than a stableful of Godzillas.

Dwan's economy is not simple mechanical expediency, but something closer to courtly austerity. Although he repeatedly holds his camera still, avoiding reverse shots and similar ploys, I almost never get the impression that a set-up was done that way merely for budget's sake. His single takes are often filled with some of the most elaborate sustained tracking shots done by an American director apart from Cukor. His austerity, I say, is a positive trait: not simply the will to deny, but to deny in order to assert — even indulge — himself; wherein he is an artist and, I suspect, a damned near unique one in Hollywood today.

His one sensuosity is that of grace: choreographic movement to which sets, actors and all other components are subordinated. He must have fairly opulent production values, as he must have elaborate plots, in order to subdue them. His films are as textureless as any I can recall: as often as not, the actors seem to have turned in their flesh for something resembling balsa-wood. The few erotic moments in his films come and go vaporously: even Rhonda Fleming in an 1870's bathtub seems fully corseted and petticoated.

His handling of violence displays the same austerity. Though he never skimps any necessary violence — the plots of *Tennessee's Partner* and *Slightly Scarlet* are saturated with murders, bombing, bludgeonings — Dwan leaves remarkably little aftertaste of violence. Even when showing violent action detail by detail, he controls the milieu so stringently that the bloodshed seems replaced by urbane, sardonic dispassion. One of the best scenes in *Slightly Scarlet* is a basically routine sequence of a gang-girl being cuffed by hoodlums, whereupon they are raided by the police. Dwan does the whole sequence in what seemed to me, at most two takes; keeping the camera at prudent middle-distance while the slapping gangster delivers his blows with a foolish-sounding "Ah! — *Ah!*" Then, when the police boil in, a slight shove pitches another hoodlum on his face. The control and vivid eccentricity of these businesses pinpoints — in every sense — the violence, so that it becomes as graphic — and remote — as next-door gossip.

Dwan prefers seemingly stolid actors who, at appropriate moments, can deliver schist like glints of intelligence or vivacity. He uses these performers, often, by turning them into ensembles of arms and legs, which he then deploys according to his perceptions of character and bodily rhythm. Arlene Dahl gives what is possibly the most eloquent performance of her career in *Slightly Scarlet;* where, as an alcoholic nympho, she was given a cursive walk — like a nineteen-twenties fashion model — and oversweeping gestures, as to a secret clock synchronized with no other in the world. Dwan's star performer is John Payne — a one-time Jimmy Stewart surrogate, who, after the wartime forties, returned to films with a look of sour harassment, and bearing of an All-American gone faintly rancid. Dwan — in *Tennessee's Partner* and *Slightly Scarlet* — turned these features to expressions of ironic opportunism and stoic bitterness. Payne's presence, as well as that of not-yet-Governor Reagan — co-operated with Dwan's talent to make *Tennessee's Partner* a melancholy, lyric and quite de-sentimentalized expansion of the Bret Harte tale.

Dwan's pictures repeatedly induce the feeling of one era — that of the twenties silents — being carried over into another, virtually intact. His ability to point and place a shot or scene, enables him to use very old devices with the freshness of combined directness, wit and necessity. In *Slightly Scarlet,* the device of surrounding crime lord Ted DiCorsia with darkness whenever he appears, is plyed with such aptness, control and visual acumen that you don't realize how Dwan — by reverting to the expressionist films of the twenties — has outstripped the similar but more pretentious gimmicks of its near-contemporaries — Wyler's *Detective Story,* or Wilder's *Sunset Boulevard.*

I think, too, that Dwan brought from the twenties — and possibly to the detriment of his career — the personal immersion in craft, prior even to art, which held such premium, then, among the best film-makers. From such immersion, he transmits the sense of the actor, on screen, manufacturing the film from his body, silk-worm-like; the story flowing as inevitably as any non-natural work possibly can. In response to a 1963 interview issued by *Cahiers du Cinema* to various American directors, Dwan wrote: "I want to keep making films until I die", and "any working conditions are alright for me. Obstacles are merely challenges for me to surmount." Sheer banality in many a mouth, these phrases ring absolutely true in Dwan's. "Keep making films" — "obstacles": a near-Puritanical fusion of self-abnegation, pride and love, by which art itself becomes a set of circumstances to surmount, adjust, transect. Occasions and necessities rebuilt each time. I think it was such devotion — and the lack of that ambition, or vainglory, or sense of gratuity which distinguishes some of the very best, and occasionally destroys them — which made Dwan (this is sheer inference) glad to accept the factotum's role which was flung him for years. And, in turn, that puritan estheticism, I think, induced in many watching his films, an uneasy sense of nothing to grasp, nothing that could be confiscated, no edges or naperies of personality, strangeness, or simple waste. Thus, the grotesque irony of their conclusion: Dwan is a cold, mechanical film-maker; forgetting or never knowing that films are the medium among media where devotion to mechanics can be infused with personal warmth, with passion. And — not knowing this — never recognizing the additional gratuity of boneclean American narrative art, with which Allan Dwan made pictures for half a century.

Peter Taylor's
Displaced Persons

Peter Taylor's stories and short novels ("A Long Fourth" and "The Widows of Thornton," now out of print; the novel, *A Woman of Means;* and the two most recent anthologies, *Happy Families Are All Alike* and *Miss Leonora When Last Seen*) welcome and menace the friendly critic. Welcome, because of those virtues, which I shall try to indicate, which make Mr. Taylor one of the best comic writers in America today. Menace, because Mr. Taylor, like not very many of his contemporaries, is an expert camouflager, constantly encouraging the critic to discuss the story, or stories, which seem to confront him, rather than the story which Mr. Taylor is telling. Read these stories in the *New Yorker*, say, and — with their modest, almost sedate narrative voice, their mote-like sifting of details (weather, geography, seeming-casual anecdotes of the characters' lives) they appear to submerge without a space bubble into the pancake-batter of the *New Yorker's* prevailing fiction style. Read them in anthologies, and these stories (many of which deal with southerners transplanted to the midwest, with psychic castration, with town eccentrics) seem again to depth-dive, this time into the dark hoe-cake batter of Eudora Welty, Tennessee Williams and their like. Yet, another reading must surely follow; and then, one sees that the imagery of batter must be replaced by another image — the chigger, that ubiquitous southern bug which makes its way impertubably beneath a familiar and seemingly untroubled skin, until a telltale pang discloses the unlooked-for tenant. The chigger is Taylor's comedy.

In the more conventional of Taylor's two recent anthologies, *Happy Families,* the most conventional story — "The Other Places" — offers us a little thesaurus of Taylor's comic values and techniques. A familiar, somewhat Fitzgerald-tinctured triangle: a well-to-do high-school girl, in a Depression small town; the earnest high-school senior boy friend, a very old boy indeed, who narrates; and the girl's uncle, a very different sort of old boy, disdained by his rival as a high-school civics teacher; as an amateur athlete (we first see the uncle in vignette, playing catch with his small nephews) and as an irreclaimable rounder, whom his students call "The Ram," and who makes unscheduled appearances in the gamier roadhouses. One night, this shaggy family inconvenience shows up at a cabaret to which the boy has escorted the girl and makes a gesture of gallantry, revealing an understanding between himself and his niece, which tilts the boy's world at a forty-five degree angle, and leaves him, as a man, still murmuring over it at the story's close.

Familiar, yet not Fitzgerald. Taylor's writing, dry and firm as pine-board, neutralizes any possibility of that Disneyish lushness which threatens even some of Fitzgerald's best stories. Nor, in fact — one more slowly grows aware — is it a love story at all: fear, self-pity and resentment are virtually the only emotions the boy expresses; the only emotions, not excepting love, for which his obsession will allow him closet-space.

"Obsession" — and, in fact, "closet-space" — are the operative words. The hero, like any number of Taylor's other characters, is mainly concerned with being in the wrong place, nor can he ever feel himself in the right place; whether in the girl's home, in the back-country tavern, or simply when putting on his brother's hand-me-down clothes. The story could as easily be called "The Other Places;" for the boy, time and, in effect, reality itself, have become transfixed as locations. "I carry in my head, even today," he remarks, "a sort of detailed map of the city . . ."

And such maps are standard property of many of the characters in *Happy Families*. Cousins, fathers, daughters, nephews, they are displaced persons: displaced in relation to their age, their class, their geography; in relation to the cousins or brothers or parents with which they must at least improvise the appearance of reasonable lives. Some of them are gently sinister eccentrics, like the Dorsets in "Venus, Cupid, Folly and Time;" or cherished local personalities like old Aunt Munsie in "What You Hear From 'Em?" Their lives have gently petrified around locations: little shrines, sometimes houses, sometimes towns or localities, by which they can certify the reality of their lives, and their very identities. "Why don't I go down to Memphis or up to Nashville and see 'em sometimes?" asks Aunt Munsie, referring to the two middle-aged businessmen whom she has raised from babies. "I tell you why. Becaze I ain't nothin' to 'em in Memphis, and they ain't nothin' to me in Nashville . . . Aunt Munsie, she's just Aunt Munsie here in Thornton . . ." And, when not actual locations, events; either savage, as in "A Spinster's Tale," or "At the Drugstore," or sentimental, as in "Sky Line," with the old grandmother's death memorialized by her flower-baskets, knocking at the house-wall. Like pencil-leads or fish-hooks accidentally swallowed, these events have been assimilated by Taylor's characters, becoming part of their systems, traveling to surface every now and again, but residing in the body ever after.

These people, dispossessed of the world around them, are often counterbalanced by others who seem more free or in more solid possession of the world. In "The Widows of Thornton," Taylor shows us an assortment of upper-middle-class Southern wives who, deprived of their husbands by the regimens of business and social life, compensate by concerning themselves with the lives of their Negro cooks and maids. Elsewhere, similar ingenuous parasites try to inhabit the lives of simple and instinctual people: the children in "The Little Cousins" by listening to their Negro governess's stories about her aging suitor; the middle-aged white couple in "A Friend and Protector," by bailing out and buffering and eventually destroying their hard-drinking manservant. Seldom entirely successful, seldom understood by their authors, these attempts detonate other frustrations and jealousies.

These stories are comedy because the dislocations in them are so many, and so apparently trivial, and because the people, like the envious father in "Promise of Rain," so often finger the truth without quite grasping it. They are high comedy, because Taylor is at least as concerned with perceiving and measuring as with judging; even though his destination may be morality, he refuses to miss a station-stop. And high comedy because of their modestly vigilant craftsmanship; the knobs and gears of which can be felt only with some attention beneath the seeming-softness of the casual narrative. This formal sense of Taylor's finds itself mostly, I think, in a partiality for stagecraft: he has published two plays, "Tennessee Day in St. Louis" (no longer in print) and "Death of a Kinsman" (reprinted, from "A Long Fourth," in "Miss Leonora"). The stories bulge with dramatic monologues, with confrontations, with codifying speeches (some of which tend to be too redolent of now-then-any-further-questions?)

But, above all, they overrun with voices — *heard* voices. Possibly excepting John O'Hara, few of Taylor's immediate contemporaries have made such ubiquitous and versatile use of sheer talk. Storytelling voices, voices chirring with small talk; seemingly disembodied voices, overheard in bars and through the walls of hotel rooms; voices aimless or importunate or ominous; voices representing to the characters the worlds of which these people have deprived themselves or been deprived; voices representing the impalpable swarm which threatens like a Great Bog. In "A Strange Story," the disembodied voices seem to be genuinely supernatural, although charming and foolish, if not benevolent; but they are routed by the voices of the world.

Most often, Taylor's stage techniques project the theme of identity and its absence and its falsification; revivifying what has nearly become sociological cliché. The various relatives in "Happy Families" enact the roles assigned them by their status, psychological situation, class. Old people like Miss Leonora, and Cousin Johnny, in "Guests," turn themselves into prim caricatures of the Schoolmarm and the Aged Relative — thus guarding themselves against any further dislocation by, in effect, dislocating themselves permanently from time. The theatrics deployed by Taylor become reflections of the theatrics imposed by ordinary life, by the family and by the community outlying the family.

The most intricate and insidious, also, perhaps, the funniest and most unsettling of the stories demonstrating this theme, is "Venus, Cupid, Folly and Time." The old Dorsets, brother and sister, descendants of a hustling entrepeneur family, have acquired, in their home town, that mixture of reverence and covert disgust usually accorded sacred monkeys. They exert on the townsfolk an unsavory and faintly pagan charm: Mr. Dorset, washing his car while wearing flesh-colored denims, looks to an old lady as though he were cleansing a sacrificial animal;

Miss Dorset likes to sun herself on her terrace in bath-robe, and with her hair "hanging down her back like the hair of an Indian squaw." The Dorsets hold every year a "coming out" party for the young boys and girls of the more well-heeled families. The brother and sister's repu-tation, plus the parties' unmistakable overtones of pu-berty rites, lend these events a terrorizing enchantment for the older people.

The body of the story deals with the innocent, cruelly perceptive practical joke hatched against the old couple by another brother and sister and their friend, the news-boy; and the blinding shuttle of sexual and class jeal-ousies, reality and reality-melding-into-legend, by which the childrens' prank reverses, taking on the sonorities of authentic ritual. The greatest beauty among the mani-fold beauties of this story is, I think, the way in which Taylor conducts the situation through the surprises and *volte-faces* and intrigues of French farce; allowing the suc-cession of comic disasters, as they hiss away like spit-dabs on a hot stove, to define the fiercer irony and sadness. He never for a second lets his imagination be slickered by the synthetic mysteries with which the Dorsets surround themselves and permit others to surround them: the pathetic figs which Mr. Dorset sells, the paper flowers which Mrs. Dorset makes, and with which she decorates the house in imitation of a Dionysian grove. Taylor never flinches from recognizing the banality of such pasteup fantasies, but neither does he fail to give them credit for specific weight; nor does he fail to acknowledge the au-thentic fantasy which these banalities set off: the fantasy of the past enfolding the present, and infecting it like some air-depriving gas.

Such fantasy is easy not to recognize in these stories, with their purring tone and seeming immaculate factu-ality. Yet, the more we read and re-read them, and especially the stories in *Miss Leonora,* the more they seem given to illusion and hallucination, the filtering deceptiveness of reality's planes. The narrator's dreams, which begin "Once upon a time. . ." in "A Spinster's Tale;" the poltergeists of "A Strange Story;" the procession of mysterious doubles and youthful counterparts, who appear and disappear, as though through a gaping service-entrance of time, in "Reservations" and "At the Drugstore" and others. All such phenomena are recounted with a wryness and flatness which seem to deflate them, yet actually re-emphasize them as illustrating the disarming shapelessness of life. We are used to writer after writer — some of them larger than Peter Taylor — telling us that life is disarmingly shapeless and declaring themselves not only disarmed but *hors de combat.* Peter Taylor, with his assortment of formal graces, confronts what often seems least confrontable in the real world; and — never pretending to outface the world — not only holds his ground, but makes this steadfastness a condition of grace.

This attitude toward reality shows itself in a deference toward the surfaces of life, a willingness to *receive* life, which goes beyond mere affection, and, at times (as in the excellent "Sky Line," in "A Long Fourth") beyond comedy as well. This is why, I suspect, Taylor's stage-plays, "Tennessee Day in St. Louis" and "Death of a Kinsman," seem rather bland, even juiceless, in comparison with those stories, like "Heads of Houses" and "Guests," which commandeer stage techniques. The best playwrights, however modest-seeming, like Chekhov, or however sober, like middle-period Ibsen, obtrude themselves much more boldly — on events, on characters, on language, on their world — than does Taylor, who seems much too eager not to "miss anything." His own message comes through, to be sure, in the plays, but much more patly and, for me, less movingly than in the stories, where the *felt* presence of the narrator moistens and enriches the texture. He is, simply, not a re-shaper of the reality which he sees and hears so keenly; and this may be, too, why he has not yet taken on the aggressive demands of the novel.

On the other hand, none of this is to deny the intensity of Taylor's writing — an intensity moral and even mystical (if one is willing to accept, as mysticism, not wooziness or coupon-clipping Rosicrucianism, but that hard-eyed exactness of discernment which Chesterton, among others, has called the mystic's first requirement). Many of the stories are threaded by Taylor's sense of nature, which, to be sure, he sees mainly as it is violated: the deaf taxidermist's collection of glowering heads, in "The Other Times;" the mother's grimly well-kept flower beds, symbolizing the pattern into which she forces her daughter, in "A Walled Garden;" the sour, envious father's sour admiration for the town park in "Promise of Rain." Repeatedly, the effort to house nature, and reality, within these artificial forms, reflects a bleak decline of life itself.

The very latest stories (those comprising "Reservations," "Two Pilgrims," "A Strange Story" and "An Overwhelming Question," present us with another sort of displaced person. (All of these stories can be found in *Miss Leonora When Last Seen,* which includes, as well, an ample selection from "A Long Fourth" and "The Widows of Thornton." This agglomeration makes for a less finely composed anthology than, say, *Happy Families;* yet, it provides its own compensations in richness of variety and contrast, as well, of course, as sharpened opportunity to survey Taylor's writing.) These newer heroes of Taylor's are not transfixed by the past, but spun about by a cyclotron-like present. Miles Miller of "Reservations," Rudy Banks in "An Overwhelming Question," are restless, reckless ground-coverers, whose unhoused condition defies even their efforts to domesticate themselves. The emblematic figure of these characters is Cousin Talbot Williamson, the devilish cavalier in "A Strange Story," whose house vanishes in flames, and who gallops into nowhere, leaving the community minus one "married woman . . . whose name had long been connected with Talbot's." In one story, "Two Pilgrims," the newer people, with their resentment of stasis and the past, come flush with two motoring Pickwickians whose love of history and curiosa endows them with humorous gallantry.

The technique and style of Taylor's latest stories, is, on the whole, harder, more obviously funny, more pointedly artificial than in former writing. In "Reservations" and "An Overwhelming Question," the narrative voice, once all but characterless, adapts at times a falsetto lilt of parody. And, even in these extraordinary stories, where a hard stagelight is focussed on the present, the past towers just behind, like an ominous breaker. "Reservations" begins with a pair of newlyweds on the run from the jubilant mob of their reception guests; continues with the girl trapping herself in a hotel bathroom; and weaves its way from there into a fantasia of "reservations" — evasions, duplicities, petty deceits. "An Overwhelming Question" simply doesn't bear description within such limited space, and from such limited resources, as I can offer. Enough to say that the old, rough, singlepiece joke which clothes this story, hides one of the best efforts I have seen, by an American, to justify much that has been written about Absurd comedy. The originality of these last stories — especially within Taylor's modest self-elected scope — piques our respect for him, for his comedy, for the coda with which (only momentarily, surely) he leaves us:

"Such a mystery becomes, finally, a kind of knowledge. It instructs and informs us about the arbitrary nature of most of the things we have to learn in order to walk the world as adults. Learn those things we *must*, but we possess the knowledge in our hearts that it might have been different."

Mr.
Buckley

I think that I might be tempted, at times, to forget all about William Buckley if the liberals didn't do such a good job of calling him to my attention. I never saw the momentous Jack Paar show on which Buckley appeared to refute something or other that Gore Vidal said about him. On being notified of this event, however, I recall that I tuned in the following night; just in time for what might be described, with more than usual justice, as the mopping-up operation. The exhilarating tenor-sax of Mr. Buckley's voice was absent, but Jack Paar's juice-harp wheedle was on hand, counterpointed at times by the pouter-pigeon sounds of his then intellectual-in-waiting, Hugh Downs. It seemed that after Mr. Buckley, accompanied by what Paar described as his claque, had left, Paar had made some additional remarks about him, interspersed with mimicry of the Buckleyan gestures and intonations. Contrary to everything that has been said about his bellicose independence, Jack Paar's great weakness is a kind of nattering hysteria which descends on him, in crises like this one, and incapacitates him from simply letting anything go: he seems compelled both to protect himself and to challenge his protection by outdoing his former stupidities. Now, he was apologizing to anybody he might have offended by his post-Buckley frolic. A moment later, he was busy as a cat with skein of wool, unreeling more anti-Buckleyisms, with the assistance of Hugh Downs (who couldn't understand Buckley's syntax) and Gore Vidal, a flaccid club-comic who specializes in modeling intellectual ready-to-wear.

I don't question that Mr. Buckley could have handled this guard of honor like a Martini drinker toothpicking olives. I think it's less evident that their impotence demonstrates, more floridly than usual, how drearily many critics — liberal and conservative — have failed to understand Mr. Buckley and what his powers consist of. If this age is ever accorded a name, the Age of Categories may serve well as any other. The special distinction of our present-day-categories is that they serve, not to sharpen identifications, but to blur them. In Mr. Buckley's case, the categories — Conservative, Liberal-Conservative, McCarthyite-Conservative, Radical Christian-Conservative — have been enfolded around him as noiselessly as sanitary plastic bags; blurring all the colors and specifics of his personality.

Buckley's personality — or persona — is, I think, the most valuable and intriguing component of his career. I find it piquantly comic that his liberal critics, by and large, are as ill-equipped to deal with this feature — personality — as medieval scholars would be to deal with the concept of oxygen. Less equipped, in one sense; because the present-day critics, aware of personality and its importance, are inhibited — by their principles of etiquette-as-morality — from talking about it directly. Even when, on occasion, writers like Dan Wakefield — in an article for *Esquire* four years ago — or Murray Kempton take a step in the right direction, they promptly fall on their faces, or go into meaningless pirouettes. Both these writers sentimentalize Buckley by apostrophizing him as a doughty cavalier of the right who has been undeservedly frustrated by being turned into a "house Conservative" (Kempton's phrase) and relegated to Harvard debating sessions where he is admired as a character, but is not (in some fashion neither writer has bothered to specify) taken seriously enough.

I submit this as the kind of thinking which has helped for so long to establish Harry Truman as exemplar of unpretentious grass-roots Americana. I doubt very much whether Mr. Buckley has become house Conservative for anyone, or is about to, save by his own volition. If he has not been taken seriously by college students, he is only one of a plethora of subjects which college students approach with either too little or misapplied seriousness. Beyond these objections, however, I suggest that both Kempton and Wakefield indulge a fundamental confusion of liberals who write about William Buckley. They take too seriously what does not deserve to be taken so seriously — his ideology; and they do not take seriously enough what is the most intriguing and valuable thing about him — his tactics. In his article on Buckley, Mr. Wakefield recounts (am I correct — with a certain measure of awe?) Buckley's retort to Wakefield, who asked him when he felt the Africans would be ready for self-government: "He was thoughtfully gazing down at the table, and he glanced up with a quick smile and said, 'When they stop eating each other.' "

Well, this is not wit, by any definition of mine. I have no idea of how literally Buckley believes this remark, and, to authentic wit, "how literally" makes all the difference. It is really just a cheap joke, reclaimed by — what? By the movement of parrying and deflecting. Jack Paar, on his recovering-from-Buckley show, fumed about "Buckley's fancy footwork"; without, of course, getting near the suggestion that you might use this to define Buckley, and not merely demolish him.

In criticism, truth is not so much located as invented. I'd like to apply this observation to Mr. Buckley, by saying that I believe his most important achievement to be that of a comic figure: not a buffoon; not a *hanswurst;* not a foil (although he depends frequently on the persona of a nineteenth-century dandy). I mean, a comic personality in the high — and now neglected — sense: someone with more rationality and perception on tap than the people to whom he is opposed, or with whom he is aligned; who is, therefore, amusing to his perpetual audience (everyone exposed to him) in a way they cannot quite define; but who is also amusing in a way he cannot define, because of his deficient self-knowledge.

A choice illustration of Buckley's comedy in motion — the only way it can be observed — is the famous contretemps with Pope John and his adherents; which also demonstrates the fatal liberal penchant for trying to rush Buckley dead-center when he has already skittered off to right field. Buckley put down the encyclical "Mater et Magistra" as a "venture in triviality" (true, the editorial was unsigned; but I reserve the right to imagine the editorial office as both unified and multicellular, like a coral skeleton. I reserve, too, the right to point out that *National Review's* editorials frequently represent so many miniscular Buckleys, born, like Alexander Pope's sprites, upon the wind); finding that the Pope had over-emphasized social reform and other secondary issues, while neglecting the menace of communism and the disintegration of morality. The reverend fathers, on *America*, the Jesuit weekly, padded after Buckley as though they were all teaching parochial school, and had heard ungodly whoops from down the hall. Eventually, they managed even to compound their original gaffes by dropping *National Review's* advertisements from their magazine. Mr. Vidal, a belated Swiss Guard, came puffing in their train presently on the Paar show, characterizing the Buckley squib as "vicious", and suggesting that Buckley is a defective Catholic. None of these well-meaning people betrayed any suggestion that they perceived the editorial to be, not so much an attack on the Pope or papal policy, as an operation in leverage. Buckley was attacking the fortuitously-timed encyclical — a meager and platitudinous performance, from the few excerpts I read — to deflect the charges of his liberal fellow-Catholics that he was a delinquent Catholic; and in a ricochet motion, to deflect the charges of the Paul Blanchards, that American Catholic thinking in politics is almost of a piece. And he did this — through a rigging of inflection, supposition, and generality, in an engineering job which the reverend fathers — missing yet another chance — failed to call "a venture in trivialization".

Nothing, I'd suggest, demonstrates better than this the main feature of Buckley's comedy: his sleight-of-hand talent for giving the illusion of movement to a static situation. This talent is shared by the masters of comedy — Molière or Meredith — and their characters — the Misanthrope or Sir Willoughby Patterne. Mr. Buckley partakes of both author and character; more intelligent than the insular Sir Willoughby, very much less profound than Moliere, or the Misanthrope. He borrows, piecemeal, from all of these, the darting vim which informs the plot complications and coincidences and incidental business of *Tartuffe* or *The Egoist*. The fundamental comedy of Meredith and Molière, of course, is that — true-blue pre-Buckley conservatives that they were — they dedicated this busyness to the services of an enlightened status quo. Eventually, the obnoxious or eccentric outlander is either routed or reformed. The broken-fly-wheel tempo turns out to have been nothing: the distractedness of everyday.

Since his emergence in American culture, Buckley's accomplishment has been to lend an appearance of shuttling urgency to the almost-sedentary posture of American conservatism. His coming has soldered a long-time break. Before Buckley, there were in America many intellectually virile conservatives, but they tended toward the dry. Typical of them, in the early Fifties, was the imperturbably arid prose of James Burnham. On the other hand, the livelier conservatives tended to be goofballs and semi-illiterates: the Rankins, Bilboes and Fishes. Buckley brought to popular American conservatism — along with other gifted trouble-shooters, like Noel Parmentel, Russell Kirk and Brent Bozell — a humming action, both authentic and mock-up, which, in its own way, re-created the pyro-technics of old-fashioned preachers, or the more prominent literary figures of the 1920's.

The movement of leftist radicalism is an extending and converting movement. The movement of conservatism is a containing and ingesting movement. Conservatism, in short, is essentially a holding action: it is, I think, the natural trend of many poets, just as leftist radicalism is the tendency of many scientists and engineers. This in no way detracts from the value of authentic conservatism; except to lessen the ready pungency of melodrama which leftism offers the uninitiated. The emotional come-hither of conservatism is stepped up enormously when the holding action is holding *against* something; when what might otherwise settle into lap-smoothing complacency, becomes a defense of values against an enemy; whose presence exerts the refreshing effect of a complementary purple introduced into a drab-green living-room.

Needless to say, I hope, I don't suggest that the Communist menace exists as a sales pitch extemporized by William Buckley and a few others. I should like to suggest, though, the tantalizing uncertainty Buckley evokes: the comic uncertainty of not knowing where his genuine dedication ends, and where the public mask which he has fabricated from it begins. Comedy takes place in unrelenting white daylight: everything is wakefulness; with the inevitable result that wakefulness, like sleep, breeds illusions and false impressions. There is no question of hypocrisy about William Buckley; as with Sinclair Lewis, and other 1920's author-comedians, there is only the question of artifice, and how large a claim it has on personality.

Examining a *piéce célèbre,* like the "Venture in Triviality," you find yourself able to sympathize with Alice Through the Looking-Glass. A lot of Buckley's contentiousness and daring seem to exist in the sideways glance of the beholder. Looking head-on at the article, you find it not only piecemeal and runny as argument, but in no way as demolishing, say, as the piece which *Dissent* ran on Pope Pius XII at his death. The resentment is unmistakeable; its offensiveness to the editors of *America,* who are surely not oblivious to papal criticism, is hard to nail down. Only when you look sideways at the article — letting your eye go a little off-focus will help — do you begin to detect the invisible cross-references to all the other editorials in *National Review;* do you detect the temors of insinuation, the glintings of superciliousness; the elements of tone and style that have nothing to do with intellectual argument, but everything in the world to do with communication. This is Buckley's force: a centrifugal force, which sends arguments flickering away from him even as he seems to catch them up.

Like the characters of Molière and Meredith, Buckley is an adept at using reason so that the keenest edge is always turned inside, and the heavier edge — the chopping edge — towards his opponent. This suits him pre-eminently for the high-school exhibitionist's atmosphere of the debating stage, where credit-card violence and sworddance argument are requisites. I trust that everybody who has been watching "Open End" or "Under Discussion" has long since surrendered the notion that debate has anything to do with enlightening or clarifying issues, or anything except the virtuoso practice of violence. The end-product of debate is not education, but ballock-jam. The violence is not adulterated, as in the wrestling shows, because the illusion of action, as opposed to the wrestlers' bloated grandstanding, is self-consistent; and the fact that the action is professedly intellectual exempts it from the need to accomplish anything constructive.

On the debating-stage, Buckley reasserts his claim as legatee of the comedians; the comedians, in this case, of the 1930's; which featured Cary Grant, Brian Aherne and William Powell in films as trim-lined and sleekly negligent as the architectural designs of that period. These actors were like lifetime lobbyists for the progressive school system. Their supposed daring and rebellion were all insured against the risks of daring and rebellion by the fact that, insufferable as their antics might be, everyone — even rivals and enemies — recognized them as children; thus providing their lives with the insularity of Peter Pan's treehouse.

Buckley also has in common with these fancy-steppers that he plays the role of the disinherited. Powell and Grant seemed continually to have been turned out of their rightful station, into the roles of chauffeur or "Forgotten Man". Buckley too gives the impression of limitless power and prestige which, quite unreasonably and ridiculously, finds itself at leisure. This, of course, refers to the conservative movement as a whole, but it is also Buckley's personal *metier*.

Never is this more sharply focused than on the panel shows (Indeed, the nearest thing to a Buckley fiasco I have ever witnessed, on a panel show, was the much-bruited *tête-à-tête* with Mailer. This took place under the supervision of David Susskind; and I blame mainly Susskind's sausage-fingered promotion techniques for the disastrous juxtaposition, of which I could bring myself to watch only a half-hour. Buckley tried to out-hamfat Mailer, Mailer tried to out-sidle Buckley, even to peppering his speech with Buckleyesque "uh" 's and "ah" 's. The net result recalled to me that insufficiently-cherished comedy team of radio, Claude and Clarence, the Stroud Twins). Buckley owes no little to his opponents: usually, conscripts from the *schmuckerie* of establishment Liberals which includes Wechsler, Schlesinger, Schmessinger, et al. The square-cut rhetoric and Christ-mongering quasi-morality of such people makes them to Buckley what the chorus of allies and opponents was to the Misanthrope and Sir Willoughby. Their central handicap is that they seem to have been standard-cut in compliance with a public image of good manners, social-mindedness and general temperance. It isn't that Buckley is intemperate or ill-mannered, by comparison: it is just that he gives the impression of being these things, or their opposites, when he prefers to be; according to the regimen of his personality, and not a dummy self.

Moreover, it is a personality which thrives on language: an element to which most of Buckley's confrontees react like scuba-divers divested of their breathing-apparatus. This may, indeed, be Buckley's most original donation to American conservatism: redeeming the validity of sheer language as an element of political philosophy. Without the dry acumen of Burnham's prophecies, without the bony force of Wilmoore Kendall's metaphysics, Buckley's style seems, even on the printed page, to encapsulate the Buckley voice, the animate Buckley. To his opposition, he seems to announce: "This (language) is my kingdom. I do not insist that you abide in it; indeed, you contest my occupancy at your own risk. But even if you remain outside, you must recognize its compact validity; and recognize, too, that this compact validity makes my kingdom as unconfined as the desert labyrinth of Jorge Luis Borges' monarch."

Buckley on these shows expresses a kind of subdivision of the heroic type whom Harold Rosenberg discussed in *The Ressurected Romans:* the individual from outside, who pre-empts a role of dynamic responsibility. Buckley presents — indeed, has helped evolve — the comic hero; who seems entitled to power and renown; who never quite gets them (first comic reversal); but who (final comic reversal) incessantly goads you with the impression that he has walked away with more than he came in with.

Writing this, I remember a session of "Open End" on which, opposite Buckley, William Van den Heuvel proposed that the liberals, in the 1950's, had done more to the detriment of Communism than the conservatives; since the liberals had endorsed and furthered the Marshall Plan and other aid plans, which many conservatives had opposed and hindered. Buckley retorted by asking: What had the liberals done, not to contain Communism, but to abolish it? To help not only the non-Communist countries but those people (and here, Buckley's voice took on that evangelical thrum already noted by Mr. Wakefield in *Esquire*) in the hell of Red China, or Czechoslovakia? Poor Van den Heuvel fluttered a bit that no consistent policy existed for, etc., etc. He did not even suggest that the liberals, in helping contain Communism — a movement which survives by advancement — *were* helping those wretches in the hell of Iron Curtain captivity. And yet, you question at last whether even such a relatively sensible rebuttal would have made any difference; and, indeed, what *kind* of difference it would be supposed to make. For Buckley's weapon is not wit, nor sarcasm, but irony; and irony expresses the ironist's confidence in his sense of geography; what his vested experience and thought have told him about the world. Irony is conservatism's natural weapon; no less because so many conservatives, in this country, have been delinquent at using it. Buckley's position is monolithic; whereas the position of the average American liberal, I suspect, is eclectic and extempore. They seem to live in a hobo jungle; since their philosophy is so much one of extension and amelioration, they must state it at *every* opportunity. By contrast, Buckley — assuming that his position is consonant with reality — lives in a manorial castle. What makes his position so dubious intellectually is exactly what makes it ideal for battle maneuvers.

It also equips Buckley ideally as a running assailant of liberal cant and fallacy. In a sense, most high comedy returns to one sort of humor: that of *reducing ad absurdum;* and Buckley has exercised this humor to its most murderous extent on the double-think and lacunae of liberal journals and oracles. Apart from a number of honorable journalists, the liberals in this country tend to apply double-think *in excelsis* to matters of what evidently affects them as prosaic detail. Reality seems to impress them, at times, as something too vulgar to confront plainly, but quite capable of being exploited. Buckley has never done better work than in the two-inch editorials which take advantage of the other side's gliberalism.

In contrast with the tragic heroes, the deficiency of Sir Willoughby — or of the narrator in Ford's *The Good Soldier* — is a deficiency of feeling: that membraneous edge of response through which the hero deals with his fellows. I cannot escape the sense of this deficiency in Buckley: a failure of feeling which is a failure of understanding. I say this, fully prepared for the remarks which seem to be reflexes of some of his admirers: remarks featuring the terms, sentimentalist, bleeding-hearted reactionary; plus the assertions that Buckley does not wear his heart on his sleeve, which is not to say that, etc., etc., that because he is fluent and incisive, this does not entitle him to charges of coldness. I can say only that my reaction is based, not on Buckley's fluency and incisiveness, but on what is not present in addition to these qualities. I get the feeling that Buckley's idealism, which demands a bellicose anti-Soviet stand, is as chillingly bare of moral understanding as the opposite positions of those pacifists who have decided that the whole world — including the world of nature, presumably — should declare a moratorium on violence, no excuses. The moral vacuity of both positions reflects a moral confusion: on the *Liberation* left, a confusion of faith and reality; on the Buckley Right, a confusion of irony and reality.

I wonder too whether this deficiency of feeling doesn't also reflect a boyishness which Buckley depicts in many ways. The need for the debating stage, with its redolence of school; the snippets of Latin, the college-humor siftings which fly-speck passages of genuine humor, in *National Review*. All those repeatedly suggest a kind of schoolboy, insular and vulnerable at once, who inhabited the stories of Evelyn Waugh, Walter De La Mare and Saki; who inhabited, too, an air-pocket of mischief and make-believe which seemed all but impervious to the world of affairs. The oddest thing about such a man, is that he should be acclaimed both as rebel and authority, in a country, and at a time, when both phrases run dirt-cheap; and by people many of whom seem not to recognize the comic nature of his rebellion, or the comic field in which he is genuinely authoritative.

Lord
Have
Mercy

Let us pray for the survival of common sense, which has just been given the business — again — by the Warren Supreme Court. You have probably read about the Court's sturdy refusal to let its monolithic justice be seduced by a bunch of children who wanted to recite their (non-denominational) thanksgiving prayers before eating, in school. Yes, it is a petty incident, although not a trivial one, I think: a difference exists between the two words, of which, sometimes, we need a law like the Prayer Law to remind us. I also know — how well! — that the Law's the Law. James Agee, I recall, once assembled a few slogans which, he said, might bear witness to the death-throes of a civilization. Wherever Agee may be, I've got another for him.

My original objection to the Prayer Law still goes: it is dangerous for any law to aim at sparing hurt feelings. Indeed, the *right* of people to have their feelings hurt, is one of the few rights which, in recent years, has survived reasonably intact the Law's ever-increasing pharisaical nosiness.

Still, the trigger for the Prayer Law would seem a humanely valid one, a shame and a challenge to any professing Christians: the at times ferocious abuse of atheist children, of Jehovah's Witnesses, or Jews, or other members of minority or peripheral religious bodies, by other children, and sometimes parents, who knew the privileges and protections of their self-designated religion better than its responsibilities. These classroom persecutions take place daily all over the world, in any school in which a single faith prevails; against all manner of minorities, including, in some locales, Christians. The universality of such nastiness, I should not have to point out, does not reduce by one iota, the responsibility to deal with it, of anyone professing a creed of love.

Did the Warren Court confront this responsibility? I think not; neither the responsibility, nor the congeries of opportunities which its challenge comprised. The Court could have, on the most obvious level, encouraged the cooperation of local authorities in frustrating mob action, whether the mob consisted of seven and eight-year-olds or forty-years-and upward; thus indirectly, too, spotlighting occasional religious bigotry and preference among those local authorities. The Court could have fostered inter-denominational education in the classroom: as introduced, for example, during appropriate sections of the history and geography lessons. It could have promoted these admittedly rudimentary but, I think, potentially effective measures, if not through direct legislation, then through oratory, for which the Warren Court, surely, has never been embarrassed. By so doing, it could have freed the qualified people — the local teachers, police, civic leaders — to pursue their job of teaching, and enforcing, elementary respect of human beings for each other, while thwarting the hypocrites and haranguers. And, at the same time, the Court could have performed the function, easily as important, of illustrating, for Mrs. Murray's children and all the other little dissidents — the real function of the Law; not of lending illegitimate strength to any ideology, including that of the outsider; but of insuring order, and within the most reasonable bounds of that order, freedom to observe one's beliefs or non-beliefs, peaceably.

We have seen how the Court met that challenge and

those opportunities. It met them by censorship; which, at its most innocuous, is a lazy or autocratic man's substitute for education. The act of censorship, resulted from the Court's garbling two rather distinct interpretations of a single word: Church. The original stricture, in the Constitution, against a universal Church, represents, as would seem clear, a two-edged protection against the exploitation of the Church by the State, as a mechanism of political extortion; and exploitation by the Church of *its* powers, for interference in the political activities of its constituents. It seems to my politically illiterate eye, that the pivotal concept here, is the double provision against the potentially ominous persuasiveness of Church and State, *as institutions*: "institutions" being interpreted in a sense at once fluid and amenable to, indeed, demanding, definition. In a very important way, too, it seems to me that the "religion" clause strives to protect both church and state against the rigors of institutionalization. And stiffening this function, is the very flinty assumption that Church and State, as institutions, subsist on power, and are self-evidently on the lookout for more.

It seems to me that the Warren Court has garbled this no-nonsense concept of Church with the *metaphysical* concept of Church: the expression of religious devotion, spontaneous or otherwise, by one or several people, publicly. Thus, the Court, with no little audacity, begins with an assumption which many devout *and* educated people prefer to regard as a question; answerable, if at all, only after the most excruciating and repeated debate: i.e., that everybody's belief counts for Something. To which, of course, Willmoore Kendall has attached the addendum (which he phrases more painstakingly than I am doing) that by this assumption, Something must mean, not very much.

The Warren Court, then, has, in effect, denied the

Church its identity as an institution; by holding that a Church or religion can exist just as validly in the form of a single, non-denominational, totally ideologically innocuous prayer, recited by a five-year-old girl in nursery school — aloud. Thus, it seems to me, while disallowing one form of power to the Church, the Court has preposterously magnified another form of power: that of myth, of charisma, lying within the bailiwick of imagination and conscience. Where, then, can this Court-buttressed protection of its citizens against a phantasmal church, extend? Or, rather, where can it end?

I wouldn't venture to say, but I can propose a motto for those who may feel as I do: "Beware the sentimentality of judges." For the Warren Court's present strictures against "religion in the schools" all are unified, it seems to me, by the fondate of sentimentality in which they repose. The worst kind of sentimentality; far worse than the kind which treats those more-or-less innocent school prayers and songs as the girders of our democratic structure. For *this* sentimentality, under the guise of reasonableness, essays to deal with, not simply intangibles, but indefinables by any apparatus which lies at the Court's legitimate disposal. And because they are indefinables, the Court, I am afraid, has already extended a dangerous protectorate over individual freedom: the kind of protectorate which, in the thirties, Czechoslovakia, and, in the late forties, South Korea, learned about; and which Viet Nam is learning about now. And, even though its strictures may so far have been niggling annoyances, the Court—in extending its boundaries to the subjective conscience—has shackled Church and State with shackles that may require a painful smithy, later on.

The
Prayer
Law

I
Prayers and Meditations

No Catholic recusants are being deported from Pier 13 next Monday. Our school curricula will not immediately be granting elbow room (amid whatever seventh graders are allowed to read) to the collected works of Ralph Ingersoll, Joseph McCabe and Clarence Darrow. Bishop Pike is not expected to incinerate himself in the middle of Sepulveda Boulevard this coming week. Should the laws of probability and human nature hold intact, none of these occurrences should ensue from the Supreme Court's ruling against school prayers, which has recently been dramatized anew by the Becker Amendment proposal (in approval of which Monsignor Sheen and Governor Wallace found themselves, so to speak, receiving communion together). The eventualities I speak of seem only slightly less likely than those proposed by some of the prayer law's supporters, who have hinted that a monastic tyranny was being imposed on our schools, and the careers of a thousand budding little *Realist* editors being ruthlessly curtailed.

Too many bewailers of the prayer law make it quite obvious that the sacred thing being violated is, their sense of personal comfort; to which their concept of religion has long been a foam-rubber cushion. What the law *has* violated (regarded by some as sacred) is, common sense; because the law is petty and niggling. The kind of petty and niggling law which attaches itself, barnacle-like, to the underside of many an issue more bulky and important than the law itself. Moreover, it has attempted to displace what is at least an aborted idea, with a vacuum of any ideas.

The central error which seems to have determined the law's enforcement so far—an error not likely to be noted by our legislators—is, its over-protectiveness toward the children. The most striking example of this—the most unexpected, too—is, the free-thinking lady who sought to protect her little boy from the pernicious noise of the Lord's Prayer, by appealing to the law against "establishment of a universal church"; obviously not accepting the premise that a future prophet of atheism could ask no better introduction to his career, than thus confronting the errors of organized religion head-on. More to the point, is the question: Should any child, or adult, of any persuasion, be encouraged in so much respect for the law? Al Capp has said that a child should healthily regard its parents as its enemies. Isn't it more beneficial to any American, today especially, to regard the law as a mechanism, a weapon, the beneficence of which depends on how it is used? Can any good ensue from encouraging an American to believe that the law is dedicated to salving his feelings by allying itself with his most childish sensibilities? The value of hurt feelings is, that they proclaim the independence of the individual from institutions, whether these be hostile or benevolent to his sensitivity. For this very reason, hurt feelings are a lousy basis for any legislation.

The attitude toward the children themselves, expressed by the Supreme Court justices, is much the same as that projected in the novel, *Lord of the Flies*: a book, dealing with the supposed deterioration of "civilized" school boys on a desert island, which says nothing about the backgrounds of the boys, or their minds, or their feelings about the western conventions of which they have divested themselves, or to which they cling. By thus presenting the children as mental ciphers, much profundity is implied without being unveiled. The present law, sharing this oracular vacuity, ignores the truth that children are not "public" in the same sense as are those adults to whom the law primarily addresses itself. Children, even sitting together in a classroom, are "public" in only a superficial way. Partly, they are unanalyzably private; and partly, they are inventing their own public, their own society.

For this reason, children from, say, five through twelve, often need rituals and ceremonies as markers for the world which they are learning about, and shaping. This truth brings to mind the sanguine comment on the prayer law of certain clergymen; who said that, after all, it was merely eliminating a "sterile ritual" (How often have these two words been used as Siamese twins!) which is not relevant to vital contemporary religion. Waiving the possibility of taking a poll among six-year-olds, to determine their opinion of how many rituals in their church or Sunday School impress them as vital, let us question the probability of the clergymen's expectations. What they would ask, apparently, is religious instruction which can instil in a first-grader, a religious fervor known to the little heroes and heroines of 19th-century Sunday School pamphlets. In fact, the fascination of ritual for children of a certain age has nothing to do with religion, and very little to do with whether or not adults consider the ritual to be boring. It is a way at once of recognizing order and of not taking it too seriously. And, indeed, the ceremonies of pledging allegiance, and prayers, and songs in assembly, all constitute one way of measuring and identifying the small novelties of one's world. The presence of prayers in a school no more makes of it a church, than the presence of the president's portrait makes of it a headquarters for the Democratic Party.

Will Herberg, in a recent series of three articles of *National Review,* has rebuked the clergymen I speak of; saying, that the authority of God is all-important to any concept of democratic government, and that the importance of this authority counteracts the supposed aridity of the prayer rituals. Mr. Herberg makes many cogent points, but also manages to beg the question no little. *Can* you affirm authority, and do reverence to it, by mentioning it again and again? What I remember of Bible readings suggests that God is a little more demanding on that score than his spokesman, Mr. Herberg. Nevertheless, he collides with an important point: the reason why the prayer has become remote and a little archaic, even though no challenge to religious or atheistic freedom. When I attended school, the prayer seemed a little like a vestige of an earlier period in American education, when schools were more isolated, more naive and, in certain ways, more central to the community than they are now; when they were supposed to be pantheons of authority: the tripartite authority of teacher, home and God; not the God of our churches, or of radio sermons on Sunday; but the God of schools; Whose presence was as formal, as mysterious, yet, seemingly, as appropriate, as the monthly appearance of the man from the savings bank, who lectured us in the auditorium.

This began to recede long before the arrival of the prayer laws, this formal and dream-like child's notion of authority; nor has the loss been insignificant; because the loss connoted the widespread evaporation of the concept of *manners,* gestures of grace in the best spiritual and social and esthetic sense of the word: one's respect for what is unknowable not only about God, but about one's fellow man, and, above all, respect for the distances between people which only such respect can bridge. This concept of manners is now being revived by the Negro demonstrators led by Rev. Martin Luther King and others; the fulcrum of whose campaign is, that grace which overarches differences in taste and background and ethnic patterns.

Rev. King and his followers remind us of the truth most grievously neglected by the prayer laws, as well as by many educators and ministers: that God is an idea, and that this idea, within recent years, has been gaining, not losing, in vitality and relevance to ourselves (indeed, the prayer law may achieve the very opposite results to what its proponents desire: that is, it may at length succeed in forcing educators to define education-as-religion; and ministers to assess the power of religion to educate). Education and religion are drawing closer together daily, as demonstrated by the recent words and actions of the late Pope John and his successor, Pius; the increased liberalization, forwarded by Father Kung and others, of the Catholic Church; above all, the performances of Negro ministers like King, on behalf of education in its most elementary and most radiant sense. Religion as idea and education is begging to be redefined, despite the occasional clownishness of its spokesmen; and despite the constipative tightening of education.

No law can comprehend or generate these ideas; but law can prepare us for their fulfillment; and law can retard them. Not that the prayer law prohibits discussion of religion, or meditation about religion; so we have been reassured on frequent occasion by its apologists. But neither is the ruling calculated to encourage the lazy and timid; whose imaginations and intelligences work so industriously on behalf of non-action, counting on the law as their intercessor.

II
Some Prayerful Suggestions
How can religion and education be better reconciled,

with proper deference to liberal sensibilities? Probably the best way would entail following to its last logical degree the approved Judaeo-Christian technique of heaping coals of fire on your enemy's head; which is to say, giving the liberal educators exactly what they profess to want, as distinguished from their sometime practice. A few of the more benevolent supporters of the prayer law have said, that of course it would not forbid "free discussion" of religion, multi-faceted experience, etc. Very well; the following suggestions might serve as a prospectus for a pamphlet, designed for consumption by both sides, and alternately titled: "Doing Good to Those Who Despitefully Use You," and "Progressive Education for Liberal Educators."

1) *Religio-Athletic Recreations: Miracle Plays, Mystery and Hanukah Plays, Religious Games, etc.,* all of which could be arranged and staged and supervised during play periods; the less elaborately the better, unless the kids opted for trappings and costumes. The improvisation would be all-important: to make these plays an expression of children's doubts and questions and resentments about all they had heard of God, or been taught in Sunday School. This could give psychodrama cards and spades; and, even at worst, it would resist the falsifications and masking which imperil similar productions in Sunday School. The Mystery Plays—recreations of Old Testament stories—and Hanukah Plays might be preferable to the Miracles, some of which are rather openly anti-Semitic. Yet—who knows?—by the time any such thing could evolve in our educational system, even the anti-Semitic plays might be feasible, to the benefit of everyone; even as the *Prioresse's Tale* of Chaucer, or the unexpurgated Huck Finn, could be feasible and beneficial today. Another suggestion: improvising incidents from the religious-centered Negro demonstrations, and

similar contemporary Mysteries, or Miracles. The religious games would have to be freely invented, or improvised, and could, perhaps, be combined with the plays.

2) *Guest Appearances by Religious Authorities, for Non-Denominational Classes.* Thus: Well-qualified Rabbis, Priests, Pastors, Monks or Nuns, the genuine scholars and shepherds, would make guest appearances in classes of various grades; teaching the prescribed curriculum, but according to their own methods; interpolating explanatory material, stories, etc., about their own parochial schools and yeshivas; about the relation of education to their own particular faith. This thing of guest-appearances has been done, relatively successfully, within my own experience as a pupil, with army officers, fire-chiefs and Quentin Reynolds; there is no reason why the best-qualified religious teachers could not bring it off with compounded interest.

3) (For lower grades) *Have Each Pupil Who Prays, Recite His Favorite Prayer, Which Will be Discussed by the Class.* This has been done within my own archaic experience, but only meagerly, as I recall, and with considerable embarrassment and holding-back on the part of many children. Probably only the most sublime level of pedagogy could insure no embarrassment; but I suggest that it could be done much more richly and less painfully, by the teacher delivering a very patient and detailed explanatory introduction, telling what prayers are, and giving plenty of examples; by suggesting that those kids who use prayers at all, try reciting one another's prayers; by talking about the differences between prayers for children and prayers for grownups; by conducting exercises, with the class experimenting with the sounds of prayers, getting the feel of words, mouthing them as in speech exercises, telling why they liked or disliked the sounds.

The Heaven
and Earth
Of
I. B. Singer

A recent news item quoted I. B. Singer's remark that
the theme of all his fiction has been "the creative urge."
An all-too-unpretentious remark, I think; and, as such,
all too likely to be dismissed as the self-deprecating platitude of a nice chap who probably doesn't speak English
too well, anyway. Actually, the imagination has ever been
the true protagonist of I. B. Singer's fiction, from *Gimpel
the Fool* to *Short Friday;* but the imagination as recognized and rendered by a preeminently religious writer.
In the stories of his first English anthology, *Gimpel,* or
the excellent short novel, *Satan in Goray,* imagination
manifests itself as the protean mysteriousness of life.
Singer's basic theme is the tension between this life, paradoxical, freakish—and the Law; in which—he emphasizes
again and again—reposes the only stability man can know
before his passage into the other world.

Singer is not, by this token, a merely moral or didactic
writer, but a religious artist of the most seminal kind. He
does not set out to instruct man in how to live (the part
of such knowledge that can be taught, is already available
in the Law; the other part is unteachable); but rather, to
help men comprehend their world and its relation to
God. This religious vertebra of Singer's writing is what
lends his stories their all-important *distance:* not aesthetic
merely, but the sensed distance between earth and

heaven; between the shifting planes of this life and the sure nucleus of God.

This mighty paradox of the veiled Certainty vs. the elusive concrete endows Singer's stories with their enchanting plasticity of tone. In his superb short novel *The Unseen,* for example, he glides from domestic quaintness to domestic farce; thence to grotesque pathos, and finally to unnatural horror. It also accounts, I think, for Singer's pleasure in masks, including the mask of the Wise Old Story-teller, which he dons for public appearances. In the supposed autobiography, *In My Father's Court,* the mask filters out the most personal, most subjective elements, leaving us a series of gem-like fables. All worldly behavior is mask, against the single face of eternity.

The single message that may be distilled from *Gimpel the Fool* and other stories of that period, is that one must keep faith with the mystery of life. "Life is freedom of choice, and freedom of choice is mystery," postulates the old Rabbi in "Joy," his own heart both uplifted and sobered by a recent glimpse of the next world. This, the challenge and affliction of life, is also its blessing and *raison d'être;* and his recognition of this—the covenant between this world and the next—and his fidelity to it, make Gimpel a saint, rather than a standard *schlemihl.* "It could happen!" is Gimpel's unfailing answer to the world's deceit; his talisman, not of credulity, but of authentic charity. He would have lightened the heart of Melville's Confidence Man.

By the token of Singer's faith, skepticism is not a self-protective distrust of any certainty, but a recognition of reality's rich elusiveness. Imagination is the staff of such faith: the insect-like, more than cerebral attentiveness to every stimulus which Singer writes about, and which he writes from. Not the sovereignty of his art controls this attentiveness, but its submission to the world's fullness and to its boundaries. Thus, his love for seemingly passive wanderers, whose passiveness is affirmation. Thus, too, his recognition that sin is essentially the paralysis, the truncation of life; the abandonment of faith in favor of security. Hell, as a friendly imp confides to us in "The Mirror," is eternal sameness; and hell is invoked on earth by people who elect for the sameness of continuous pleasure or safety, or who attempt an impossible symmetry of both worlds. In the hideous aftermath of his Indian summer romance, the middle-aged landowner of *The Unseen* finds himself kept by the wife he had deserted, in their attic, in a macabre travesty of the old domestic warmth: a living anachronism. A masterpiece which deserves to share "Gimpel's" fame as its black counterpart, *The Unseen* concludes with Singer's most piercing image of hell: moral inanition become palpable.

Singer's novel, *The Magician From Lublin,* presents us with a similar, yet fundamentally different sort of alienation, and a different role for the imagination than we have seen in the earlier stories. The result may be the most quietly disturbing of his novels. At the outset, it is drily realistic, more cosmopolitan in tone than much of the previous writing. Yasha Mazur is a relatively sophisticated professional; not a magician in the cabalistic sense, but a sleight of hand artist, juggler and acrobat extraordinary. A philanderer, with one mistress in the neighboring gentile village and another among the Warsaw aristocracy, he finds his attachment to the Jewish community and his plump, devoted wife, becoming daily more tenuous; yet, cannot entirely abandon them. God, to him, is a presence Who manufactures the world's marvels, yet is sublimely indifferent to its people: a sort of cosmic Yasha, whose detachment is not to be bridged by the Law. Singer writes about Yasha in a series of intimate set-pieces, not unlike the closeup sequences of a film. Although the richly visualized backgrounds of his earlier stories continue, there is little of their roaming in time.

Aware of life's impermanencies, Yasha wants to possess whatever he finds good in it, without the stabilizing pediment of faith. At length, he finds his synthetic universe fraying and shredding. He makes a desperate attempt to re-assert his powers with a clumsily disastrous experiment in burglary. Madness and suicide make unexpected appearance. Then, the half-anticipated eruption takes place, not as revelation, but as metaphor. With a bound, the narrative propels us into the future, where we see Yasha in self-imposed hermitage; as uncertain as ever, yet, persuaded, at least, of the void in which he has been living; and resolved to free himself of this world by relinquishing his share of it.

This—the story of an intelligently self-conscious man, convinced of life's instability—is, I think, a significant turning-point in Singer's fiction. Heretofore, the prevalent view-point, the dominant imagination, have been those of the community and its folklore: the narrative voice, as in "The Wife Killer," that of the story-telling gossip — subtly amplified, at times. Yasha's testimony of the world's shiftings, is not affirmation — like Gimpel's "It *could* happen!" — but evasion. Nor does Singer allow us to confuse Yasha's quasi-nihilism with his own view (although one or two of the novel's reviewers made a point of missing this point). Yasha anticipates the protagonists of Singer's most successful stories. In his next anthology, *The Spinoza of Market Street*, the title character — a bilious Polish intellectual — marries his devoted charwoman in a gesture of resignation when his pantheistic creed no longer sustains him. And the Jewish doctor, in "Wedding in Brownsville," having miraculously escaped extermination, finds that his separation from his fellows

— first enforced, then prideful — has apparently placed him outside of the barriers of life and death, like a Henry James revenant.

As the latter-day saints of the *Gimpel* stories have their counterparts in the passive sinners, so the alienated characters of these later stories are counterparted by rebellious daredevils: those who, perversely and desperately, try to reshape or merely disrupt the very matrix of the world. In their dashing or thundering bravura, these figures seem nearer to the lineage of Jacobean drama than to the Yiddish types of Sholem Aleichem or Perutz. Such is Reb Itche Nachum, of "The Fast," who is outwardly pious and self-demeaning, but actually turns his devotion into a lever for self-pity and vengeful rage. His fasting is itself a demonic outrage against nature, and against the religion he pretends to serve. And, at last, the vehemence of his jealousy will become palpable; avenging him, without his knowledge, on the woman who rejected him.

In the stories of *Short Friday*, the force of the imagination becomes a force indeed: a natural energy, like electricity, which can overleap the conscious will. And yet, this enormity of the imagination merely reasserts the individual's dependent place in the community. Which is to say, of course, not the social community only, but the community of nature itself. If there is any kind of mysticism in this, it is the truest kind of mysticism: that is, the most earthly-rooted kind. Singer is saying, I believe, that no more than Heaven, may the world and its realities be violated or mishandled. He is more concerned than previously with the tragi-comic reversals by which life avenges and restores itself. Even a prank can resound as a major upheaval, as in the slight story, "Big and Little"; or the wonderful story, "Teibele and Her Demon," in which a situation of Petronius — or, operetta — evolves, through Singer's amalgam of warm earthiness, delicacy and sympathy — a a lyric romance, enchantingly poignant as anything he has written.

This masterpiece is equalled by the stunning tour-de-force of "Blood"; the heroine of which, within the tiny scale of her Polish village, is as horrendously insatiable as Lear's daughters, or Vittoria Corombona. "The cabalists know," begins the story, "that passion for blood and the passion for flesh have the same origin, and this is the reason 'Thou shalt not kill' is followed by 'Thou shalt not commit adultery.' " In the person of Risha Ehrlichman, the twin lusts find unexampled union. The formidable wife of a doddering, gentle Jewish landowner, she becomes fiercely attracted to the ritual slaughterer whom she forced her husband to employ on his estate; and, making love to him, finds her brutal carnality further inflamed by the blood and writhings of dying animals. Eventually her savage fantasy extends itself to corrupt and madden the town.

Despite the obvious potential luridness of his materials, Singer distinguishes himself here, as much as anywhere in his writing, by his sense of scale: not only the tightly marshalled color of his style, but the humane perspective which keeps him from romantically over-indulging monstrousness and phantasmagoria. Seen empirically, he stresses the more trivial of Risha's sins: the corruption of ritual. But this sin against religious form is not to be seen empirically. Rather, it is to be seen within the world which Singer not so much creates as perceives: a world in which the laws of God and nature are as one. In his fidelity to this world, perhaps, I. B. Singer belies my previous distinction: a religious artist *and* a profoundly moral one.

Critic
Going
Everywhere

Manny Farber's criticism is an extension of his painting, of his talk. *Extension* is the theme of his work. The
fretful energy which births his virtues and sometimes
faults, is an energy through which work covers ground:
the terrain existing only to be covered, not occupied, not
(for too long a time, at least) staked out. Thus, the work,
painting or movie criticism or art criticism, advances
horizontally, in all possible directions, never seeming to
exist for a simple progress from A to B; and getting away
as far as possible from any pivot, any centripetal force.
The criticism which Farber published to so little notice
in *The New Republic* (1941 through 1946) and *The Nation* (1948 through 1952) and in *The New Leader* during
the later fifties, and in *Commentary* on occasion — all
prophesied, from the forties on, the main directions and
motifs and attitudes which only now are being recognized as defining contemporary art at its most important.
And Farber prophesied, not through jeremiads (although
a lot of his writing can be taken as such — superficially, I
feel); nor rubrics, but through a crepuscular swirl of
observations, images, wise-cracks, puns and remarks, frequently uncalled-for (in the sense of unauthorized; seldom in the sense of unwarranted). A style that transects
all the boundaries, supposed and otherwise, between reviewing and criticism, because Farber perceives criticism
as a constant review, during which the reviewer sits in no
box, remains at no post, but runs his ass off to keep up.

This last, I think, may be a foremost reason why Manny Farber has never gained the audience which attaches (often on the basis of his poorest, most self-indulgently fancy and sentimental work) to James Agee. Agee at his best was an assessor, a summarizer of art, who sensed that behind many of his subjects was that which either refuted or out-stripped his attitudes. The testimonial of Agee's worth was the cleft in his self-regard, which his perceptions occasioned: the desire to *be* the provincial which his limitations decreed; warring against the desire, never entirely articulated, perhaps never entirely admitted, to be something considerably larger and wilder. And in the cleft, I think, he found that partnership — a partnership of accord, never of actual collaboration — which carried him and Manny Farber through parallel careers on *The Nation* and *The New Republic*. Yet, it must be noted, that during this time, when Agee was in the ascendant, Farber's work was still tentative and teacherish (although the conventional language is constantly buckling to blasts of angry opinion; and during his last years on *The New Republic,* with the reviews of *Song of Bernadette* and *Open City* and *The Well-Digger's Daughter* and *Henry V*, the language and sentiments begin to jostle and wrench into the familiar voice.) Only when Farber took over as movie critic on *The Nation*, in late 1948, after Agee's resignation in favor of screen-writing, does the critical writing fully display the exasperated alertness, the seeming assurance (which, however, encompasses so many distractions), the combative skepticism which contribute to the most original and valuable film criticism in America today.

It's easy but still a considerable mistake, to infer from this — or even from reading Farber's criticism — that his work is essentially "negative" in any of the popular modes of cynicism and opposition and darkness. What really, valuably alarms about his writing is not its negativism but its wildness, its seemingly utter lack of commitment to any ideological post or critical stand. This I recall, was what most alarmed me on first reading his pieces on Huston and Carol Reed and Stanley Kramer, in the late forties. Leafing through bound copies of *The Nation* in the stacks of Brooklyn College library, I was most put on the defensive by the lack of center to Farber's attacks on these men, who then seemed to so many like magnetic poles of artistic and social virtue. Thus, Farber's criticism, the most direct of its age or of many ages for both stating and practising his attitudes, seemed to me an attack on center itself; and, much more disturbingly, an attack which never assumed the brasses of crusade, which couldn't care less (it seemed) who supported it, which couldn't have more firmly resisted proselytes, since the attitudes stated or expressed in one article, would be recast or outright contradicted in two weeks. Farber's pulverizingly clear-sighted appraisal of John Huston (when Huston was scarecely less than Lorenzo the Magnificent to so many critics, Agee included) can serve as a tract for film critics of two decades, *not* because he wants to destroy Huston (he points out many genuine virtues which survive in Huston's work in these out-of-favor times) but because he wants to know what the hell Huston is all about, which is to say, what explains the contradictions in Huston's work between a rather cold, cleanly-focused craftsmanship and a yeasty pretentiousness (mixed with a still-less-becoming opportunism and sentimentality) which has dominated in films like *Moulin Rouge* and *We Were Strangers.* Nor will Farber settle for any of the slogans, paradigma, bargain-counter poetics, with which critics ever-increasingly try to settle all arguments. *He wants language to do the job of explaining*. And anyone who thinks this an easy request, has no notion of what language has become since the forties, or in whose hands it has found itself, or rather, lost itself. Nor any idea of what explaining really means.

Manny Farber's command of journalistic rhythms and, rather too often, journalistic means, somehow never hide the truth that he is a painter who writes. He uses language as he uses paint, as a medium of unfixed exactness: precision which is repeatedly merging and changing, having to be refocused and renewed. There is no metaphor in his writing: the outright metaphors which he seems repeatedly to employ in a conventional way, are generally used as ironic wise-cracks, to demonstrate (a) the false extravagance, the human improbability, of what he is writing about, and (b) the distance between such confusion and the resources of any self-respecting language. His images are the self-mocking images of western tall talk; and I do not cite them for the same reason I have not heretofore quoted from Manny Farber, seemingly one of our most quotable writers: it is far preferrable to read the articles themselves, which join and separate and rejoin the phrases in endless web, justifying them at every turn. He uses metaphor mockingly because, unlike the solemn users of metaphor, he enjoys no confidence at all about the limits of the world. And unless a man can enjoy such confidence, he must hold himself, if he be artist or critic, accountable for every inch he covers: constantly measuring and constantly leaving the measurements behind. This is the lesson which, notably among poets and painters, has only in the last few years begun to affirm its truth. Artists have become makers of maps on which there can be no more *terra incognita*. Land is unknown only because one has not yet reached it. When you reach it, you know already all that you can know, which is to say, all that the present time allows. It exists, but it cannot continually exist, save through the act of moving on, thus extending it through one's movement. Farber, I say, has long recognized this. His recognition is itself hard to recognize, at first, because, in the forties issues of *The Nation*, he must write mainly attacks: attacks which, I repeat, seem more devastating than they are, because Farber does not intend to devastate. He wants only to move along, and this purpose must prove anathema to the unmoving, and the unmovable; which forms so much of the most popular art and writing; most particularly in the center-seeking forties and fifties, but scarcely less since then!

The lesson which Manny Farber brought home to me when I first read him — against all the resistance of temperament and persuasion which I could summon, against all the partisans which I then found at my side — was, the bulk and crowdedness of the art world, and its inseparableness from the world all of us know. The clamorous geography of this world informs everything he writes, or paints, and — still more important — so does his sense of himself as a pedestrian witness to this world — as anything but its Cortez! The categorical arrogance of his tone is always being qualified, if not countermanded, by his humor, more robust than ironic, reminding the reader of how large and unfinished is the job which a serious critic assumes. In Farber's writing, a single artist or artwork lets in a throng of artists, who, in turn, have to make their own space against the audiences, or against the sheer physical data of the world. Read him on the Krolls' furniture, or on Matisse, or the paintings of James Brooks. Thus, the seeming shapelessness of his articles, in which the implication of the opening sentence might be totally bypassed by the dissection of the artist's work (see his obituary piece on Val Lewton, as well as his later tribute to Lewton's film, *The Leopard Man*.) So, too, his "failure" to "develop" ideas or motifs, in the *conventional journalistic sense*. His genuine development of his perceptions takes the form of brocading them, augmenting them with other observations and aphorisms — not trying to persuade audiences, but testing the durability of those observations by leading them throughout the world. A painter's mode of development.

It is startling to realize — so radical is so much of his tone and stance—that Manny Farber is deeply conservative, yet he is. And, like the best conservatives, he counterpoises the richness of the world against the modesty with which we must use it. We cannot own art — whether the work or the activity — by fiat, he seems to be saying in each of his articles. All we can do with art is produce it — an endless traffic of behavior — and all we can own are the boundaries of ourselves. Thus, his admirations: filmmakers like Sam Fuller and Robert Aldrich, John Sturges and Anthony Mann (all of whom Farber was first to evaluate for American audiences.) The common denominator of these artists (or artists like Brooks, Hopper) is not their masculinity (although manliness is an essential component of their work) but, their dedication to their art; *not* as a replica of themselves, but as an emanation of themselves, a current of that behavior which at once links them to the world and dissolves them among the things of the world. Manny Farber has discerned and embodies this dedication.

I think that his most important weakness is an over-respect for certain journalistic values — mainly, the most secondary sort, involved with making his writing more emotionally accosting, more punchy. The greatest harm in this deference, I think, is its impingement on his genuine abilities and needs — mainly his acute appreciation of *surfaces*, which is of course crucial to the art I have tried to characterize. Often, when he seems most journalistically canny, Farber is simply using what is most pertinent to his best purposes — i.e., convincing his readers and spectators that the "depths" of art, if that mean the values of art, lie in its surfaces: that there is no floating capital in art, but only the cash on hand, the hard currency. However, the journalistic element of his writing, and his own aptitude for it, too-frequently encourage us to read faster than we ought to and less often than we ought to. And it conveys on occasion a swagger, an assured glibness to Farber's writing which belies the real content of his criticism — wherein he is constantly thinking through his observations and the terms which he gives them. He is most painterly in this, that he adds and revises on the spot: without any apparent need for retrenchment, for recapitulation, for reappraisals agonizing or otherwise. Sometimes, however, the too-consummate rhythms of his writing, the too-easily-appreciated wisecracks, encourage us to overlook the characteristic abrasiveness and good confusion.

Yet, these weaknesses never really put off anyone willing to meet Manny Farber as a co-participant of his world, which is the world that shows itself to us today.

Ed
Dorn's
Transients

Edward Dorn's most recent book, *The Rites of Passage*, is best to be understood and appreciated, not as a novel, but as its subtitle characterizes it: a "Brief History." More precisely, an autobiographical chronicle: not the evolving accretion of a novel; but a ribbon of time, a succession of episodes and vignettes and interpolated reflections by Dorn. Not that it is desultory; with his familiar tone of mock-leisurely vigor, his gravid warmth, Ed Dorn bears witness to the importance of each event. And — although *The Rites of Passage* is to be distinguished from the excellent poems in his first two collections, *Hands Up* and *The Newly Fallen* — this sense of bearing witness, through one illumination after another, lends his new book its kinship with his poetry.

The setting, and theme, of *The Rites of Passage*, is a landscape of impermanency: the Cascade Valley near Puget Sound, with its populace of fruit-pickers, loggers, impoverished Indians: people who are passing through, or who are trying to forage the rudiments of a home or daily work. A country of incessant transition, which Dorn announces on his first page with an image of the weather:

"Every aspect of the land and sky is smudged. The cold, fine, substance, more than mist, not quite rain, naturally haunts the atmosphere as it moves in slightly blown waves back and forth across the land and the islands."

"More than mist, not quite rain," the crepuscular haze

shifts through the daily lives of three families which Dorn's history comprises. Each family finds itself among, yet apart from, the other tenants of the Valley. Piecing together a kind of domesticity, all are impelled, by temperamental restlessness, discontent, or the simple pressures of weather and joblessness, to move and move again. Jim McCarty drinks himself out of paychecks, laces his barroom conversation with references to Nietzsche, Jack London or Florence Nightingale, fights and boozes, in his foul automobile, with his Esquimau wife, Ramona. Hendersson, former kept man and convict, is trying to recreate a frontiersman's existence by poaching deer on the lands adjoining his shack. Recalling prison, he notes that

"When the sun comes up it comes up different in prison. . . . It's closer in prison. When you're on the outside the sun is a long way off. There are many convicts in prisons all over this country that are awake right now. It's still dark but they're awake."

The impingements of an ever-contracting space weigh upon these people, with a weight which Dorn conveys to us, often as successfully as in his most remarkable poems: "The Open Road," with its "particles of men/who are the outriders of golden dreams

> "and who wake to a grey morning
> finding themselves
> that their homey
>   delvings gleam
> only with cotton batting lions
> trotting no more breathlessly
> than they"

Or, "On the Debt My Mother Owed to Sears Roebuck," "The Tepee at Tomah," and the most extraordinary tribute to "Ledyard: The Exhaustion of Sheer Distance:"

> But what I wonder at times,
> being only from Illinois is
> did you count the stretching corridors
> of spruce on that trek coming back
> as we used to count telephone poles

No need to speak of Jack Kerouac, in such a context: Dorn resists false romance as effectually as any contemporary American I know; while not yielding a gram of respect for the restlessness of these people, whose concern with the rudiments of living is too pressing for such restlessness to provide a mere exercise in self-bedazzlement through sight-seeing. That space which, in southwestern America, may still seem boundless, is, in fact, bounded virtually everywhere, Dorn perceives; most of all, in men's imaginations, their wills. So are the lives of Navajos bounded, in William Eastlake's novels, by the civilization of tourists, fugitives, professors and poets. So the world of Claude Squires' odyssey, in Douglas Woolf's *Wall to Wall*, is fringed by used-car lot and sanitarium.

Carl Wyman — the third and most complex of Dorn's family-men — embodies this sense of fettered yearning. More than the romantic Hendersson or the semi-primitive McCarty, Wyman stands apart from the valley's existence, although forced to seek work, even as the other men, in logging camps and on farms. He is repelled, on the one hand, by the McCartys' improvidence and filth, and on the other, by the callousness of Hendersson's rebellion. For his own part — the son of a put-upon tenant farmer — Wyman recoils from the commonplace violence and ugliness of farm life, and from the more vast horror of wastefulness which these casual unpleasantnesses embody (a sequence of chilling lyricism, too long to quote here, describes the boy Carl's reactions to a chicken being decapitated). Wyman's viewpoint, I hardly need underscore, is that of a very particular, rather than a "universal" or "typical" intelligence; yet, it is Wyman whose humane, although essentially helpless, sensibility rallies the images and currents of the book around its emergent theme: the struggle — no less gallant because it is only fractionally willing, only imperfectly intelligent — of hard-driven people against the *wastefulness* which engulfs them and repeatedly infects their lives.

Although only occasionally does Wyman react straight-on to their struggle, and his, his very presence focusses the situation, and enriches it. For example, his recollections of the farm, with its incessantly replenished excreta — livestock and human — provide the book with its most important imagery: imagery of excretion, in a score of forms — tubercular hocking, masturbation, defecating — which culminate in the awful terminal image of a man being expelled "like the wadding in a gun," from a flooded tunnel.

I have no intention of suggesting that *The Rites of Passage* is in any sense coprophilic (in any sense, that is, except insofar as Dorn's acceptance of the least questionable human needs and occasions, is never far from love). No more do I wish to imply that these images and motifs are at all conspicuously "brilliant," like little flags marking the author's conquest of Human Experience. Dorn's nearly perfect tact, always riding abreast of his vigor, repeatedly enables him to see without exploiting: imagery, metaphor, even overt comment at times, appears to surface, as through the merest change of emphasis.

I wish to underline Dorn's tactfulness — the perceptible distance which he always (sometimes, I feel, only half-voluntarily) assumes from his writing — because this quality appears to me central to both prose and poetry.

Here, particularly, because in this book, Dorn is testifying to a world through which, by nature of the chronicle, he and his reader must pass as hikers, or as pilgrims: a world over which he exercises no right of conquest. It is a mistake, I feel, to think of Dorn's poetic voice as droning (a reaction I have heard several times; based partly, perhaps, on Dorn's evident admiration for William Carlos Williams). If he drones on occasion — almost always purposefully, if not always successfully in his purpose — he can speak with elegance, grave or mocking; with staccato intentness; with tangy lyricism. For all these tones, separately or in combination, I recommend the poems mentioned and quoted above; plus "The Land Below," or "Hawthorne, End of March, 1962," "The Song is Ended for Nellie L," "Trail Creek, Aug. 11, the Reason of Higher Powers."

In *The Rites of Passage*, Dorn has deliberately relinquished his poetic self-possession. Here, his voice is not charged with assembling the world in the form of poetry. It would be misleading to call his style more limited than in the poems: its function is different — noting, appraising, sometimes perhaps a little too often, interjecting comment. The plastic clarity of this style never seems an act of self-denying will: Dorn as much as tells us that making one's self accessible to the world is as important as remolding what one can of the world. Yet, he never recedes altogether from our notice; Carl Wyman is his outpost in the valley of passage.

The prose reflects, for all its temperance, a deliberateness that a reader, not knowing Dorn the poet, could mistake, at times, for distrust of language. Ellipticism is never his purpose: if an extra word is needed to nail in the meaning, better that nail than that the structure tumble. Once or twice, it *does* tumble, however, simply from too many nails; and every so often Dorn's carefulness seems that over-carefulness which follows on too-hasty thought; an impression not much helped by the frequently poor proof-reading of this edition.

But the overall excellence of this book, is the way in which it reticently, yet by no means modestly, strives to *locate* author and reader in a present-tense world, a world as yet unencapsulated by metaphor, for which (at least, so Dorn and others temporarily succeed in persuading me) the best medium must be an intensified journalism, itself a re-affirmation of prose as significantly apart from poetry. I see Dorn's "Brief History," here, in company with Hubert Selby's *Last Exit to Brooklyn* and Gil Sorrentino's *The Sky Changes*, to appear in March, which I have just read, delightedly, in galley proof. Such writing represents, it seems to me, no "trend" (at least, I hope not; for a trend would ultimately mean mere imitation, which could mean only a return to that tackiness from which Dorn and others have wrestled their new journalism). If whatever writing follows from it, should include the equals of Dorn and Sorrentino (just as likely, it will be led by them and others) why should American readers and writers not be hopeful?

Over
the
Cliff

In the decade since I wrote *Cliffhanger Comic,* about
Al Capp's *Li'l Abner,* the most crucial event by far in the
Yokum saga has been Abner's marriage to Daisy Mae.
This occurred in 1951, as the result, I take it, of those
"public pressures" which are so often misread, as they
were in this case. For Abner's implacable virginity was —
next to Downwind Jaxon's permanently averted face in
Smilin' Jack — the arch tease of the comic-strip world.
Too, it was central to that secrecy which gave *Lil' Abner*
its tone, its unity and — beyond the rather specious satire
and fantasy — its fascination.

The trouble was that obviously, for Al Capp, this
permanent virginity conditioned Abner's world: a world
permanently suspended, a cliffhanger world, equally imperilled by the prospect over the cliff, or that of level
ground. Capp, after considerable wobbling, settled for
over-the-cliff. I can only assume that he thus decided to
take seriously the doowah long circulated about the "self-
contained world" of Abner; than which a world less self-
contained would be hard to find off the stage of the old
Palace. *Li'l Abner* was all missing walls, open ends and
breakaway chairs. Its glory was its two-dimensionality,
not the cheesy fantastic-realism accorded it by academi-
cians and other sentimentalists. Capp's very imagination
— I'm not talking about ingenuity — lacked one wall.
Billy DeBeck, who divorced Barney Google with such
brusque and jovial aplomb, might have met the chal-

lenges of marrying off Abner, assuming he'd have considered Abner worth his time. Capp, who built a career on making shift with his stunted and fractured inventive power, found his strength in mockery of his characters' humanity. To make Abner's marriage (a) funny, (b) humanly persuasive, would have entailed an imaginative coup of which he had never shown himself capable; not to metion a total refutation of his strip's basic premise. His reaction was very nearly as interesting: he wrenched the typical parody of his strip into something more openly acrid and rancidly grotesque than had ever appeared theretofore. Those strips following Daisy Mae's wedding with Abner are probably the strangest, most distasteful and most idiosyncratic comic strips to appear in America at that time. Immediately, on the honeymoon, Abner was entrusted by Mammy Yokum with an enormous phallus-shaped ham — the Family Ham — which, like the family pig, Salomey, was inviolate (one of Capp's typically askew introductions of his Jewish background; another being that the Yokum family subsists on pork chops). Li'l' Abner's solicitude for this monstrous, vaguely animate ("I kin hear its heart beatin'!" he reassures himself, when the ham has been struck by the railroad engine) talisman, comes between and his bride in every respect, including, of course, the most agonizing. The eerie, travestied sexuality of these episodes caused several panels to be banned by local papers.

Like so many primitive societies, Dogpatch in upheaval was attended by all manner of prodigies and portents. Foremost among these: Mammy Yokum "gave birth" to a younger brother for Abner — a blonde, even-more-lumpish near duplicate named Tiny. Mammy had produced Tiny while visiting a neighbor — then had absent-mindedly left him, deeming the experience an attack of indigestion. Obviously, Capp, his *jeune premier* deposed, felt pressed to rush in a surrogate Lil' Abner. But the most striking feature of his ploy was the naked ugliness of its grotesquerie, and the bilious contempt implied in it. Mammy Yokum's standard role, of course, had been emblem and (Capp's usual jugglery) caricature of motherhood — as institution, not as biological process. But beyond that, the grotesquerie and scorn of the episode — neither element unfamiliar to Capp's readers — took their heavy, mordant tone from the rawness of Capp's importunity: he *had* to do this; and, for the first time, his desperation seemed remote from sport, from daredevil enterprise. The pressure which he had acknowledged by marrying off Abner was simply too hectoring, too obvious. And it was the pressure not of commercial expediency alone, but of biological reality: that reality which he had flouted so long. His sole retaliation against this triumphant reality was a snarling disconsolate mockery of marriage and birth. But that act of retaliation was many-sided. For Daisy Mae, for instance, honeymoon frustration was the lightest affliction. During successive months she became monstrously fat (through compulsively eating mad mushrooms); lost all her hair; broke her nose and was forced to wear a sack over her head. What made these — well, yes, assaults — so singularly shocking, beyond the hyperbolic dilemmas of other episodes, was, first, their common physical basis — heavily outlined by the contorted natualism of Capp's drawing style — and the common implication, which seemed only then to have dawned on Capp, that, as marriageable, reproducible creatures, his characters were also perishable: they could die. Marriage predicated death; therefore, let her, the one most responsible, bear the ugly brunt of physical liability.

Once again: Abner's marriage rent the veil of teasing ambiguity, which had sustained it, bodying forth its origi-

nality. Except for *Little Orphan Annie,* no comic strip —
probably — was so distinguished by what it did *not* say,
did *not* show, *Li'l' Abner's* power came from its underground rivers of hostility and repressed sexual energy
and irony, which — thanks to the shagginess of Capp's
narrative, the gnarliness of his drawing — were *felt* more
than they were specifically perceived. If the content skittered away from sexuality, the drawing — the winding
black line, the use of silhouettes — squirmed with sexual
implications, straight and kinky. When the drawing soft-
pedalled violence, the dialogue played it *fortissimo.*

Throughout, Capp's tactic was giving with one hand
what he took away with the other. As a mama-figure,
Mammy Yokum was both benign and haggish, often
simultaneously. Capp derided the situation of an urban
Jew exploiting hillbilly primitives, not only in the use
of "in" Yiddishisms, but by oblique references — sar-
donically reversed — to Jewish culture. Thus pigs — or
the pig Salomey — is taboo for dietary purposes in the
Dogpatch canon; although the Yokums subsist on pork
chops, the source of which is never identified. Domestic
virtues are fondled and chaffed in the Yokums' sweetly
troglodyte household. This repertoire of ambiguities and
withheld secrets, all refers to the anality of *Li'l' Abner;*
which, I think, has flourished its sexual hangup as bla-
tantly and as indefatigably as any family-oriented strip.
Buttocks in every guise and situation (no office scene is
complete without a curvy secretary stooping to that bottom file-drawer); excrement (Senator Phogbound, the ma-
nure expert; outhouse jokes in quantity sufficient to
wrinkle Chic Sale's brow); corporal punishment whenever indicated, even tentatively. Recently Capp's tastes
have obtruded themselves so as to cloy even the connois-
seur: one episode, a couple of months ago, had Salomey
pursued by a foreign delegate named Rumpelmayer, who

yearned for roast rump; was referred to on an average of once an episode as "our greatest asset"; with a cataract of similar puns, calculated to beggar the combined memories of the above mentioned Chic Sale, Pat Henning, and any team of Minsky's writers.

Anality means the separation of experiences, each safely packeted, so as to have the best of each: as in *Li'l Abner,* squalor and dirt and ugliness (but also, the Noble Savage in his shaggy purity) alternating with luxury, glamor, svelte beauty (also, selfishness and megalomania). Anality means the harboring of secrets, the inviolate cache. All such symptoms are rooted in anxiety about the body, and about its vulnerability to the dirt and pain of reality. When Capp married off Abner, he imperilled the separation of experiences: Abner's insulation from sex, and its piquant side-products. He sacrificed his cache — the mystery of Abner's continuous virginity, and how far it could be placed in jeopardy. And he included in the package a sacrifice graver and less reparable: the sacrifice of his emotional commitment to the strip, the creatively anxious involvement, which one felt as a transmitter-wave day after day: that gambler's enthusiasm and mock-cynicism, *Li'l Abner's* real warranty of youth. When Abner married, it was like a departure from Shangri-La; he and Daisy Mae did not grow up, but they grew very old.

The ultimate result of this impasse was that Capp should turn "conservative" — a conservatism as meretricious as his liberalism of a decade ago. For conservatism in its valid forms, entails giving — giving, with full acknowledgement of the giver's boundaries, personal and proprietary. Capp's reaction against his past liberalism was entirely self-protective — a scrambling makeshift of identity, to replace the identity which has been jeopardized by his vast concession.

That is half the trouble — his conservatism now has no more integrity than his libralism then. Then, too, he opposed big business and establishment meddling — remember General Bullmoose, and Bet-A-Million Bashby? Senator Jack S. Phogbound was lanced against quaint provincials as much (at least) as political reactionaries. Only a Swift could sustain the change — or what has remained unchanged.

And Al Capp is no Swift — the other part of the reason mentioned before. The strongest instincts of Li'l' Abner — discernable by the most casual or lowbrow reader — were duplicity and self-insulation. And their justifying force was a devil-may-care excitement and abandon. Now, Capp is still playing to popular response — but with all his cards face up. I agree and sympathize with many of his present-day sentiments, and still turn up some amusing episodes — Pappy Yokum's experiences with today's judicial labyrinths — but good conservative satire — and most good satire is fundamentally conservative — requires a more solvent more enterprising bile. Conservatives must be more concerned with principles than the liberals — and Capp never showed concern with any principle between self-preservation and genital preservation. Joan Baez as Joanie Phonie, just isn't enough.

Reading it mainly in sorrow and embarrassment, I recall the awful bleak dignity of *Little Orphan Annie* in its last episodes, when its author, Harold Gray, was dying of cancer. Would such dignity ever be imaginable for Li'l' Abner? Is it ever imaginable for the old who frantically pretend to youth?

The Land of
Grace and Isolation

Now might well be none too soon to write about the writing of William Eastlake, two of whose novels—*Go in Beauty* and *The Bronc People*—have long been out of print, and whose third, most recent novel, *Portrait of an Artist with Twenty-Six Horses,* has been hustled to the graceless old age of remainder counters. The three novels are linked by their common landscape—Southwestern America, particularly the checkerboard territory of New Mexico—and the reappearance in each of George Bowman, rancher turned Navajo trader, with various members of his family. In the different sorts of emphasis which they accord common themes, in their variations on recurrent metaphors and symbols, these three books might be regarded as the contributory panels of a triptych.

Go in Beauty, the first novel, corresponds to the central panel in its catalogue of details and themes of Eastlake's landscape which is actually two landscapes. The New Mexico prairie, with its striped meccas, sinister arroyos, red Morrison formations, all contain and reinforce an invisible landscape: the community of Navajos, with their dessicated but not moribund culture, spiritually living out their years of fullness in monstrous incubators.

This terrain might well suggest why Eastlake's novels have found so little of their deserved reception. The American Southwest is too blatant and too monotonous— it is too obtrusive as a *setting*—for many of those contemporaries of Eastlake who deal with the afflictions of consciousness, and whose only concern with setting, usually, is how to make do with as little as possible. For these writers and their readers, Eastlake's involvement with his landscape might easily suggest the term "regional writing" which, in turn, might easily suggest the literary equivalent of those papier-mâché miniature landscapes enclosed by glass spheres.

Yet such terms convey nothing of the most impressive paradox in Eastlakes' first novel: the way in which he achieves his fullness of landscape through a sense of *distance* from that landscape. *Go in Beauty*, in a very real sense, is a novel of distances: the psychic and physical distances, from the Indians and from each other, of George Bowman and his brother, Alexander, who wants to write a novel commemorating the historic Southwest of their grandfather. Alexander falls in love with George's wife and leaves with her to travel through Europe, becoming a successful regional novelist. A drought descends upon the Navajo territory—the result, the Indians feel, of Alexander's desertion and George's failure to forgive him.

From this point—through a procession of vignettes illustrating George's efforts to express his forgiveness, and Alexander's increasing agony of nonfulfillment and separation—a seemingly conventional triangle story swells toward the bas-relief dimensions of fable. Despite occasional overindulgence in the wide gesture and glib sententiousness (two faults which will become more pronounced as Eastlake's virtues intensify) the fable succeeds; basically, because of Eastlake's wise candor in admitting that, beyond a certain point, the Navajo community is inaccessible to his imagination, except through the language of indirection and metaphor. Part of the Navajo's collective life is two-dimensional spectacle, much of it for white men's eyes; the other, major part must be barely articulable in white men's words or to white men's minds.

Eastlake plainly recognizes and acknowledges this, and counters his limitations by presenting the New Mexico territory through a battery of images, delicately caricatured Indians and white men, and pattering, insidiously stylized speech:

> *Why really, I hate to say this but you think everybody on the big reservation is crazy. You think their religion gives them no togetherness with nature, has nothing to do with medicine and is for the ignorant and superstitious. . . . You think they think what is good for the big car is good for the country and what is bad for the big car is good for the enemy. Why really, I hate to say this. . . .*

So speaks the old medicine man, Paracelsus. Also in *Go in Beauty* we encounter the first example of that imagery which will often preoccupy Eastlake: images of spying, of people watching scenes and tableaux or simply, one another's behavior; of passive onlookers; of a reality constantly verging on stage spectacle.

Eastlake's approach to his subject is distinguished by his own sense of apartness from the Indians. This psychic remoteness widens his compass to accommodate a skepticism and moral ambiguity in which overreverence is counterbalanced by exact perception, plus mockery; in which Indian shrines are seen as futile museum fixtures or tombs. Central to *Go in Beauty* is the house of petrified wood—"neither wood nor stone"—in which the brothers' grandfather lived, and in which George Bowman, as trader and semi-recluse, passes his hours: a retreat and a tabernacle, but also a hiding place for George's own spiritual evasions about his relationship with his brother; and, almost, a moral sepulcher.

Perhaps because of the sense of distance from the

Navajo landscape Eastlake's writing in this first novel is very attentive to the externals of land and of people. The countryside of *Go in Beauty,* while rich in symbols and metaphors, is not itself a metaphor; Eastlake's scrutiny is too close for that. The kind of distance I have been describing is not the aesthetic distance, the receding and returning of the subject, through which metaphor gestates. In his second novel, *The Bronc People,* the gestation has occurred. Here, the landscape houses a coiled irony. A precocious Negro boy, whose father—a scholarly recluse—was murdered and his ranch burned by white marauders, has been adopted by George Bowman and his second wife, who have settled on the father's land. The boy has become good friends with Bowman's son (who is himself bedeviled by the memory of an adored rodeo star, whom he has seen smashed nearly to death during a performance).

Here, Eastlake's graces—his feeling for concrete imagery, his command of prose rhythms which redound almost to slackness, then whip into sudden compressed statement —produce a fusion of richness and stripped concentration which makes *The Bronc People,* the most beautifully organic of the three novels. The Indians play a much more dynamic role than in *Go in Beauty* where, despite their importance, they seemed not entirely assimilated into the situation of the Bowman brothers. They function both as chorus (the book opens with a scene of red comedy: two Indians watching, from afar, a range war, making the listless running comments of inveterate television viewers) and as featured players—but always as magnetic stations to the moral atmosphere of the story. To Eastlake's vision, the Indian community encapsulates the sort of grace manifested in the passion and strength of his own writing. Grace: but not Hemingway's grace of chivalric honor and stoicism, nor Steinbeck's odd benediction on the squalid. Even the Indians' passiveness exercises dynamic influence: like a magnet rallying iron filings, their social and spiritual suspension seems to call to itself the frustrations of white outsiders. A missionary, stupefied by their genial indifference to his God (they use a funeral as occasion for a social dance, and wonder when the bier he refers to is going to be served) realizes that he, in the near-paralysis of his will, is more dependent on them than they on him; and, with a final gesture of surrender, draws them to him at last. The Negro boy becomes aware that the gall of his dilemma resides not in his being persecuted (the whites are kindly, the Indians accept him as a different sort of white man) but in his being, like the Indians, stultifyingly overprotected.

The moral paralysis of the whites is counterpointed not only by the Indians' grace, but by the spaciousness and luxuriance of the desert. Eastlake knows how to deflect this grandeur well before it becomes romanticism (as in *Go in Beauty* where he compares a striped mecca with a crumpled flag); here, he poises the largeness of his setting against the pizzicati of the dialogue between the Negro and white boy. In this way, he brings out perfectly the specific gravity of the boys' dialogue: their world, personal but by no means trivial, weighed against the geographic world in which they move. The boys seldom speak directly of their problems yet these problems are sensed through the conversation like far-off hoof beats, the vibrations of which are felt before the animals are seen. Against such nervous shuttling, the background acts alternately as stage-setting, ominous bystander and *deus ex machina;* its massiveness contrasting in turn, with the boys' tensed facetiousness and with the half-concealed wirings of anxiety or bitterness, so that all effects reinforce one another without embarrassment to any.

Compared with *The Bronc People, Portrait of an*

Artist with Twenty-Six Horses shows Eastlake widening and complicating the vision of the second book. *The Bronc People,* in basic form, was a relatively conventional novel: the frustrations of the boys were shown, or withheld from view, through a score of permutations; but their common situation was the dynamic, question-scattering situation of a novel. *Twenty-Six Horses* is more episodic and naive seeming than *The Bronc People;* it is, in fact, a sophisticated reversal on both *The Bronc People* and the more naturalistic *Go in Beauty:* an allegory of human self-destructiveness and, set against it, the ubiquity of moral choice.

The book consists, for the most part, of a succession of *fioretti*-like episodes—they could easily be the stanzas of a ballad, or the story-telling links of an Indian necklace —all threaded, as in *The Bronc People,* by two boys' resistance to their fathers. Here, George's son, Ring, is troubled by his father's having taken into his hogan a Navajo girl, a former acquaintance of Ring, who was involved ominously in the death of an Indian boy. Ring's friend, Twenty-Six Horses, has left his father, a one-time communal leader, now deposed by the white man's influence, whose wife runs an unsuccessful pseudo-white restaurant.

These intersecting situations are screened by a foliage of more or less contributory incidents, dialogue, thematic variations. This multiple perspective is one of Eastlake's more important techniques; he has a dexterity which is probably as much indebted to ballet as to drama, which he exhibits when moving toward imminent violence, then shying from it, then unexpectedly, at another time, closing with it (the brilliantly fluctuating episode of the rodeo performers enroute). In *Portrait of an Artist with Twenty-Six Horses,* this technique is strained more severely than in either of the two earlier novels, in the interests of the allegorical scheme. And, on behalf of this same scheme, Eastlake calls more strenuously upon "typical" themes and situations (the Indian boy leaving the reservation for the first time; the rodeo performer losing his nerve) of Western myth, legend and first-to-fifth-rate literature. These cliché situations, deliberately selected, have served Eastlake in the past to illustrate the tensions between imagination and an almost unencompassable reality which is always proliferating myths and clichés. And Eastlake nearly always, in some way, reverses these seemingly trite situations, or paraphrases them brilliantly. But occasionally his oblique, diminuendo methods produce something close to *reductio ad absurdum* (the episode of the Nazi, for example, reminds me of Edna St. Vincent Millay's less fortunate World War II poetry; and is, in any case, less successful than the comparable episode in *Go in Beauty* about the foreign-car festival supervisor).

The real situation, the real theme of the book, is not so much the common distress of Ring and Twenty-Six Horses, as another variant (its skepticism not perfectly concealed by the sweetness of Eastlake's voice) of the original theme of grace, which *The Bronc People* brought to fruition. This variant might be expressed most succintly as "hanging on," or in Synanon's phrase, "Hang tough." The central situation is almost literally a "cliff hanger"; and the book proliferates images of suspension (the old medicine man's horse balking on the crest of the hill; the rodeo riders' Lincoln teetering on a bluff) which, with a mixture of seeming crudeness and sophisticated evocativeness, portray a variety of people suspended between affirmation and self-destructive resignation. As usual, only the Indians manage to reconcile affirmation with seeming resignation.

The completion of Eastlake's theme is resurrection: a kind of resurrection which might well exhaust the credit extended to religion by many imaginations. Eastlake's token resurrection is a phony magic stunt concocted by the two boys and tendered by them to the dying medicine man, so that he can enter heaven with good evidence of his magic powers. The point is that the magic's falsity is redeemed by the life-conveying power of its art. Indian magic and Indian art merge in a single turquoise-hued strand to furnish the reassurance of Eastlake's world, much as I. B. Singer's God furnishes the solidity for his world. The very spiritual suspension of the Indians and whites provides the unmoored condition in which this art flourishes; and even the imagery of suspension becomes exultant in the book's titular symbol: the Indian boy's painting of the twenty-six horses which comprise his name; which hover, taunting and encouraging, on the mountain's face.

My main cavil is simply that Eastlake's techniques, having achieved suppleness so rapidly, may be conceding too much to neatness and patness and facility. Even the *fioretti* episode structure, so promising in itself, has an oddly contradictory glibness; and very often in this book the art of the short-story writer, the art of revelation through image and metaphor, seems to threaten the art of the novelist, which is involved with permutation, the proteanness of experience. These doubts murmur—as yet, only murmur—against my enthusiasm.

In any case, it is our good luck, if not Eastlake's, that *Portrait of an Artist* can still be bought from remainder shelves for some 49c. May it be Eastlake's and our good luck that he have continued vigor and gifts, to build campfires around which great themes can dance.

Noble
Savage

Recently, I've enjoyed reading three of the "Doc Savage" pulp novels which Bantam Books has been reprinting in paperback. They afford, not the cowardly—and self-depreciating—pleasure of "camp" (a distortion of Susan Sontag's meaning), but the liberating fantasy (however occasionally wadded with pulp magazine crumminess and nonsense) of Dashiell Hammett, or at times, Chandler. Many of them were written, in fact—I found out recently—under the pseudonym, Kenneth Robeson—by Lester Dent, a contributor to the blue-jawed *Black Mask Magazine,* in which the contemporary American private eye largely originated. I hadn't read *Doc Savage* in its original pulp format, during the thirties and forties: the only pulp heroes I was at all acquainted with, were *The Shadow*—whose adventures I admired for the ingeniously staged stunts (a description of thugs doing an office hold-up with a clothing-store dummy) and intricately staged fights (one such free-for-all, in *The Black Dragon,* as I remember, involved a Japanese ceremonial sword, the wooden sheath of which cannot be broken until the sword is to spill blood); and *The Spider,* of which I remember only two issues—so unbelievable and abominably written, it seemed to me even then, that I suppose I never read any others. Only recently, however—in Ellery Queen's 1965 anniversary magazine, I read one of Dent's *Black Mask* stories (printed by Queen under the title, "Tropical Disturbance," and by Ron Goulart, in his anthology *The Hard-Boiled Dicks,* as "Angel Fish") which featured a Florida adventurer named Oscar Sail. As described by Dent, Sail is long and lanky (as are several of the supporting cast in the Savage stories) and somewhat piratical-looking, being dressed entirely in black, with black-painted sneakers. Sail, however, functions as a nautical private eye—extricating a beautiful girl from the cross-traffic of a treasure-hunt by competitive bandits—and he moves with the weightlessness of an elemental through adventures which—as in Hammett's writing—bulge, with their own bas-relief, the familiar-looking planes of reality. In this story, as in much of the Doc Savage writing, Dent's use of violence is constantly restrained and purposeful, and yet sensational as well—in the superior sense of "genuinely surprising." The acts of violence—even more, the insistently conveyed apprehension of violence—are the lubricant of Dent's plot-machine.

Doc Savage is as much an elemental, as mythically-imagined, as Oscar Sail or any of the outstanding pulp and boys' book heroes. His name suggests the "noble savage;" his epithet, "The Man of Bronze," carries inflections of the Old Testament warriors, as well as the Mayan and Aztec civilizations. In appearance, too, he is something other than a latter-day Anglo-Saxon, with his constantly bronzed skin and gold-flecked eyes. Like tribal heroes, he possesses the full encyclopedia of physical and intellectual skills (with emphasis on the sciences). But the name Savage is combined with "Doc:" the popular name for a benign healer; and the pattern of Doc's knight-errant adventures, with his retinue (who are also supposed to be scientists, but might as easily be called Little Savages) are, if not non-violent, at least consistently non-murderous. The bullets they fire merely anesthetize; as do the "poisoned" sword-canes brandished by the group's legal expert.

In his biographical note for *The Hard-Boiled Dicks*, Ron Goulart mentions that Dent devised a master-plot for his years of pulp manufacture. I should suppose, from the four Dent stories I've read, that this master-plot centered on the Quest: a treasure-hunt, engaged in by the good guys, the heavies (usually, several camps, or competing factions in one camp) and some essentially innocent by-stander, through whose hands the treasure passes, thereby endangering her (always, her). This situation, of course, works to the utmost advantage of the pulp hero, since it enables him to function at varieties of violent action, without imposing on him any *obligation* to be violent (as would the revenge plot). The pulp hero, as mythic hero, constantly renews his extraordinary nature by contending with extraordinary events *which he has begotten*. He rides those djinn which he has called up. Yet, a merely functioning hero would be automation. For me, Doc Savage and the Shadow and the Continental Op possess a residual magic which consists, in great part, of creating magical situations from the vortices of their hidden personalities—then, at last, dispelling those shadows for new ones.

It seems to me significant that none of the heroes I have mentioned, wear masks, *a la* Batman and Robin. Any masks, of course, would be superfluous, since their personalities are masks. The Shadow, as an elemental of darkness, wears a black costume which enables him to camouflage himself (unlike the filter-voiced hypnotic stunts of the radio version), and occasionally, briefly like any pro, wears disguises. But, of course, the Shadow's cloak and slouch-hat are extensions of him. He is not "really" Lamont Cranston, as on radio; Cranston is merely an alternate identity. He is "really" the Shadow, *tout court.*

Just so, a mask is a kind of apology to society: a way of saying (a) you see, I recognize myself as an outcast *by your terms,* and (b) of saying, please accept me as not-

really-Bruce Wayne, or Richard Wentworth, or whoever. The men I have referred to, concede no gesture to society. The only "normal" lives they know, are lives for which the wounds in the surface of reality are constantly re-opening.

I should add, that Doc Savage is less consistently successful than Oscar Sail (even in that one story) or Hammett's heroes; simply because Doc, as a series character, was devised for that peculiar age-range of early teens to early twenties, and that peculiar amalgam of metropolitan toughness and hero-seeking naiveté, which characterized the pulp-audience of the Depression. As a series character, Doc has to wear his heroism—has to wear, rather, the events which beget his heroism—more loosely and flashily than do Sail or the Op; has to insist more on gratuitous virtue than those men, whose common virtue was sparked by one abrasion after the other. From all I can tell, Dent had a firmly-packed imagination, a sense of trimness, which must have been repeatedly embarrassed by that repeated need to gawp about Doc's superhuman skills. A slightly less encumbering convention was the need for an entourage: about four or five less-catholically-endowed scientists, who bandy thirties' slang and squabble among themselves like the characters of any innocuous boys' gang series. But they, at least, are occasionally interesting when they are required to blunder (as Doc never does) or suffer (as Doc cannot do).

But when Dent becomes involved with closely-observed action, and/or hanky-panky, the lower-grade hokum evaporates like the imagistic blood of their gun-duels. Dent evidently relished quick-change reversals of character, or mysterious behavior, suddenly explained. He savoured these whirring toys as no mere jaded retailer of magazine fiction ever could have. My favorite of the three books I have lately read—*Fear Cay*—is almost pure

Black Mask, for great stretches: the opening section, a cataract of delightful flim-flam, carries its participants from a shyster lawyer's office in and out of several shooting-frays, to a disastrous reception for a Hollywood starlet, to the swamps of Flushing, where a hanged corpse is resurrected briskly enough to contribute its share of the fighting. *Quest of the Qui*—the latest re-issued by Bantam —is nearly as good, with its Icelandic pygmies (Dent's evocation of Iceland cold is as theatrically vivid as his descriptions of tropic Florida) and one, to me, unexpectedly scary scene in which one of Doc's aides is nearly frozen to death. *The Thousand-Headed Man,* which takes the Savages to Malaya (in pursuit of a dandified Oriental villain, who is hyper-solicitous about his gold fingernail protectors: no good at all in hand-to-hand combat!) is more hammy and strenuous than the others. But, as I say, they pleased me with a modest fullness of pleasure, which I had long since ceased to expect from pulp writing; not that much honest pulp writing can be found any longer.

The
Fire

"What perhaps was most pathetic about
the Morrison and LaPorte suicides was the
futility of such attempts at martyrdom . . .
within the ample means and methods of
U. S. democracy, a human voice means
more than a human torch . . . 'The mark of
the immature man is that he wants to die
nobly for a cause, while the mark of a mature man is that he wants to live humbly
for one.' "

Time, Religion Department, mark you;
November 19, 1965

Well, it's always nice to know, courtesy of *Time* magazine, how not to be a successful martyr; not to mention
(courtesy of *Time* plus Wilhelm Stekel) the difference
between maturity and immaturity. At that, I might observe, it was pretty daring of *Time*'s Religion Page to
select its bit of terminal wisdom from one of the age's
leading heretics; especially when substantially the same
wisdom was available from the dialogue of the average
TV drama.

I have read a number of pronouncements, steeped in
that peculiarly retrospective maturity which *Time* so
admires, on the deaths of Morrison and LaPorte: the
Quaker and Catholic Worker who burned themselves to
death in protest against our conduct of the Vietnamese
war. Intermingled with it is large measure of that compassion which, in its all-encompassing scope, does not
balk at acknowledging that men like Morrison and La-

Porte were moral cowards; so long as the compassionate ones can thereby forgive—i.e., overlook—the disturbing implications of Morrison's and LaPorte's common fanaticism. *Newsweek,* writing about LaPorte's death, even put in a good word for the Catholic Workers; while in *Life,* a few issues back (I wish I had the copy before me; but the words aren't that easy to forget) a Mr. Loudon Wainright, who is somewhat the house expert on suicide over at *Life* (having written a previous article on the subject, a month before) declared that the issues of Vietnam had to be "chewed over"; whereas the unobliging Morrison "chose to die." This unaccented conclusion by Mr. Wainright suggested, somehow, a tactful shrug, a murmured "If that's how you want it—"

The tenor of such—what to call them? reactions, arguments—seems to be merely that Morrison and LaPorte were suicides, like many others. Mr. Wainright's philosophic consolation was commended, in the next issue of *Life,* by a psychiatrist in charge of an organization devoted to rescuing prospective suicides from their actions. I do not mean by this observation to disparage suicides, although the few with which I have been familiar have seemed to me dreadfully mistaken; the silly popular reaction that they take the "easy way out," is refuted, for me, by the several attempts I can recall having made, earlier in my life: anything but easy, as my survival may indicate. At any rate, for whatever my opinion may count, I think that most suicides are probably mistaken: mistaken in that the unhappy people believe they can somehow possess, somehow absorb, the violence with which they are striving to rend the texture of a life they feel they despise. They hold to the hope that they can cling to their actions; but the characteristic of any violence is, that it detaches itself from the man committing it. This is why the term "impersonal violence" is a redundancy. A violent act, once done, cannot be drawn back as on a line, cannot be controlled; it can be controlled only while it remains a contemplated act.

Yet, the essential fallacy—and the essential nobility—of Morrison's and LaPorte's actions, was not that of the average suicide, I think. I can only hope that I do them no injustice—and that I am not being merely portentous and pseudo-mystical—when I say that I think death, as such, was only a secondary consideration in their terrible gestures of protest. And the irony of statements like those I have cited, or the *Herald Tribune* editorial which Nat Hentoff has dealt with, in *The Village Voice*—is, that these people do what they charge Morrison and LaPorte with having done: they pretend that death is only a separate compartment from life; that death does not permeate life, as we know it does; that death exists, indeed, only to be forgotten by the living for as long as they can manage to forget it. And, believing thus, the people of whom I speak, commit the grave error of regarding Morrison's and LaPorte's deaths as *someone else's* death; thereby assuming that the manner of dying, makes irrelevant the purposes, the structure of actions, which culminated in suicide; presupposing, in effect, that the suicides were *never* conscious and responsible and, living men. So that—blaming Morrison and LaPorte for disavowing their share in other people's lives—the accusers disavow their share in the lives which Morrison and LaPorte have left them.

For, as ultimately mistaken as I believe them to have been, I also believe that Morrison and LaPorte's deaths were perpetrated as acts of faith in life, and faith in the people who would carry on life, and carry on, too, some of the most hideous aspects of current life, i.e., the events of modern warfare about which we read daily. No matter how much one can sympathize with the original motives of America's participation in the Vietnamese war, no one, I think, can conscientiously deny that, against the horrible, willful and often gratuitous violence performed by both sides—the Viet Cong and the South Vietnamese, plus the United States—such motives could have been fully redeemed only by a near-miracle of clear-sightedness and charity and honesty, surely unheard of in most contemporary warfare. At best, we can only hope, immediately, fractionally to redeem the professed reasons for our entry into the Viet Nam war against the Communists. And even such fractional redemption can only result from a far more positive decency and intelligence, a far more vigorous determination that the worthy purpose of anti-Communism will *not* result in our playing ducks and drakes with the lives of helpless people—than, many of us feel, our administration has so far begun to demonstrate.

I do not mean, indeed, to comment extensively on the politics of the Viet Nam war, since I am in no wise qualified to—nor, indeed, were the deaths of Morrison and LaPorte especially relevant to the political behavior of America and the Viet Cong. As dreadful, and, in a very important sense, as presumptuous as they were, their actions were as humble as anything I have heard or read pertaining to Viet Nam. For they, I believe, were trying, agonizedly, to make intelligible—not bearable, not at all; but *intelligible;* and that, by no means in terms of the intelligence alone—the unspeakable, barbarous and insensate violence in which all parties have engaged since, I presume, the war's beginning; often, as though expecting such violence in itself to coalesce into a policy, or give rise to one. Reading in daily newspapers about the bestialities committed by muggers, thieves, rapists, racist fanatics or brutalized police—I have felt, from time to time, like doing the same thing which Morrison and LaPorte did; feeling at that moment a oneness such as I have not often felt, before or since, with those people who were simple bystanders, onlookers; yet, were touched by even relatively mean, rat-vicious violence, *as* violence. I cannot say, even now—nor would I care to guess—how much of sanity, of selfishness, of cowardice, of sheer inertia, or of some atrophied faith, combined to stop my hand. Yet, how much more of this must Morrison and LaPorte have felt? Quakers and Catholics, men whose work as pacifists, whose temperaments, whose vocations, made them *recipients* of the world in which they lived: who found themselves, like bladders distended out and out by scalding water, filled with the unfocussed violence from which they could not for an instant disallow themselves.

So, it really seems to me, they tried to make metaphors of themselves; to force upon their countrymen, a vivid awareness of how arbitrary, how ragged, was the reality which morally impinged upon them. Vanity, surely, to feel this way, and to place such faith in their fellow-Americans' response to a single, desperate action. Yet, we draw, it seems to me, very glib distinctions between Morrison and LaPorte and the Christian martyrs, say; who, we are quick to point out, sacrificed their lives only when they knew that no other action was possible, or only when they knew that the faith would not otherwise survive. Were they really so (by present standards) clearsighted? Has the future of *any* faith so depended upon the life of a single man as to satisfy Herr Nietzsche's requirements for martyrdom (standards by which, at any rate, he exonerated himself)? How many authentic war heroes would survive the strictures we apply to Morrison and LaPorte, if we knew about their motives and instincts all that was to be known? But the difference, of course, between war heroes and the kind of madmen with whom we deal here is that, for those who have not fought beside them at any rate, the heroes often provide a reassurance: that death flows seamlessly into life; their lives being swallowed up in our own. We go on for a little while about the high example of their sacrifice, and how we must all live better; while actually, even at the time, congratulating ourselves on being worthy, even in our unworthiness; and persuading ourselves with no excessive delay, that all "they" want is for us to go on as we have been.

The deaths of Morrison and LaPorte were not heroes' deaths; yet, neither may we easily swallow them; and perhaps that is all we can ask. That, and a reminder, and warning: that burning one's self to death may not, to be sure, be the worst form of self-destruction. Compared with the piecemeal death of the soul, the slow daily murder of the heart—in the name of calculated indifference, apathy or even noble stoicism—reducing one's self to ashes may seem an act of grace.

Pontius Pilate
on the Bench

"Under a new law, adopted this year, juries first arrive at a verdict of guilty or not guilty, and in a conviction, are permitted to recommend either death sentence or life imprisonment."

From the *New York Times*,
October 12, 1963.

"Have fun. You called me a killer. Sleep tight, gents."

Francis Bloeth, the second man to receive the death sentence under the law quoted above.

In a sense, the most disheartening reaction to the New York State law, quoted above, will be the probable question of many liberals: "How much difference can it make?" The law is an atrocity against jurisprudence, human intelligence, any coherent notion of human conscience. Yet, we have progressed; an issue of conscience, one of the most awful and probably one of the most needless which we in America must constantly face, has been transferred from the holy tabernacle to something resembling a board of directors' meeting. The phrase, "capital punishment," is, and always has been, an obscenity in the mouth of anyone under God Himself; the obscenity is now a little less awesome, and a little more crass. So—many people of sanguine reflexes might ask— just what has been lost?

The answer is, a great deal. It has been, probably since

the 19th century, a self-deception to suppose that capital punishment with its evil absoluteness could be reformed "gradually": a more flagrant, more ugly self-deception than the "deliberate speed" theory of civil rights reform. Even if the law were executed a thousand times more fairly than it is now, even if every convicted murderer could look forward to appealing his case a hundred times, the imminence of the final sentence after the hundredth appeal failed — the fact that this sentence was accepted as a possibility — would pervert the meaning of the "due process" which had gone before.

The evil of capital punishment, plainly and simply, is that no one who prescribes it, or administers it, can possibly control it; can possibly make restitution of what they take away. This is the answer to those liberals who argue that laws like the one under discussion are, "at least," a fractional advance toward civilization of our laws. Lives *cannot* be taken, or saved, fractionally; and the lives taken by the death sentence are not particles of the corporate state, but individual mysteries, no matter how bestially or how splendidly they have been used. The state cannot pride itself on sparing a life as long as it takes another life the following day. It can credit itself only with madness; which may or may not be less degrading than fanaticism.

The death sentence may have meant something else, however cruel and ferocious, when God's participation in legal matters was taken reasonably seriously; so that execution, while an act of vengeance, was also a holy ritual: the judges and public saying, in effect, we cannot pursue further this evil riddle, we commend final judgment to the Great Judge. It was, of course, no better for the victim; but perhaps a little less bad for the souls of his judges and executioners, who may thus have recognized, on occasion, what a mystery, and abomination, they were invoking.

With the disappearance of God, everything has become abomination; abomination crass rather than mysterious. Every department of the law is debased; because the death sentence, no matter how insane the principle behind it, becomes, by its very gravity, the center of our law. So, in fact, the death sentence becomes identified with the enigma and grandeur of death itself. So, in fact, with the disappearance of God, the death sentence has become equal in its solemnity and irreducibility, to the will of God. Like God's will, it can be temporized with, even cheated in small, unimportant ways, but never, ultimately, denied. And, indeed, it enjoys one advantage over God; Whose will, while immutable, is often concealed. The results of the death sentence are always unmistakable.

So the death sentence, like a cache of decaying meat, sends its reeking sweetness through the most innocent sections of the law. And the people who submit to this law passively are as subject to its corruption — even though indirectly — as those who participate in its administration. Every law — particularly every evil law — has two lives, the one which it enjoys in the statutes, and the one which it enjoys in the imagination of the public, who see refracted in it their anxieties, ideals, hatreds, hero-worship. The death sentence holds out, to every citizen, the promise of personal revenge; the fulfillment of that yearning for a cruel and impossible power, with which the most decent men may sometimes console themselves for the humiliations and importunities which civilized laws occasionally impose. And the more fair and reasonable every other law, the more exacerbated one's resentment at the need to deaden one's instinctive feelings, by submitting to a law which so closely reflects the strictures of one's own conscience. And the sweeter the aroma from the possibility that one day you might legally destroy your fellow man. In this way, the death penalty becomes, for all honest laymen, the explanation of all other, milder laws.

It might be protested that the present law can at least be acknowledged to have stripped the death penalty of its more sacrosanct pretensions; that no excuse now exists for seeing it as any other but what it is. The judge, for example, has for some time been little more than a glorified arbitrator, whose authority is nearly as atrophied as that of the King of England. Then why not transfer the authority outright, in token as in reality, to the jury? And why not give this dismissal of one more illusion credit for what it is?

This sounds true as far as it goes: nobody could ask for a more devastating *reductio ad absurdum* of institutional law than the spectacle of a man being told "We want you to die" by a jury of his supposed peers, consisting in fact of hair-dressers, insurance-salesmen, and notary publics, in an assemblage which may have no resemblance to the intellectual or economic level of the prisoner on trial; and just as little resemblance to the gathering of neighbors decreed by the Hebraic Law, which this procedure charades.

And yet, at bottom, such realism is only a more virulent euphemism. The continuation of capital punishment is a matter not of mere ignorance, or madness, but of hypocrisy. And while ignorance or insanity may be tended, hypocrisy must be cauterized, as events in the South and the North have recently demonstrated. The issue here does not reside in the secondary illusions represented by judge and jury; but in the fundamental illusion that legal killing can have anything to do with law or morality. Madness is a fight against reality; hypocrisy is a fight, not only against reality, but against one's consciousness of reality. The only way in which the pivotal illusion of the death sentence can be removed is by changing the reality in which this illusion is embedded.

And will we sacrifice so little, in sacrificing the token authority of the judge? A murder trial, simply because it deals, usually so flagrantly, with intangibles, often lends a much-stronger-than-usual metaphorical importance to the ceremonies of judicial procedure. And, in this divesting of the judge, the most important loss — uniting the metaphorical and the real — lies with the dismantling of authority. Here, precisely, the worst fatuities of modern-day liberalism and modern-day conservatism shake hands with each other: in the contempt for authority which is expressed symbolically, here, in the discountenancing of the judge. For a rough, but serviceable parallel, see the treatment of the late Pope John by both liberals and conservatives: as insensitively possessive, or as callously disdainful, as though he were a toastmaster at an Elks' luncheon. And in the office of the murder trial judge — as in the office of the Pope — authority appears as the embodiment of human conscience. The judge demonstrates the price which passing judgment exacts of any reasonable and feeling human being: the price in solitude, in exacerbation of conscience, in the recognition of distances between the judge and the victim of judgment, which no one can ever entirely bridge. And these agonies of authority will continue, for every humane judge who sits at a New York murder trial. (This is not to deny the existence of judges to whom *any* decision is equally a gall; and who will welcome this blessing on their inertia.) Those who had intended, with this law, to eliminate the judge's innate authority have not done so, simply because this authority has been for so long more symbolic than actual; and, because this symbolism will be perpetuated in the conscience of every honorable and reasonable judge; even though from now on his only meaning, to the intelligent onlooker, must be not as a tragic figure, but as a figure of pathos.

For the new law does not *shift* responsibility — how

can it, with a responsibility which the law never possessed? — but truncates responsibility, the responsibility of human conscience. To find a suitable metaphor for such a law, one must resort to Camus's essay. "Notes on the Guillotine," in which the instrument of "punishment" is also a perfect image of contemporary justice. This headlessness of the current law, is why those arguments sound feeble, which say that at least the new law will confront the layman — as represented by the jury — with the moral cost of capital punishment. The most obvious question for such an assertion is: How can the law propose to regulate people's attitudes, when the law cannot change the situation which shapes those attitudes? People of naturally sensitive conscience have always been repelled and perplexed by the necessity of voting "Guilty" on a murder jury. Less sensitive people will probably not be affected by a law which confronts them, not so much with the horror of execution, as with its aura of personal power for the juror. And even if every other juror serving on a murder trial were to undergo conversion as the result of his experience, would this justify the hypocrisy of a law which deceives its citizens about their power over their fellows? Even more so now, it would seem; since, now, the emphasis has been shifted from the necessity of the jury reaching a decision, sifting evidence, considering probabilities of truth or falsehood — to the necessity of a jury passing a sentence.

To reach such a decision means not a distribution of judgment, but a division of guilt. To reach a verdict of "Guilty," and pass sentence, on behalf of a completely fictitious community, cannot resemble a board of directors' conference, at which a fluid theme is debated and ideas contributed. The death penalty is not an idea that can leave free the mind of anyone involved in it.

An additional consideration, by no means the least

important: the currency of popular imagination is the law, good or bad. And a law with the temptations of this one for the best of men, can establish itself in the popular imagination with frightening speed: congealing in the mind with the publication of each successive verdict. For those who have not taken a part in the trial, the law cannot seem so different from the previous law; so it will be, except for those who actually serve. And, except for the extraordinarily humane and courageous, they will probably never have the opportunity to use whatever they may learn. In most cases, they will probably never want to serve on such a jury again.

Heretofore, in America, the jurors have been the holy blind of legal process; like the blind man, the juror personified complete receptiveness to experience, and complete respect for the plausibility of surfaces. Juries' only necessary virtues have been collective good sense and discretion, and a lack of either vengefulness or sentimental partiality toward criminals. The phrase "jury of one's peers" can be taken to mean that the average juror should be at least as free to make decisions as once was the man being judged.

Can this be true any longer, in the state of New York? For the revised construction of murder jurors' responsibility entails not only an average man's receptiveness to actuality, and his sense of community, but the metaphysical intelligence of an ethical philosopher. It demands not merely the jurors' willingness to be fair and compassionate, but their willingness to resist a positive invitation to be judicial murderers. The old system, at its best, ignored complexities, to its benefit, permitting the jurors to function completely within their roles. The new system imposes a monstrous *non sequitur* on those roles. And what kind of jurors can this insure in future, assuming that the conscientious people available must be reduced proportionately by the terrible absurdity confronting them now?

To sum up: the greatest moral fallacy afflicting Americans today is the belief that we are familiar with death; that we can take possession of death through our imagination. The death penalty has long perpetuated this fallacy, by imposing a specious order on a fact which recognizes no order, which is essentially extraneous to human intelligence. Now, in the current jury law, we have the final ferocious parody of itself by this civilized superstition: the belief that we can pay off legal murder, through refining ceremonies, through strengthening the appearances of control and equity. So we propitiate an insane situation, by paying graft to reality; or, rather, by trying to force reality into the symbolic molds provided by the law. In such a situation, the price that reality exacts is far more drastic than we are willing to pay: and no amount of enlightenment, short of enlightenment by truth itself, can satisfy this price.

A Vote of
No Confidence

The most shocking aspect of that epilogue to his career, it seem to me, is the feeling that he always needed me more than I realized. *Me*: i.e., his audience. In the bleakest and grandest moments of his seeming isolation, Westbrook Pegler had handcuffed himself to his reader; and now, the reader sits about a foot away from Pegler's campfire, with that black rotunda just outside.

Pete Hamill did well, in his recent *New York Post* column, to mention Pegler's vagrant debut in the white supremacist *Counsellor*, of Louisiana. The excerpt which Hamill quoted was an astonishing fantasia about the adulterative presence of Jews (or as Pegler spelt them, "jews") in the Hearst syndicate. It was pricked out with references to the "sheeny superstitions" of Hearst columnist George E. Sokolsky and the duplicities of manager Richard Berlin; who once, according to Pegler, informed Pegler that he, Berlin, had "rolled on the floor" over a Pegler attack on the Anti-Defamation League; but that the "Jew Klux" — allegedly clamoring in Berlin's ante-chambers — would have to be smoothed down with the "Eli, Eli bit." Hamill did well, I say, to mention it; and — in writing about Pegler's removal from his vocation, and from life, with evident sympathy and ruefulness — he did, I suppose, as well as might be expected.

Yet Hamill's remarks seemed to me clogged with the romantic sentimentality which marbles the comments of that other former-Pegler-fan-now-Pegler-mourner, Murray Kempton. Kempton's observation, cited by Hamill, that only someone whose wife loves him as Pegler's wife loved *him*, can "argue" with Pegler, is a bit of high sentence equal to Kempton's ex-neighbor, Mary Worth. Hamill neglects the conjugal angle of Pegler's journalistic career, but deplores Pegler's antagonism to Walter Reuther and organized labor, and Pegler's need to find a reason for the world's afflictions; leaving us free to infer that such philosophical aberrations might easily lead to anti-Semitism and an outcast's life.

This kind of reverse hero worship ("His ideas were all wrong, of course, but by George, he walked tall in his day!") condescends excessively to Westbrook Pegler's attitudes (I mean, of course, the attitudes of the Roosevelt-and-labor-baiting 1930's and forties) which, while anything but sophisticated, or even thoughtful, were in some ways very shrewd and sensitive, lending his work a drive and solidity it might otherwise have lacked; and condescends, too, toward Pegler's weaknesses: a mental flaccidness (apart from his rhetorical skill) and a temperamental passivity; which, so far as I can tell, from perusal of his 1930's writing, was turning up in his work long before his career showed any decline. If one feels impelled publicly to write a man off, well and good; but one owes him then, it seems to me, the respect of looking at reasons with a humility which precludes sentimentality.

It strikes me that neither Kempton nor Hamill have mentioned the malignancy of Pegler's daily occupation; when he wrote, first for Scripps-Howard, then, in the forties, for Hearst, a daily opinion column. As I see it, such a column, besides fiercely exhausting, must be the most essentially *unnatural* of journalistic tasks. Unnatural, because it depends on the illusion of eternal life, which the columnist, day after day, must sustain (It is understood that I'm not now referring to theatre, music, or other such specialized columnists, who are fortified by at least some compartment of the world.) This eternal life is not, of course, like the immortality of the epic hero; for such immortality, in Homer or the Roland legends, was really the epitome of mortality: its mutability, its courage, its vulnerability; while the columnist's eternal life is of a piece with that of the TV serial hero: i.e., a perversion, featuring infallible virtue, immutable astuteness; fortified by the crassest, and least negligible, virtue of all; the brute ability to survive Thus invigorated, the columnist, like the TV hero, becomes, for his public, through the erosions of time which nevertheless may not kill him, either insufferable irritant, or an affable convention. He appears to be — must appear to be — independent of time, a cheerful circuit rider; whereas in fact, he is more a sharecropper of time, working always on the margins of events.

Westbrook Pegler learned very early in his career, apparently, how to make the best of a potentially pulverizing mechanism. I've been reading some of his thirties' pieces, in *The Dissenting Opinions of Mr. Westbrook Pegler*, and *'Tain't Right*: two collections published in 1936 and 1938; noticing again that singular passiveness which struck me, occasionally, in the 1940's columns he did for Hearst. Even toward the beginning, he seems to have found — or sought — as little ego-capital in his vocation, as any American journalist of the time. Judging by the anthologies they furnished, those thirties' columns were probably as varied in subject-matter and tone as any work Pegler ever did, before or subsequently. He attacks the Ku Klux Klan through a Klansman's imaginary diary ("June 8 — Awful tired all day. Out all night flogging Hyman Cohen, the clothes presser . . . Heard addresses by Kleagle, Kligrapp and Great Exalted Kludd.") He presents a moving, chilling sketch of a "Sick Town:" Eastport, a glum wilderness of debris and lethargy, after the administration cancelled the Passamaquoddy Dam project. He shies at the New Deal, in a fable about a poker game, and proposes a fund for rehabilitating alcoholics, to be garnered from the monies spent by drunks at bars. And yet, whatever the subject or the political slant, Pegler's consistent tone, his basic voice, is self-effacing to evasiveness. He repeatedly adopts *other* voices: the voice of the Kansman; that of George Spelvin (in what I always found the most boring of his productions; not, as Oliver Pilat proposes, because Pegler and Spelvin were so much alike; but rather, because Pegler was imaginatively incapable of projecting himself into a two-dimensional democratic low-brow). When he *does* speak in his own voice, the writing is candid as clear water. He frequently jibes at his more portentous fellows; suddenly cutting short the diatribe, and the column, with a blunt dismissal, like: "This is getting plumb ridiculous." Compare Pegler in the thirties with the urbane sententiousness of his colleague and ex-friend, Heywood Broun; or with as much as you can bear to read of his later colleagues, Lait and Mortimer. There is almost no ostentation, no intimation that "Everything's under control, folks." He evidently acquired very young the knack — more likely, it was an astutely-recognized need — for keeping to the perimeter of events. That knowledge enabled him to scout a column from a phrase, a scene, a Disney cartoon, an incident seen or heard about. And always he treats the column, not as a power conferred, as an office, but as a handy location, a place to be. Even in *The Dissenting Opinions*, you receive the image of a man to whom things happen, *a man who is done to*. At that time, however, his sense of his audience remained solvent: the audience was still to be accosted, confronted with Pegler's *specific* experience; was not yet merely a huge, implacable extension of his writing. So, his passiveness doesn't interfere with humane declarations, tartened by melancholy:

"We somehow do not think of women at all in considering the down-and-outers. They are scarce in the breadlines, they rarely are seen begging in the streets. And they are not recognizable in crowds by the same plain signs which identify busted men . . ."

Hardly brilliant, barely "distinguished" by any of the obvious counters, this passage represents, to me, some of Pegler's very best writing; and some of the best writing in American journalism; precisely because he is *attesting* to misery, not pretending to rectify it through grandiose sentimentality, or epigrammatic social prescriptions. He feels himself a subject of a situation to which he can perceive no end; and this sense of participation, immensely hard for a newspaper columnist to convey, it seems to me — is what Pegler brings his audience; not by disclaiming the distance between himself and them, but by never forgetting it.

His style, not so pressing as later on, was, and is, second only to that of Ring Lardner as a contribution of American journalism to writing. Pegler lacked Lardner's wit, or his almost excruciating sensitivity to the nuances of popular speech. When Pegler pretends to be somebody else, the effect is of false-face rather than of disguise: he never shared Lardner's curiosity about language, or the people using it. But the voice which Pegler achieved, is a miracle of flexibility and precision, as distinguished from reportorial accuracy. His attitude toward elegance was never the nervous half-patronage of Hecht or Gene Fowler, who repeatedly used Fancy Dan circumlocutions to get a cheap laugh (mixed with admiration, of course). Pegler's elegance comes from galvanizing very simple words, or from repeating such a word, to set the beat for one of his disarmingly loose-gaited occasionals. A piece on six-day bicycle races (as stock-piles of philosophy for his more ambitious colleagues) is a howl, in great part from his marimba-like repetition of "think." The untiring lope of the sentences — giving place to unexpected fussiness over some minute qualification —furnishes us, at times, with wild Chicago comedy, always stitched with the already-familiar cruelty: ". . . The designers of the (Chicago) Stadium played the boys a cruel and cynical trick. They canted the Stadium lobby in a steep incline to the door, so that when the boys stand around and rock, they rock themselves gradually down hill and presently out onto the sidewalk. The Garden lobby is a flat lobby, and so are the floors in Washington, so the boys do not rock themselves away."

The reader is borne on a skein of absurd suspense, to the minor key ending. A kind of singing governs Pegler's articles: the words, or rather their sound, is often the most substantial feature; he seems constantly aware that he's delivering nothing else to his audience; nor does this trouble him at all. There is no sustained thought in any of his pieces that I can recall, unless (but are they "thought?") one counts the several exposé series that he did in the forties: on Willie Bioff, the West Coast labor racketeer; on Henry Wallace and his guru pen-pal. He demonstrates very little inventiveness, ever: the poker-game column, the column (quoted above) on punch-drunk fighters and politicians, depend on the basic idea, and the stylistic riffs he performs with it. Nor are there the visual effects, the metaphorical spangles, that you can find in his trashier disciple, Ruark, for example. His writing shows no artistic or intellectual structure, although it displays plenty of form — in the sportsman's sense of that word: grace modelled by playful intensity, to discharge the artist's purpose.

But that reedy, ingenious, faintly Irish voice carried

farther than it is credited. I don't think Hemingway was much of an influence on Pegler; I find more of Mark Twain in the repetitions, the surprise climaxes, the loose-buckled colloquialism. And, in turn, Pegler's application of these devices has, I think, influenced not only Ruark, but a generation of sports columnists who found, not only in the sports columns themselves, but in the subsequent occasionals, a persona to unify and confirm their observations; and a kind of view-finder for the world at large. Jimmy Cannon, in the forties' *New York Post*; Bill Slocum; Ruark's imitator, Richard Starnes; Starnes's imitator, Jimmy Breslin, Breslin's second-stringer, Dick Schapp . . .

Yet, however much they benefitted from him, I think that none of Pegler's admirers and imitators were able to reprise his original contribution: a unique feeling for the *looseness* of everything — current events, human behavior, ethics — lying outside the sure, but hardly snug, enclosure of his column. He never had much sense of complexity — having neither the ability nor, I believe, the will to locate relationships among the prisms of experience — but he was remarkably sensitive to contradictions and distractions; and even a simple-looking article will hum with their exciting pressure. For, sensitive as he was to contradictions and distractions, he was also unafraid of them; so that, even in the open-hearted essay on busted men and women, he must, with a cat-like twitch at the end, score off Edward VIII, a regal down-and-outer, for his opulent pension. In one of his best pieces, in the Birch Society magazine *American Opinion,* he takes the part of a labor czar — Jimmy Hoffa, no less — against a still more odious adversary, Bobby Kennedy. The apparent self-contradiction, here, signifies his response to a deeper contradiction, of Kennedy's pretensions by his occasionally cleat-footed practises. And yet,

I'm sure, Pegler himself never saw it that clearly. To confront contradiction requires a sense of irony which, in turn, entails more confidence in one's mastery of the real world, than Pegler, evidently, ever felt or could feel. Long ago, I warrant, he submitted himself for good and all to the reversals and paradoxes and blow-ups of the world, in a way all but unthinkable for a man resolved to contribute some sort of order to the world. His column is the only stable place, and none too stable at that: like a shanty built within, say, three feet of the river's first tide-marker; the waters, dappled with rubbish, pouring through the shanty's two rooms every other day or so; but never quite dislodging it. And there's always the salvage. Perhaps only a daily syndicated column enables a man so regularly to recognize the variability of life, without facing it.

Those columns of the thirties and forties, in which Pegler attacked the Roosevelt Administration (following a roseate group of articles, the first of which was forthrightly titled "Honeymoon Weeks") are widely accepted by Pegler's Liberal pall-bearers, as advance signs of intellectual sclerosis. I don't agree, even granting much to find fault with, here as in the earlier columns. Apart from my belief that much of Pegler's sentiment against Roosevelt's arrogance and frivolousness, was correct; I think that his sallies against the Administration offered Pegler a terrain outside of his own column's precarious cabin, which — if only for a limited time — stood him in excellent stead: sharpening his wits, endowing him with a purpose beside mere self-sustenance. The purpose I refer to, was that of reaction: a word which has been used often enough as smear, but which I prefer using as identification. Pegler reacted — or better, *counter-reacted* — against everything about the national set-up, which caused him pain or consternation. This "everything" was multi-faceted and, fairly often, contradictory: as I've indicated, he never seemed much attracted to complexity of thought ("Mine are not deluxe thoughts," he concedes, "but they are good and sturdy and give satisfactory results . . .") He had, however, a jabbing response to specific provocations: he seemed to react with his skin more than any other columnist, and his brutally chummy characterizations of F.D.R. and his ménage (Old Moosejaw; La Boca Grande; Bubblehead Henry; Old Wienie) created an entourage resembling the pestilential secondary characters in comic strips.

Pegler's skin, I dare say, was always the most important ingredient in his critiques of men and affairs. Time after time, through all the knuckly playfulness, the Roosevelts and Wallace and Ickes seem to cause him something like the sensation of too-tight garters, or a socially inaccessible itch. This ability to ache and chafe from others' foolishness and corruption (and, occasionally, misery: late in the thirties, when his career as anti-liberal troglodyte was well under way, Pegler wrote the then-famous essay on the fate of Jewish children under Hitler; as well as a piece on the destitute swamp-dwellers of Ocheekobee, Florida, nearly equalling the Eastport sketch) is probably the most important trait he had in common with Swift and Juvenal; not that skin-reaction isn't, in my opinion, a thousand times more meaningful a criterion for satire than highly puffed and guffed "moral vision" (Juvenal's bipartite moral vision — get rid of the faggots and foreigners/pay me more money — is slightly more restricted than the liberals' version of Pegler). Appreciably often, as in the piece on Ickes, he gets masterful results from a combination of sportsfans's argot (which he used far less gravely than Hemingway) with a (probably Irish) ability to deflate by aggrandizing:

"I may not be so hot when you put me in with some of

those mainevent ideology blokes and Fancy Dan econo-
mists, but give me Ickes any time. He was made for me.
Santa Claus brought him for me . . .

"I murdered him out in Chicago during the Democratic Convention when the Party of Roosevelt and
Humanity renominated the Great Indispensable under
the social and political auspices of a gang of political
porch-climbers and who else but Harold the Pure in
Heart?"

What he's doing, of course — and the technique became ever more accommodating over the years — is, scaling *down* the Roosevelt Administration, so that its
members (as well as George Meany, William O. Douglas,
Justice Frankfurter) are conscripted into his troupe. His
handling of Henry Wallace is consistently brutal: Wallace comes through as Punchinello combined with Dum-
mer August. This is why, I now feel that the various
distortions and slanders charged against Pegler, and,
from time to time, proven, were less serious than they
may have appeared: for Pegler pretended less than any
columnist to be a Mass Information medium (although,
of course, he did occasional straight news stories, like the
series on Willie Bioff. And (but this is part of the price
exacted by that eternal life for which he opted) the
boundaries of the column become ever more important
over the years, so that the column at last is not so much a
place, as an aperture before which he must appear, every
day. For a man in many important ways so reticent, Pegler announced his limitations more forthrightly and
more eloquently (although, often enough, unconsciously)
than any of his contemporaries. The stories he told about
F.D.R. and Mrs. Roosevelt, and Wallace and Quentin
Reynolds (all defamatory of the subject's honor, or pro-
priety, or good sense, or sanity) were probably accepted
by Pegler himself, were probably believed by him, on the

occasions when he used them; but the effect they create is of folklore. He seems to entertain no real hope that these horrendous legends will effect any exposure of Roosevelt or of Labor, because — just as the personalities come to resemble comic-strip characters — the evils which they circulated become, in his swirling, spiralling prose, as timeless, that is, as separate from reasonable time, as the episodes of a comic strip: one more scurrilous story melting into the arcana of yesterday.

He had no terrain, however. Swift and Juvenal's best work embodies, not merely aversion to the world, but love-hatred for it: the taste of the world inflames their membranes, like the effect of white *chalah* on the murderous peasant, in Lamed Schapiro's story. As their satire advances, it alters the moral and intellectual shape of the terrain outlying it; and, in turn, must devour more. Pegler is a reactionary; the great satirists are imperialists. That is why his exercises in sustained irony, like the piece about the Klansman, or a testimonial to the "kindliness" of imperial Germany, seem heavy-handed and unpersuasive. He lacked the confidence in his own turf, the assurance that he could prevail over the world, the certitude which gives irony its necessary leverage.

Nor, I think, was he ever truly a conservative, in the sense in which other fractious, eloquent old men— William Carlos Williams, Edward Dahlberg, Graves, Frost, Ezra Pound—have honored the word. Even at their most antagonizing—when you're on the point of saying, well that's that, he's had it, or I've had it—these men, in poetry and printed statement, never relinquish their holding action: clinging to reality and, at the same time, exemplifying reality for us, generously. For no matter how wayward, they are all generous, with the liberality of poets; which is conservative to the bone. I remember some remarks made, some seven years ago, by William

Carlos Williams, on an interview program; in which, perfectly soberly and without rancor, he explained how many Jews, in his opinion, antagonize gentiles by their aloofness and unethical dealings with them. No question of "justifying" such an opinion; rather, the opinion substantiated Dr. Williams: his candor, his good and unassuming provincialism, and, indeed—for he made his remarks while refuting Ezra Pound's patchwork anti-Semitism—Dr. Williams' generosity. It is impudence even to consider apologizing for this man.

By comparison, the awfulness of Pegler's references to "jews," mentioned above, is their lack of *any* passion, generous or otherwise. One senses no imagined assault by khaftans, beaked noses, rabbinical beards. Pegler is sporting with the theme of confusion: the absurdity of a professed Catholic surrounding himself with ideological aliens. The men of whom I have written, even in moments of the most bilious misanthropy, regarded their audiences as extensions of themselves: not merely a waiting "public," vast and nebulous, but a particular image of a "good listener," not merely a reflection of the artist, but a guide to subsequent work. For Pegler, during the most productive sections of his career, the audience seems to have been a crepuscular swarm, Out There. He was always jealous of preserving his identity—the one thing, evidently, he truly cared about "conserving"—yet, that identity seems never to have been rich or complex or satisfying to him. Rather, it seems to have dwindled over the years, into a talisman, like the magic bone worshipped by aboriginal tribes; while the public outlying his columns becomes more shifty and nameless and menacing. Indentured to a daily column, one finds oneself ever more obliged to open one's self out; to publicize, thus simplifying and making innocuous, one's eccentricities and tics. Pegler recognized this very early in the game, I am sure. When he wrote to a critic: My real name is Westbrook Pegler; what's yours? There is more in the cry than mere glib, sloganeering xenophobia; though the fear of foreigners, of all immeasurables, entered into his writing again and again, increasingly in the forties and fifties. They were hateful, of course, not from what he "knew" of them—like the professional racists—but from what he did *not* know. The worst aspect of Pegler's jibes, is that their real target is an audience for which the "jew"—that handy symbol for stupefied despair —is the most articulate emblem.

During the forties, particularly, he learned to make a gambit of confusion. His political-toned columns often resemble test-pattern screens of bewitching zig-zags and scallop-shapes. The idea or proposition or catch-phrase which leads off the column, finds itself a-skitter on the edge of first one, then another spiralling sentence. The game is, keeping intelligibility right-side-up. He writes a zany-exotic parody of O.O. MacIntyre ("Lookalikes: Will Hays and Irwin S. Cobb, Fannie Hurst and Charles M. Schwab, Irving Berlin and Gene Tunney.") His feelings toward George Spelvin and His Missus always came with at least two handles, as far as I could tell; as often as the Spelvins retail folk wisdom, they seem also to be Pegler's mouth-pieces for sheer incoherence: sausage-chains of those flag-waving imbecilities which Pegler most specially despised, and which the Spelvins habitually unwind before an imaginary Congressional Committee, headed by Senator Nilly (Ind., Ind.). The wooziness is compounded by the vagueness of the Spelvins as characters: they display none of the fine-point of even Ring Lardner's most loosely imagined people.

Yet, after all, it isn't Lardner with whom Pegler demands comparison, and contrast, any more than the great satirists of previous centuries; but rather, another American artist, who successfully channelized a sluggish-flowing river of black bile; who, sinuses droning like a fat, lethargic hornet, quietly proposed Boredom as content long before Miss Sontag had years or opportunity; who (and, even now, ahead of Ionesco and gaining!) celebrated the voluptuous inanities of speech, in monologues (often counter-pointed by the regular thuds of overcome dowagers) about how his pet snake rescued him from burglars by rattling for a constable; or, about a Negro midget named Major Moe, who once attacked him with a two-inch assagai sword . . .

But that other captious, eccentric, anxious and abrasively gifted man, W. C. Fields, worked in a more free, more accident-prone medium; he was capable, even in his last years, of conducting inspiriting tug-of-war with his audience, which he had defined, sculpted. Above all, he learned how to salvage that which he found worth salvaging of his identity: in a mask which seemed as obvious as a Los Angeles thoroughfare, but produced the subtleties of an unhealthy summer.

Pegler's graces were the inmost vulnerabilities of his audience, rendered in chemically-unstable art. But around such an art, the public—which the writer has never tried to overcome—can only give back, as refrain, the prophecy of Chesterton's *Lepanto*. The sky does grow darker. And the sea rises higher.

Square
John

It seems a pretty safe bet that Spencer Tracy will never
know the humid raptures of a "cult"—born partly of
public relations, partly of collegiate yearnings to recap-
ture their elders' innocence, partly of authentic admiration, partly of faddishness both scornful and possessive—
such as momentarily enfolds Humphrey Bogart. Bogart
produced a highly serviceable mask—the Bogey mask—
from his image of himself, his screen appearances, and his
audience's willingness to underwrite and enlarge upon
what he offered them. Tracy, in his over-three decades'
career, seems not so much to have offered his audience
any masks, as to have been offered them: the bluff, somewhat loutish Irish charmer; a sardonic Gatsby, wire-walk-
ing between faintly-criminal low-life and great place; a
mellow, pseudo-tough vis-à-vis for Katherine Hepburn;
and finally, the most public mask of all: the Elder States-
man, white hair uncombed, pleated jowls unstraightened
since previous use by Bernard Baruch, Robert Frost and
Carl Sandburg. Tracy, I say, has never entirely filled any
of these masks (although, in a way, the latter one seems
least inappropriate; if only because it has never de-
manded a point-by-point fit; and, too, because Tracy,
since his film debut at the age of thirty, had made a second career of growing old.) His acting, a kind of sculpture, reminds me of Lipchitz's counsel to a young artist
who wanted to sculpt an elephant: "Just hack away everything that doesn't look like an elephant." Tracy's elephant is Tracy. The part that doesn't look like an

elephant is, as often as not, the portion of the film which surrounds him.

He seems to have begun his film career—*Up the River,* for which John Ford summoned him to Hollywood, in 1930—with his acting equipment and his stewardship of it, substantially intact. The role was a comic paraphrase of the part which so impressed Ford on Broadway: "Killer" Mears, the convict—rebel of *The Last Mile;* and subsequently, Tracy did at least one other variant of the criminal-rebel: Tom Connors, of *Twenty Thousand Years in Sing Sing.* You don't notice anything very different from his acting of twenty or thirty years later—anything notably rough, or misfired. Despite the skimpiness of the scenario—a paste-up of episodes from Warden Lawes's book—Tracy, flanked by one of those crystallinely sensitive and-unmannered performances of the younger Bette Davis, is a consistent delight. There is the slightly nasal city tenor, which, angry or prideful, can ring with as hard a brass as any in films. There is the tapestry of gestures: rocking on his heels, massaging chin and jawline with a forefinger, as though testing the durability of his wrinkles, or diagramming new ones. His head tilts with humility, shrewdness, or prowling irony. All the same as later on; and particularly the weight—psychic and sensuous—with which he rams in the bolts of the role. A performance as conservatively forceful as sculpture or carpentry. Anger sets the key for much of this acting, and he is a virtuoso of anger: clanging bravado (when he flings down a pair of ill-fitting pants in the prison haberdashery) or choked fury (his specialty) when he storms into an apartment for a showdown with a shyster lawyer. Yet, he invests the same weight in the scenes of tenderness with Davis, or in the pale, wary voice with which he says "Okay, okay" to a chewing-out by the warden (Arthur Byron). These piano effects, with their obligatto of tremulous anxiety cutting the thick aggressiveness, show the same consistently focussed will: some-times, as in *Captains Courageous,* too nakedly, so that you feel a breach between Tracy and the part: as well as too-vivid a feeling of what he senses the character *should* be: sweet, heroic.

In many important respects, I believe that the films Tracy made for Fox Studios, his first employers, included the most interesting pictures of his career, and his most persuasive aggregate characterization. I'm thinking espe-cially of those pictures in which he played a man on the high wire between a world of either extreme low-life or actual crime, and a world of respectability and, beyond it, opulent power. I've never seen him in what may have been the most distinguished of these films: *The Power and the Glory,* with a screenplay by Preston Sturges and direction by William K. Howard. Tracy co-starred with Colleen Moore as a railroad working-stiff who becomes a transportation magnate; and—recalling the melancholy power of William Howard at his best; recalling, too, Sturges' screen-plays for *Diamond Jim* and *Easy Living,* let alone *Sullivan's Travels* or *The Lady Eve*—I can't help but think that it may have been quite remarkable; and wish that Tracy might have found himself in at least one of Sturges' Paramount comedies, rather than the marinated Lunt-Fontaine things that he did with Hep-burn, Kanin and Gordon.

As it is, the most interesting of those success-chasing films that I can now recall seeing, is *Dante's Inferno;* which ought to have been much better, but offers the splendid presence and intelligence of Henry B. Walthall (who, I think, appeared to better advantage as a sound film actor, than he did in, say, the silent *The Birth of a Nation*); a remarkable set-piece, in which Doré-derived scenes from the *Inferno* are counterpointed by Walthall's voice and a wailing, wordless chorus.

Tracy plays, again, a success-getter: this time, a carny

worker who becomes a voracious amusement tycoon; and whose gambling yacht is finally visited by Dantesque Providence. Although the terms in which the character is presented, seldom rise above competent moral soap-opera, the character itself is striking. For, as it melds with Tracy's performance, although apparently in pursuit of success, the character of the hero seems subtly attuned to failure. Even when he is being most jocular and friendly, most go-getterish, Tracy imprints the performance with a vocabulary of irony and willfulness and calculation, which shows up under the screenplay's light like an invisible ink. He is, of course, from one viewpoint, no more than co-signing the theme of the screenplay: not so much a cautionary tale, as an inspirational sermon for Depression proletarians (And you thought *this* was what you wanted! And you thought Daddy Warbucks was a happy man!) But, after all, Tracy's best contributions to films *were* produced by the Depression. The insistent feeling conveyed by his performances (by no means unique in film acting, but especially haunting from the sense of form, the vocabulary of contradictions, which he brings it) is that picture after picture represents just another phase in a *cumulative performance,* which Tracy is building in his various roles, and, often, independently of the surrounding film; like a hobo helping himself to the materials of a housing project, for use in his shanty.

This reminds me of the converse to his morose go-getter's role that of the down-and-not-quite-outer, who makes a nervous pact with respectability. Here, his most extraordinary film, perhaps, was a Columbia film: *A Man's Castle,* directed by Frank Borzage; in which Tracy, a gruffly mellow drifter, adapts Loretta Young, an Irish wayfarer, to keep house for him in his Central Park Hobohemia. What possible alternatives existed for such material, apart from the rowdy sparring of *My Man God-*

frey, or the wistful cuteness of Robert Nathan? Yet, *A Man's Castle* is at once a most appealing romance, both succinctly lyrical and delicately sensuous; *and* an unexpectedly wry comedy, whose avoidance of LaCava slapstick underscores its imminent bitterness. At the last, the improvised domesticity doesn't take, and Bill is off again, this time with the police somewhere behind; but, also, with Trina well in tow.

Domesticity is touched by restlessness, restlessness, in turn, is fortified by human stoicism. These qualities and their relationships were typical of the American Depression, and, as such, were, I think, embodied in *A Man's Castle*. And the film was embodied in Tracy's performance; which—distinguished by a dry mellowness which he seldom again equalled—could serve as a medallion for all that was good in his film acting. Although his subsequent work with Borzage never duplicated *A Man's Castle*, I am inclined to think that, along with George Cukor and Edward Dmytryk, Borzage was Tracy's best director; that even in the vastly inferior *Mannikin* and *Big City*, they tended to tighten and enrich each others' abilities. Borzage's real talent, it seems to me, always lay in the direction of realistically-tinged romantic comedy; and here, his aptitudes for crisply eloquent pantomime and weightless story-telling gait, are focussed with particular wit and poignance. Tracy's abilities are marshalled and concentrated, so that he melds with the character, and with the distinctive rhythm of the film. I have seldom seen his *body* used at once so tersely and so expressively. He is placed on stilts (from which he conducts a conversation with a lady friend in a top-floor apartment); and makes something very funny of loping across a stage, affably to present a summons ("Surpri-ise!") to a speechless actress. And, in the film's lyric moments (Tracy and Loretta Young, swimming together in the park lake, or watching a flight of migrant birds) the conventionally conceived, but sweetly forthright romanticism (Loretta Young, I should add, displays the nervously vivacious best of her thirties performances) converts both players into something like the mythic figures of silent romances.

After Tracy moved permanently to M.G.M., around 1936, his portrayals began to take on the loose-napped broadness of the movies in which he appeared: *San Francisco, Test Pilot, Captains Courageous, Edison the Man, Boys' Town.* Perhaps I am being whimsical, but it strikes me that in such pictures, Tracy's *face* becomes noticeable almost to the exclusion of his supplementary equipment. With a more ostentatious ruggedness, a richer fresco of wrinkles, than it displayed in the Fox films, this face rather becomes the emblem of Metro's product under Thalberg and Goldwyn and Mayer: spacious, conspicuously painstaking, intricately embossed. My earliest memory of Tracy comes, in fact, from a Metro film: *San Francisco,* seen when I was about six years old. And from *San Francisco,* I chiefly recall Tracy's face, right after Clark Gable punched him in the mouth. That tight-lipped scowl merely seemed to get longer and longer; turning finally into a trickle of blood.

Paradoxically, it is those films in which I first noticed the monolithic quality of Tracy's acting; in great part, I suppose, because roles like Father Flanagan or Manuel in *Captains Courageous,* seem to fit him less well than any of his Fox roles. As adapted to the screen by Mayer's and Thalberg's writers, these parts are neither characters, nor the types in which a firmly and narrowly defined actor could find reasonable freedom. They are, rather, like those enormous (I think, Tibetan) ceremonial masks, beneath which only the wearer's feet can be seen. And, perhaps, the most impressive thing Tracy could do with them was what he *did* do: replace them with his own mask: one which seems an enlargement of his features, but is not; one which seems enormously clear and candid; but—with only a little further scrutiny—proves to be loaded with enigmas. At length, indeed, the mask turns out to be still less a mask than a machine; in which the features can be re-adjusted, the emphasis shifted, by a sliding mechanism; yet, always remain fundamentally the same.

His most characteristic role in the middle thirties, is Square John: the role with which, among many spectators and all-too-many critics, his work and capacities have since been identified. Actually, Square John represents a transition from the success-getters—and domesticated hobos—of Fox, to the Grand Old Man of the fifties and sixties. Whereas the keynote of his early thirties characterizations was restlessness, that of the late thirties was stasis: stoicism saturated with melancholy. In fact, Tracy's typical roles of the late thirties involve a darkening of the frustration which underscores the characters of the entertainment czar in *Dante's Inferno;* the railroaded (and nearly lynched) young laborer in *Fury;* Bill, in *A Man's Castle.*

It was during this period that he became typed (in remarkably few movies, for such forceful typing) as partner to the gregariously swaggering Clark Gable, in *Test Pilot* and *Boom Town.* Tracy's role was intermittently known as "the guy who doesn't get the girl". He might with equal justice have been called "the guy whose advice is never taken," "the guy who loses the fights with Gable," "the guy on the sidelines." Square John was a morosely practical, caustically pessimistic counterpart to the soldier-of-fortune played by Gable: a more intelligent Sancho Panza. And—despite the adventurous opulence of the Gable films—the basis of Tracy's interpretation, its dark fortitude, was as redolent of the Depression as were his earlier taxi drivers and roustabouts. He seemed, at the age of thirty-six or thirty-seven, much older than Gable, or Garfield, or even Bogart; the more so, because, unlike them, his strength seemed deeply related to *inaction*. Indeed, I suspect that he was probably in demand for that very reason: that the glowering presence of Square John, grousing and chivying, undercutting Gable's more ebullient toughness, provided those late Depression audiences with the pediment which they needed, the bracing reminder of the reality to which they would have to return, but not yet; that reality whose tethered, frowning presence made it possible for them to accept the surrounding fantasy.

The fulcrum of his style, his originality—in this period, especially—is, his *reception* of situations. He is what the language of his profession calls a reactor. He has a portion with Richard Barthelmess, Jean Gabin, Henry B. Walthall, Thomas Meighan (indeed, at least as many silent as "sound" actors; for, though Tracy never appeared in silent films, his acting at best has both the largeness and inwardness of silent movie acting); and he is, in turn, at least partly responsible for the acting styles of William Holden, the post-war Glenn Ford, James Whitmore and Ed Nelson. The average of Tracy's contemporaries in the thirties can best be compared to a soldier separated from his division: his tactics combine trying to remember what he can of his commander's instructions; improvising when necessary; sending up a few flares, if indicated; and above all, maintaining something like a cohesive route. The film actor's foremost care—as the connective tissue for a gliding, crepuscular art—is to keep on top of the script, and make as consistent an impression as possible.

Tracy, on the other hand, seems to care scarcely at all about keeping ahead of the script—rather, he seems to immure himself in it, as though digging in for the winter. Instead of creating a cohesive character, he concentrates on registering the impact of every emotional encounter. Yet, this sort of craftsmanship—this dedication to the most intense and most clear reaction—becomes, itself, a sort of consistency which extends from picture to picture. Where most of Bogart's responses seem to take place within him, Tracy presents a vocabulary as blocky and clear as a mural—so much so, that we don't at first notice its intricacies.

But they make themselves felt: most often, as a kind of reserve power which is never entirely called into play. Watching him in *Test Pilot,* for example—as Gable's grease-monkey pal, who begins going to pieces when he realizes that Gable's love for flying is destroying marriage —all we may feel, while Tracy is on screen, is the excitement and biting sadness of his various moments: snarling, sulking, soliloquizing, athletically chewing gum, commiserating with Gable's wife (Myrna Loy) and with himself . . . Only afterward do we realize how close Tracy has come to creating a different character, and, almost, a different film (since his involvement in each situation subtly modifies the situation) from the gritty, gallant imaginings of scriptwriter Frank Weade. Try to imagine any of the scenes (his telling Myrna Loy: "You little fool . . . and you went and married him!"; shopping for furniture with Loy and Gable; clouting another grease-monkey; the "three roads" speech) being done by Lloyd Nolan or Preston Foster or Paul Kelly. Each of these men would have contributed something to the film different from Tracy's contribution, and, in a sense, less; but only in a sense. Might not they have made us understand the film as a whole much differently?

Because of the acting style I have attempted to define, the word "sincere," affixed so many times to Tracy's craft, seems to me especially silly, and even impudently condescending. Sincerity seems to me a peculiarly ambiguous virtue in any art, unless, of course, associated with a cluster of other virtues; and, at worst, it can offer the artist an excuse for persisting in and exacerbating his worst faults. Tracy, it seems to me, is sincere in approximately the same way the late Robert Frost was sincere. Like Frost, he was always too explicit, too much "with" his feelings of the moment, to be entirely without calculation; which is not at all to suggest fakery. And, like Frost, he seems to harbor a consciousness of his art as involving kinds of manliness, visceral hardiness, urbanity; also, by the most carefully gauged implication, frustration, defeat, internal torture. Like Frost, he has projected these traits with an insular force, externalizing them without losing their structure; so creating his own *persona* of the artist. Himself as vessel for his art.

What has helped both men enlarge reputations (which, in great part, are irrelevant to their authentic talents) is, their common sense of *form:* meaning, in this case, measure and balance. Each man gives the impression of yielding no more than is absolutely required of him, yet yielding full measure of *that;* of saying no more than needs be said, but dotting every i. This kind of form instils in their audiences a feeling of safety; of confidence that we can believe the pieties of Father Flanagan or Tom Edison the Man, or "Birches"; that we needn't fear, not seriously (though each fresh encounter revives the old fear) the frenzy of "Home Burial," the cold rejection of "Death of the Hired Man"; or, the suicidal melancholy in *Test Pilot,* the unstanchable restlessness in *A Man's Castle;* the ruthlessness in *Dante's Inferno,* or *Edward, My Son.* The sense of inner control carries with it something of benign justice: a faint *imago* of the patriarch's almost-smiling scowl. And if there is any tragedy at all about this patriarch—if the symmetry of his justice, its moderation, is really the most presentable side of a noble ineffectuality—we need not, we feel, concern ourselves with *that,* as we sit, reading or watching.

As I have hinted, I find the general run of Tracy's "library" performances—as historical or "classic" literary heroes—the least interesting of his work. Partly, I think, this is because Tracy's acting *persona,* as I have described it, corresponded too closely with the virtues of the ikonized Edison, Henry Stanley, Father Flanagan. Apparently, Tracy simply accepted this congruence most of the time. Moreover, his "reacting" style of performance often worked against him in these roles. In films like *Captains Courageous* or *Boys Town,* the events had been arranged, selected, emphasized or underplayed so as to highlight the static nobilities of the main characters; with the result that Tracy's passive style, usually disarming, had nothing, this time, to disarm. Even a second-rate actor like Paul Muni will recognize that, since nothing much is going inside the hero, it were well to set up some distractions; so that the Muni Zola, or Professor Elsner, or Pierre Radisson, will diddle the spectator with a full programme of beard-waggings; wheezes, snorts; croonings; head-scratchings, and shuffles. The most you can expect from Tracy is a something-other-than-Portuguese accent, in the role of a Portuguese fisherman. And you had better expect *that,* for no less than two hours.

This is not to say that Tracy doesn't do well in library films, whenever the script offers him anything at all to work with. In the superior adaptation of Kenneth Roberts' *Northwest Passage,* Tracy, as Major Rogers, has a moving scene of collapse when he finds a sought-for outpost deserted. Tracy's disbelief, with the final, stunned onset of weeping, is done with a directness, terrible gravity, and almost ceremonial rhythm (repeating "It's

Major Rogers—Major Rogers and the Rangers—") which might well have pleased that eminent admirer of Tracy, D. W. Griffith.

And, for at least one of Tracy's "classic" performances, both performance and film are outstanding. I refer to *Dr. Jekyll and Mr. Hyde;* which I readily admit, is uneven, containing its share of foolish or misfired things; but which has been underrated for so long, on the basis of these relatively few weaknesses, as well as reviewers' misunderstandings and distortions of its virtues, that I feel no qualms at all about slighting its defects on this occasion. Indeed: the source of many critical objections to the film, I think, was its fidelity to Stevenson's somewhat bookish and literal-minded allegory (Stevenson's *Markheim,* on a related theme, is much more original); while the film's virtues proceeded from this fidelity, plus its imaginative expansion on Stevenson. The fantasy sequences, for example, which represent Jekyll's transformation into Hyde in terms of sexual nightmare, were jeered at, on the film's premiere, for their shallow "Freudianism." Now—possibly because the over-publicized Freudian "revival" of the forties has subsided—I see no more connection between the dream sequences and Freud, than, fortunately, between their poetically graphic and startlingly fresh sexual imagery, and the usual hackwork of Salvador Dali, who, I understand, participated in their design. Ingrid Bergman, much castigated for her Swedish accent as Hyde's barmaid paramour, was, I felt on seeing the film again recently, surprisingly touching; her look of robust sensuosity emphasizing her pathetic helplessness before Hyde's unspecified, but powerfully hinted, perversions. Under Victor Fleming's direction, the visual and aural images were repeatedly evocative and moving. An experimental rabbit nipping at Tracy's finger, after being dosed with Hyde solution; the connective image of the huge laboratory key, symbolizing the experiments' dangerous esoteric glamour; the ominous distant view of Tracy wandering through Picadilly with stick and opera-cloak; while, on the sound-track, the waltz he is whistling gradually segues into the polka-tune associated with Hyde's mistress.

Actually, the film is not only a two-handled portrayal of hypocrisy; it reverses the "success stories" of the other Tracy heroes, Edison and Stanley and Flanagan. As written, and portrayed by Tracy, Jekyll is a kind of front runner for psycho-analysis (one gets the impression that the Hyde compound was a rough first try: that's science!) and a less conscious hypocrite than his original, only in his emphasis on a liberal ideal of freedom, rather than spiritual perfection. His Jekyll, in fact, united the library heroes of his late thirties films, with the tortured failures of the early thirties (the sub-plot with Ingrid Bergman, involves a similar reversal: that of the traditional "Cinderella" story).

Tracy's depiction of Hyde is, in some respects, the movie's most extraordinary feature. His voice is a harsh, chortling whisper: the voice of the Indecent Proposal. His make-up, again according to Stevenson's specifications, makes Tracy into a mad-eyed old man with a suggestion of fangs in his smile. With each successive transformation, the face becomes more wild and bestial. The last transformation—accompanied by its "motif," the magnified beating of Jekyll's heart—we watch, for the only time in the film, straight-on. Tracy's physical bearing, too, was in contrast to his Jekyll performance. His walk was a wolfish charge; and—fiendishly mobile, as against Jekyll's stiff-kneed bearing—he was repeatedly vaulting balustrades and lunging up stairs like a perverted Douglas Fairbanks.

In 1941, with George Stevens' *Woman of the Year,*

Tracy began a series of films, mainly comedies, with Katherine Hepburn replacing Clark Gable as his partner. The constant theme of these films, is the attempts by a sophisticated couple to reconcile love with their respective jobs (they are usually members of the same profession—journalism, law, politics). My summary may suggest those other comedies, in which Melvyn Douglas—occasionally spelled by Ray Milland—would cozen his boss-lady, usually Rosalind Russell, out of her front-office frigidity. In fact, the Tracy-Hepburn comedies were very different. The lady executive played by Russell was repressed; Hepburn is at once a fully womanly woman, and happy in her vocation, even when, as in *Woman of the Year,* she overdoes it. In fact, the usual comic fallacy shared by her and Tracy, is that they *try* to keep separate their two lives: the sexual and the professional. This is obviously contradicting nature (especially since Miss Hepburn's vivacious energy, a main source of her charm, is augmented by her cantering around as newspaper-woman, lawyer or golfer); and the bifurcation produces jealousies, sulks and misunderstandings. Hepburn may take up with another man (who, however, is (a) younger and (b) less virile than Tracy). To adjust the *contretemps,* concessions must be made; most of them, as usually happens, by Tracy (although, in *Woman of the Year,* Hepburn must sacrifice some of her inordinate drive). Tracy is usually the more conservative of the pair; holding fast for political compromise (*State of the Union*); strict legality (*Adam's Rib*); or athletic discipline (*Pat and Mike*). Even when, as in *Adam's Rib,* he has the moral edge over Hepburn, he must sacrifice some of his position; and sacrifice, too, some of his masculine insularity, which is counterposed to her volatile womanhood. A couple of times, indeed, Tracy must sacrifice the man's role. At the climax of *Adam's Rib,* when he and Hepburn are on the verge of divorce, he resolves things by crying. (Even the later disclosure that it was only an act, changes nothing; since popular cliché still identifies "turning on the tears" as a woman's tactics.) And in *Pat and Mike*, Hepburn—already encumbered by a starchy boy friend—cannot give herself to him until he "proves" himself weaker than she is.

But all such concessions are secondary to the inevitability of the pair's union: as predictable as a wedding-ritual; which, in fact, might be said to set the pattern for most of the comedies. Rituals of all kinds pervade these films: the re-marriage ceremony of her divorced parents, which Hepburn attends in *Woman of the Year*; the little catechism ("Who owns a piece of you?" "You do", etc.) in *Pat and Mike*, (which has Tracy uttering the responses by the film's conclusion); the objections and counterobjection in *Adam's Rib*.

If my account of an outstandingly popular comedy series sounds portentously grim, that is pretty much I feel about the majority of these films, and especially those on which Ruth Gordon and Garson Kanin collaborated, as writers, with George Cukor, as director. Gordon and Kanin have demonstrated their proclivity for cuteness on any number of subjects, not excluding suicide; and the relatively unchallenging material here provided them, by them produces results which, in *Adam's Rib*, *Pat and Mike* and *The Desk Set*, make me feel as though I were sitting through six hours of more-intelligent-than-average home movies; while balancing on one knee a portion of whipped-cream-slathered pineapple upside-down-cake. Even when I laugh, I'm aware of having to keep an eye on my lap.

Tracy's acting style in these films is an *adagio* version of the elaborate code which distinguished his performances opposite Gable. The seeming-direct, actually oblique signals, broadcasting effects which are slightly out of true with the script, are here converted to charm. Eye-rolling; purring, sometimes (much less frequently than in the Square John days!) interspersed with snarling; puckering his surprisingly soft mouth, apparently to moisten his words, and delivering entire speeches with tongue quite literally in cheek. The function, too, is parallel to that of his acting in the Square John roles; where he embodied the realism of the Depression, only rendered impotent. Here, the dangerous force is sexuality; which is rendered harmless by his intricate, sidelong charm: its playfulness and its detachment. Hepburn, by contrast, is compact of earnestness; and a quite untethered sexuality which, however, seems at times to need no partner at all.

Yet, in a few of his performances opposite Hepburn, Tracy seems divested of virtually all mannerism and excess. In *Woman of the Year* — which founders as a comedy beneath George Stevens' mosaic heaviness, but flourishes, at odd moments, through his disciplined quietness — Tracy gives a portrayal like polished bone as Sam Craig. Craig — a newspaperman whose pragmatic democracy is offended by Tess Harding's (Hepburn) strident ambition, was obviously conceived as a study in modest hardihood. Under the ministrations of Stevens and Tracy, however, an iron hostility, a twinkle of egoism, entered Honest Sam. Using his palest of voices, acting, at times, with no appurtenances save a tight, shifting mouth (many of his scenes with Hepburn amount to mouth vs. mouth contests) Tracy occasionally surprises the meandering, crepesoled script with a complex cruelty that would not be unexpected in a Molière comedy. The moment when Tracy taunts a jolly, non-English-speaking diplomat, is a masterpiece of smug meanness, which John Osborne could tick off in his mental notebook.

Keeper of the Flame is one of the only two non-comedies I know of, in which Tracy and Hepburn co-starred (the other being the lethargic Kazan-directed western, *Sea of Grass*.) Tracy appeared in it as a liberal journalist, the posthumous biographer of a national hero (vaguely Rickenbackerish) who turns out to have been a deluxe native Fascist. Hepburn played the dead man's wife. The film might be characterized as patriotic-Gothic — one of those oddities fostered by World War II — and its suspenseless pace was not accelerated by the middens of talk, both expository and flag-waving, in which the characters frequently lodged themselves. Yet, a surprising number of moments were reclaimed, it seems to me, by the waltz-like precision, wit and ruthless dispatch of George Cukor's direction. Cukor, an often-superior director, is still much under-rated, partly because of unfortunate self-indulgences like *Pat and Mike*, where his leisureliness overrides his ability to pace it; but also, I think, because his best application of his talents often occurs in the supposedly uncinematic areas of setting, make-up and costumes. Here, he accomplishes such small but never contemptible wonders, as the transmutation of Joan Crawford, in *The Women*, Maureen O'Sullivan in *David Copperfield*, or — no less remarkable because less obtrusive — Hepburn and Tracy in *Keeper of the Flame*. Tracy, playing nearly as quietly as he did in *Woman of the Year*, has a role somewhat germane to his library roles: most of his "action" consists of asking questions or delivering little speeches. Yet, under Cukor's disciplinary aegis, he never slackens into mere inertia. His very quietness (note the scenes where he asks Hepburn for permission to use her husband's library, or the one in which he discovers the dead man's true character) discloses the asceticism, the implacable humility, of a familiar liberal type. He also has a good scene — most unusual among his films, and about the only indication, in this one, of screenwriter Donald Ogden Stewart's erstwhile talent for comedy — in which he must first stupidly look for a fight with Forrest Tucker (another of the stiff-necked Yale types of Miss Hepburn's film retinue) and then, as foolishly back down. Hepburn's performance (interesting to note, by the way, how the usual conservative and radical roles of Tracy and Hepburn are substantially reversed here: Hepburn attempting to preserve the myth; Tracy insisting on the truth) is entirely without the secondary tremors which have sometimes muddied her acting. In the final scenes, especially, she displays the ruthless crispness of a particularly dangerous enlightened aristocrat: eager to do right by her less fortunate fellow-Americans, even to liquidating a subversive husband. The performances of these two, aptly supported by Forrest Tucker, Richard Whorf and the younger (about 10) Darryl Hickman, give the film an occasional piquancy which your common (and critical) sense may not immediately acknowledge.

Probably the best (in the sense of most active, most appealing and most comic) of their comedies, was *State of the Union*, directed by Frank Capra from the Lindsay-Crouse play. The formula was very much in keeping with the Gordon-Kanin-Cukor *rollatinis*; but — as against the shapeless dawdling of the G. K. C. films, Capra brought to *State of the Union* the same spaciousness, and sense of milling excitement, the same aptitude for caricature — sometimes acute, sometimes slick and bulgy — in short, the same mercurial mixture of Sennett and Disney, which furnished forth the best portions of *Meet John Doe, Mr. Smith Goes to Washington*, or *You Can't Take It With You*. Also in evidence were Capra's sympathetic dexterity at directing women (I have seldom been so aware of Hepburn's capacity for tenderness; and never so much aware of the *mutability* of her face; while Angela Lansbury, as an ogresized Cissy Patterson, is as flexible as I have noticed her in her forties appearances); as well as his often overlooked alertness to various degrees and kinds of human softness. As a dark-horse candidate who, for most of the film, is quite happy to trot between the shafts of party expediency, Tracy conveyed beautifully the flaccid, broad, soft-mouthed obligingness of the Wendell Willkie type on which the role was based. He came about as close to the publicity departments' niceguy platitudes about him — but realized with brutal literalness — as he ever did. Although the film drifted repeatedly toward the familiar sack-time comedy of G.K.C., and although its political caricature is persistently unincisive, its exuberant charm makes great stretches worth watching.

As I have indicated, the Patriarch mask, accorded Tracy in the most recent stage of his career, is more nearly mythic than any of the others. It comprises public relations dispatches; various efforts by the public and mass-communications arbiters, to tranquilize the common fear of old age, by making it into a benign and rather featureless chromo; and a parallel effort to quiet the common fear of a subtly disturbing artist, by jovially hustling him out of one's own time, into a white-haired, bewrinkled Limbo. Tracy resisted such quieting maneuvers, I think, because, as I've tried to illustrate, quietness was one of his favorite mechanisms; as was his own disquieting version of age. Also, the Patriarch stereotype permitted some measure of public candor about Tracy's personal idiosyncrasies — his drinking, his long sequesters in a secluded house owned by Cukor, his hyper-anxieties about scripts and direction; thus, refreshingly, dissolving the more vaccuous stereotype of one-note sincerity. Best of all, the aged camouflage permitted him to play a greater variety of roles than he had done in several years; and which almost resemble a medley of his thirties and early forties pictures: the convict of *Malaya*; the pious man of nature, in *The Mountain*; a daredevil priest, in *The Devil at Four O'Clock*; a sugary Latin fisherman in *The Old Man and the Sea*.

The common theme of the best or most interesting films in this period, is another, more frankly heroic and sad, variant of the frustration theme: an aging man striving to salvage, or revive, his manhood. In *The Mountain*, he sets about an Alpine rescue operation (much beset by Robert Wagner, as his incredibly younger, incredibly rascallier brother.) In *Bad Day at Black Rock*, he stands off a desert town of bigots, psychotics and ninnies, in a re-staging of the traditional western theme.

The strange advance herald of these films — it came out around 1944 — was *A Guy Named Joe*. One of the all-time cinematic oddities, this film, an aeronautical fantasy-romance, was a series of skirmishes between the generations. Tracy played the pilot boy-friend of Irene Dunne (temporarily supplanting Miss Hepburn) aith his grey hair untouched. He has his own tussles with his superior officer, Jimmy Gleason, a blustery, harmless father-figure, whom Tracy sasses. Tracy's consistent attitude toward Dunne is that of a grouchily indulgent father. When he is killed (within the first half-hour of screentime, thus guaranteeing his return as a very stocky ghost) Miss Dunne is attracted — again, like Hepburn — to a younger man, Van Johnson; who, however, unlike Miss Hepburn's Ivy League boy-friends, is robust enough to make Tracy turn jealous, and neglect his duties (as a dead pilot, he is supposed to act as guardian angel to younger pilots) by keeping tabs on Johnson and hectoring him. A really formidable father — Lionel Barrymore

—finally intervenes to end Tracy's, and the film's aerial poltergeisting.

Tracy's acting of his Old Man roles might, expectedly, have been flabby and jaded, or else raffishly hammy. Actually, in the main, Tracy's acting of the last sixteen years has been as trim and purposeful and highly-charged as I have even seen it; in great part, perhaps, because many of his films, under the late economies prevailing at M.G.M. and United Artists, were more closely woven: characters and stories more tightly interlocking. The one display of ham by Tracy that I have observed among his fifties movies, was his rather widegirt portrayal of Clarence Darrow in Stanley Kramer's *Inherit the Wind* a job which I would attribute in part to the film's content — a bellicose show-boating of the Snopes trial — and in part to the steam-whistle direction of Mr. Kramer. Conversely, Tracy delivered a performance of subtle melancholy as James P. Curtayne, the elderly lawyer of *The People vs. O'Hara* (1951). The film, a very good adaptation of Eleazar Lipsky's admirable crime novel, was kept from unpretentious excellence by an, at times, excessively naive script, which occasionally fumbled the humane skepticism of Curtayne's relationships to his clients. (unlike the novel, Curtayne is quite illogically killed at the end of the film; probably because, since he tried to buy a witness in the course of it, the Christian wisdom of film censorship thus dictated his penance.) Tracy and his supporting cast — notably John Hodiak, and two elderly Italian laborers, who contribute a few flint-like seconds apiece — were directed by John Sturges with the low-toned alertness which distinguished his pre-western films.

And Tracy contributed arrestingly solid and clean-focused performances to at least two richly hammy roles of the fifties. He played Matt Devereaux, rancher and frontier entrepeneur, in *Broken Lance*: a 1954 remake,

directed by Edward Dmytryk, of Joseph L. Mankiewicz's doughy melodrama, *House of Strangers*. The Italian-American banking family of Mankiewicz's film was
replaced by frontier cattle-men. Tracy handled a number
of barn-storming scenes (flailing at, his dishonorable sons
with a bull-whip; pleading with, and storming at, the
territorial governor, well-played by E. G. Marshall; doing a protracted death-scene while sitting upright in a
saddle) with biting vigor and exactness. Edward Dmytryk,
never more than a very competent craftsman, brought
peculiar distinction to the rank in this film; more than
compensating for his, and Tracy's, frost-bitten histrionics
in *The Mountain*.

Tracy also presented a comically gloating urbanity in
Edward My Son: a film adaptation — directed, once more,
by Cukor — in which he played the role created by
Robert Morley: a rascally tycoon who confers on his son
(offstage throughout the drama) his money, his conniv-
ing and his selfishness, but not his manhood.

I cannot claim to have seen him in all of his films, at
any stage of his career; and yet, the nature of that career
counter-balances the lack, to a certain degree. I do not
mean to say that "if you see one Spencer Tracy film, you
have seen them all." One point I hope I have managed to
make, is, that, as a succession of revolving prisms, he
brings to each performance a different coloration, a different emphasis, in a personality which has mineralized,
as it were, into his craft. He reminds me much of American artists like Frost, James Agee, Conrad Aiken. These
men can never be charged with doing less than their
vocation demands; and yet, often, I feel of their work
that their *sense* of vocation confines them; making them,
in a peculiarly American way, submissive to each job they
do; each job manifesting itself as an excellently worked
fragment, or group of fragments.

When will I see him in Ibsen's masterpiece of false resurrection, *John Gabriel Borkman* (Why, indeed, has he not been seen in the work of Ibsen, his ideal dramatist, long before now?) Pacing his attic, listening to the subterranean murmurs of hope, and to the *Danse Macabre*, played by his daughter. Flanked by his mistress (Jeanette Nolan); his wife (Uta Hagen) and the devoted journeyman-poet (Roland Culver); one hand behind his back, one finger diagramming the wrinkles which vindlcation will repay. Head cocked in the familiar attitude, listening for the trolls.

Mann's
Fate

To watch any number of Anthony Mann's films, means sitting through a heavy deal of dull artiness, erratic sadism, non-stop plotting — all familiar ingredients of the average western or crime melodrama. Yet, if you watch Mann's films with any attention at all, you find not only the action, but the artiness, transformed by a choppy, feisty narrative rhythm, and fluid use of actors, into something original and, indeed, pretty rare: the imprint of one of the most complex personalities to be found among Hollywood commercial directors, and a notable artist.

Anthony Mann's career, up until his death two years ago, followed the typical parabola of fairly ambitious directors, to the final up-curve of "important" productions like *God's Little Acre* and *El Cid* and *The Fall of the Roman Empire*. Usually, such projects prove disastrous to whatever makeshift originality has attached itself to the director's career; simply because they betray the truer and more personal notions of art — expediency, tactics, the handling of problems — which were involved in his earlier, more modest films. We are treated to the director's "principles," which are boring and servile and, heretofore at least, irrelevant to art as the film-maker's reflexes knew it. I'm sure George Stevens' *The Greatest Story Ever Told* — which I've never seen — was bad, if it was, not because it lay outside of Stevens' scope, but because, in making it, he sacrificed his personal instincts — a luxuriant sense of landscape, and of the way landscape absorbs or threatens human beings — to a stodgy, didactic notion of "important" art.

So, after a fashion, did Anthony Mann; yet, watching *El Cid,* I found this courtly mastodon become more interesting and honorable than the average pretentious debacle. The reason, I think, was that Mann — like John Huston, with *The Lists of Adrian Messenger, The Misfits,* or even *Freud* — brought to the more pretentious material his own tight, cagey sense of scale, his own sort of smallness and crassness. The other point is, that — as with Huston — artiness was always a part of Mann's attitude towards films and the reality which he rendered in them. He incorporated this artiness into his work, even before he broke through with *Winchester 73,* in 1950. Here too, a niggling constriction, a mean purposefulness, ride the stringently designed compositions, the beshadowed countrysides.

Mann's directorial resources, on which he seems to have over-prided himself, are much less inventive than Lang's, whom he replaced on *Winchester 73.* He doesn't have Allan Dwan's choreographic intricacy; his work is probably as void of sensuosity as that of any important director. He uses a handful of compositions: a favorite being two or three people — foreground, middle plane, back — flanked by a pillar, or tree, or railroad engine, or whatever, which serves as valance and pivot for the shot. When the camera travels, it is at a tight-tethered lope, usually ended by a head or hand thrusting into the foreground — a visual "shock" which usually proves as shocking as oysters in Massachusetts, due to Mann's overcalculation. The fights generally lack the familiar sort of suspense, since the camera, like a cynical gambler, is parked right in the corner where the loser will flop; besides which, the continuity is chopped up into close views of the contenders — leaving very little room for fluent motion, but much for the strenuous gaucheries and small, thrashing cruelties of serious close battle.

What became clear to me after watching some of Mann's earliest films — those, that is, in which he moved independently — *Railroaded, Raw Deal, The Black Book, T-Men* — was, that the constriction and cruelty and crassness — yes, and artiness — presented a consistent and interesting pattern. Not the sort of pattern which can be gleaned from enough of any director's movies, good, bad or indifferent — but, the pattern of a man coping with his art on his own terms.

It is difficult for critics to involve themselves with middlebrow vulgarity (not so lowbrow; not any more) and the more so when middlebrow and lowbrow are mingled, as in Anthony Mann's work. Yet, Mann lacks one important component of middlebrow vulgarity: self-indulgence. Even on big productions, like *Naked Spur,* or *Man of the West,* or *Tobacco Road,* he brings to bear the same depression economy of devices that he was using in *Railroaded* or *Strange Impersonation.* The curious, atavistic effect is of a primitive film-maker employing the hand-tooled methods, the pragmatic irreverence toward his material, of great silent films.

Among those earlier films, Mann was shrewd in choosing as his screen-writer, John C. Higgins — Mann's perfect complement. Higgins, who wrote *Railroaded, T-Men* and *Border Incident,* specialized in fictionalized documentary, which had reached a popularity crest in '50s movies, since *Boomerang* and *Call Northside 777.* Higgins contributed to the trend a particular dry dexterity at showing the intramural politicking and resentful frictions which give large-scale crime kinship to its respectable counterparts. Under his, and Mann's ministrations, the crooks in their films monopolize the human weaknesses of cowardice, jealousy, ambition; whereas the

heroes are monolithic embodiments of idealism, law enforcement, or vengefulness. Combining realistic humanity with fleet, plausible extravagance, Higgins was a
perfect match for Mann; who, under the appearance of
romanticism, countered with one of the most anti-roman-
tic of film styles; a style which chops up conventional evil
into petty meanness, vacuity and cadging; which converts
conventional good into animal tenacity which, in the
clinches — and they are many — is often hard to diotin-
guish from evil.

This tenacity is Mann's only common ground with any
orthodox romantic. In his last interview — with *Cahiers
de Cinema* — he declared his admiration for heroes like
the Cid, who unswervingly follow a single course. This
singlemindedness has found its way into Mann's movies
since his installation as director — but it is more the
singleness of the mink or stoat, which gnaws away its own
foot to escape from a trap.

What Mann gives us, in stringently formal melodrama,
is the ugly dignity of human survival through savage
obstinacy. His snapping, stalking, charging characters vie
with a Germanic Destiny, as embodied by stony landscapes in which nature and architecture and machinery
seem almost interchangeable, and all vaguely animate.
An archetypal Mann scene, in *Border Incident,* witnesses
a rendezvous in an open field between a supine George
Murphy, and a mechanical harrow, advancing on him
from what seems ten city-blocks away. In *The Tall Target,* Dick Powell — a pre-Civil War detective guarding
President Lincoln — pins a would-be assassin (Lief Erick-
son) to the path of the oncoming Inaugural Express, in
a phantasmagoria of steam and wrought metal.

Mann's cardinal images are of pinioning, binding, cag-
ing, pulverizing: so the landscape returns the tenacity of
its inhabitants. A central figure of *Men in War* is a mute,

paralyzed officer (Robert Keith), strapped to a litter. Mann binds his stories, too, with key images — the gun in *Winchester 73,* the horn in *The Glenn Miller Story* — which serve as elegant, static fetters for the episodes.

The fascinating tension of Mann's films comes in great part from the haunting sense of his raw, fecund materials being, always, slightly mis-matched with his vigilantly theatrical technique. The great open spaces are sectioned as methodically as a football field. Mann will use, quite piquantly or powerfully, effects which are circumstantial to the movie; yet emerge as arbitrary to the point of sur-realism. In *The Naked Spur,* James Stewart and Janet Leigh enact a love scene in a mountain cave, accompanied by the plunking and planking of rain in a series of tin basins. In a night-club sequence from *The Glenn Miller Story,* Stewart, June Allyson and Louis Armstrong are run through a spectrum of hues by a color-wheel. Instead of opening up the film as one might expect, these precisely-framed and syncopated effects box the scenes in which they appear, with almost the muted poetry of Carne and Prevert's thirties films.

I must qualify what I said before about Mann's lack of sensuosity: the faintly unsavory tension of his best sequences, furnishes its own sensuosity, which is considerable. Mann's fondness for thrashing, nipping action shows itself in his numerous small cruelties: he is one of the deplorably few directors who can *scale* violence. He shows what I would take as an aversion to mass violences, i.e., Indian raids, battles, etc.; at least in their usual time-consuming aspect. He uses crowds *en bloc,* as though influenced by Reinhardt. I think, too, that his scenes of violence disclose as little blood — I mean the actual splashing, oozing imagery — as any recent Hollywood films. We get, instead, Raymond Burr flicking a hireling's ear with his cigarette, or Dennis O'Keefe's progress — in gruelingly fetid montage — through a series of steam-baths, in search of a narcotics smuggler. The event of violence, or merely of painful erosion, are precisely noted as in Hammett, or in Harold Gray's *Little Orphan Annie.*

Much of Mann's sensuous tension comes from the way he counterpoints rigid design with the small authentic fluencies of acting and mood: the unexpected delicacy of an artist whose formal vocabulary is not merely a token of distance, but *a vocabulary*: something to communicate with. Like Huston in his best films, Mann focuses on voices and faces; overhauling the actor's commonplace vocabulary by shifting emphasis to the more intimate and less familiar. Murphy, in *Border Incident,* could not be farther from the chipmunk-grinning Mayor of 42nd Street: Mann has brought out the jabbing anxiety of Murphy's song-and-dance style, and concentrated on the morose watchfulness in his thickening features. The same picture contains a remarkable appearance by Howard DaSilva, as an effetely pretentious, cowardly gang leader. I've seen DaSilva good, bad and indifferent, but never so free of mannerism as here: the thick-lipped mouthing which often threatens to choke his performances is completely absent in this portrayal of bland, quietly apprehensive softness.

Watching Mann's films in close succession, one realizes that the conventional and frequently boring values of western and crime films have been subverted by an octupus-armed sense of form: a sense of form which frequently works to build up one's anticipation rather beyond the ability of the story content to satisfy. An Indian attack, in *The Naked Spur,* is delivered as a pile-driver of half-naked bodies, ramming down a rocky slope again and again, the camera sidling to and fro at its usual discreet distance; until, somehow, they are routed. A shooting-match is presented with the same deceptive bluntness; none of the usual suspense-begging variations, big close-ups of reactions, etc.; but an intercutting of distant figures, rock shelf, and pistol-volleys as elegantly co-ordinated as piano arpeggios; until, eventually, one realizes that orthodox suspense, and its graitifications, have been deposed by beautifully oblique narrative rhythm.

Mann occasionally pays off on such carefully built expectations with felicities of mood and atmosphere which, not infrequently, appear as striking coda scenes; like the opening of *The Tall Target*. The film, about a conspiracy to assassinate the newly-elected Abraham Lincoln, opens with a splendidly somber high view of the railroad terminal, and the ornate black bulk of the Express in the foreground; a scene accompanied by no music save the premonitory ringing of the engine-bell. This coda-scene spills itself throughout the film (co-authored by Geoffrey Holmes and Joseph Losey, who was to have directed); in a suffocating evocation of plush, gas-light and Nemesis. The generally ordinary *Glenn Miller Story* concludes with the phantasmal beauty of the fatal plane moving, green and silver, through thickening fog.

During the early fifties, Mann replaced scripter John C. Higgins with Borden Chase, who has done excellent genrework (*Man Without A Star*, co-authored with D. D. Beauchamps), but is slower and softer than Higgins, and given to one of the least-delectable narrative devices of present-day westerns: John Ford's *Stagecoach* legacy, the *Cross-Section of Humankind* (whore, desert-rat, jovial outlaw, army officer) all promenading their humanistic platitudes on a quasi-allegorical pilgrimage. Chase has enough humor and inventiveness and hard perception of western landscape, to redeem a lot of such pious boomph (*Bend of the River*, *The Naked Spur*); but Mann's next writer might have proved ruinous: Philip Yordan, a most ambitious pulp-writer with the inexhaustibility of an Elizabethan genius. Yordan has infinite resources of disaster and garrulousness which, together, tend to act as a boa constrictor on any script-material which crosses his path. He may begin with a flurry of rape, mutilation, mass-shooting (mules or men), beating; then, proceed from there, with a happy heedlessness of form or continuity, spraying his debacles with an Accent sauce of liberalism and other pseudo-philosophical dressings; on and on and on and on, until one feels the only way properly to conclude is, after the two hundredth or so shooting or barn-burning, to have Porky Pig poke his head out of the screen with the usual: "Deedeeduhdee th-that's all, folks!" Yordan's slack-girted pretentiousness would seem to be what Mann least needed, precisely because such coarse pretentiousness seems so close to Mann's unworthiest aspirations. Yet, between them, Mann and Yordan managed to come up with some occasional punchy episodes (in *Man from Laramie;* plus, in that same film, a good piece of homosexual-tinctured villainy by Alex Nicol); and a near-triumph in what might have been the apex of disaster; their adaptation of Caldwell's *God's Little Acre.* For all Caldwell's trashiness — the scrofula-patches of sex and slapstick-melodrama — *God's Little Acre* contains a genuine, almost cadenced, dialogue of animalized men and women and their environment. And in this content, Mann found the fulfillment of a theme which, for once, he did not have to elide or disguise: a scruffy, randy, and yet solemnly rhythmic struggle by nearly pulverized humans to survive, if even as stoats or possums.

Mann again demonstrated his almost-unique appreciation of Robert Ryan as a character actor: a beautifully straight performance as TyTy Walden, with no trace of Spike Jones smirking, not even when plainly bidden by the original. Buddy Hackett, as the perennially hopeful Sheriff Pluto Swint, offered a marvel of self-discipline: diverting the manner and energy of his night-club characterization into a perfectly self-contained grotesque. Until the last twenty minutes, when it went a-glimmering into some pointless fights and no-more-pointed pieties, *God's Little Acre* was remarkable for the dance-like movement which Mann and Yordan and their company set going behind every sequence, quite fluently and appositely. Two cardinal scenes remain as my witnesses: the sequence in a Georgia street, at night, when the family goes searching for TyTy's brother-in-law, Will Thompson (Aldo Ray's best performance that I've seen): TyTy sitting in the car, while, from the bar where the others have gone, a piano tinkles an obligatto as haunting as the plinking rain in *Naked Spur*. And soon after comes the triumphant scene where Will, in a mingled excitement of sex and rebellion, tries to turn on the power in the shut-down mill where he has worked. This scene, too, could have been awful simply for the echoes of "big film" crowding it. Yet — aided by an erotically chugging Copeland score — Mann walks the sequence down its artistic gauntlet with perfect tough control and — excepting, perhaps, some too-Rockwellish faces in the waiting crowd of workers — an air of never having heard the names Einstein or Ford. The erotic movement of this sequence — Will's wife sitting in the kitchen, framed by the window — Will and his girl-friend Allyson, their erotic, anxious walk framed by the huge building, then the machinery of the mill; and finally their ascent to the catwalk, and the lights going on — all combine for an eerie, exhilarating, horny mixture of sexual and revolutionary excitements, which make solvent the gimmicks and evasions of previous Mann films.

Of *El Cid*, I can best refer the reader to my opening

comments: despite its saraband pace and monotony of its central character, the film embodies an almost savagely serious directness of Mann confronting his material. His own penchant for austere design, and aversion to spectacular massiveness, make him resort to small, personal kinds of inventiveness which unexpectedly liven the film and, still more unexpectedly, its performers. Charlton Heston's embattled sinuses are, for once, charged with a wolfish energy, emphasizing the glum stolidity of his face and his body (which habitually seems armor-plated, anyway). The two champions buffeting each other with shields is worth watching for, as is the silhouetted spiteful dialogue between two brothers at their royal father's funeral; as is a delectable comic note, Her Majesty Genevieve Page's little scowl of indignation, through a Moorish grill-work, at Sophia Lorne's relentless vendetta.

In discussing an artist whose work, when discussed again, will probably be too decked with categories, including self-elected ones, for much accurate appreciation, I haven't mentioned his most extraordinary accomplishments; the resuscitation of Jimmy Stewart, from the aged adolescence of Mr. Smith et. al., to the middle-aged energy of *Winchester 73, Bend of the River, The Man From Laramie*: roles which cultivated, rather than disguised, Stewart's spasmodic hostility and edgy stubbornness. Stewart's typical performances for Mann provide, together, a sort of coat-of-arms for Mann's achievement: habitual mannerisms never relinquished, yet providing a background for quite personal and original insights and energies.

Obit
of a
Sort

Our last newspaper strike — a prolonged stage-wait for
the Afternoon Cameleopard — saw the death of New
York's best newspaper, which could not have had less
portion with the fate of other New York journals. Jack
Green's newspaper — which was called only that, and
published according to no schedule but Jack Green's
inclination — showed us all what a good newspaper today
must be, and sometimes — perhaps, during a fifteen-
minute pause in union-publisher negotiations — we shall
start thinking about the lesson. For *newspaper* was an
authentically provincial, an authentically local *newspaper,* 95% of whose content was Jack Green's empirical
shrewdness, wit, prejudice and candor. Its very appearance incorporated Green's voice: printed on 9 x 14 sheets
of durable beige paper, mimeographed in a soot ink of
Green's own composition. Looking at those staid, down-
right, serviceable rectangles of tiny print — rather like
peering upon a city from helicopter level — you get the
sense of Green's own conversation: that light, rather dif-
fident tenor which — at nearly always the same level —
acts as a conductor for any opinion, hence any emotion,
which happens to be his. The same applies when you
read the text, unpunctuated (save when he quotes someone) and uncapitalized. The purpose of the very familiar
typographical device is not only to disarm the reader,
but to liberate Green's voice, by eliminating the most
familiar and most innocuous-seeming, therefore the most
inhibiting, conventions. Here, as in all of Jack Green's

writing, necessity calls the turn, no matter how large or small the results.

Newspaper, during its twenty-issue, ten-year life, was genuinely an extension of Jack Green, whereby he first explained the world to himself and, consequently, himself to those who read him. "Explaining" is, perhaps, less accurate than "accounting." Green's prevailing bent was for figures and statistics, with especial delight in columns and catalogues. "Fire the bastards!" his ambuscade against those reviewers who had attacked or slighted Gaddis's novel *The Recognitions* — was a three-issue (I think) relentless breakdown of what occasionally seemed like every ignorant snipe that had even been taken at Gaddis's novel. Yet, every line of it was pertinent, simply for re-affirming the value of such tabulation, and the monstrous relevancy of every seemingly "trivial" swat, in a world where unacknowledged distance has multiplied the necessity of measurement.

What Jack Green does is build his world and himself through the medium of *newspaper*. Unlike a few other recent personal journalists, he seeks order; not that order which is supposed to endure eternally, but an order which yields only grudgingly to whatever challenges and buffets confront it. *Newspaper*, even at its seeming-wildest, serves that order; reflecting Green's conviction that the idea of clarity is all-important, no matter how often remodeled the form.

This, it may be recognized, is merely another way of saying that Green is a conservative; not in the obvious sense, but then, how often is the obvious sense the index of authenticity? The heart of Green's conservatism is the conviction — to be found in such of his contemporaries as Gil Sorrentino, Fielding Dawson, Edward Dahlberg, Charles Olson — that a man has certain boundaries, in the recognition of which lie his dignity and his capacity. These boundaries insure nothing, save, possibly, his ability to move, and to measure those boundaries against the boundless erratic fluidity of the world. We are to maintain our *sense* of boundaries, rather than these particular boundaries; not in the fool's superstition that therein lies stability and normalcy; but in the persuasion that this is the only way to know anything about the world; and to combat what may be the foulest myth of our time, the myth of immeasurable distance.

Not a few of Green's strengths and weaknesses are illustrated by the roster of his literary preferences, which he cites in newspaper #20. Pirandello, Beckett, John O'Hara, Simenon, William Gaddis, William Burroughs, Ayn Rand . . . It seems at a careless survey like a hopeless conglomeration. But not, of course. To read even a sampling of the authors on Jack Green's list, is to appreciate recurrent specific strengths: a small-bore precision and hard alertness, which do not suppress but re-inforce the writer's sense of fluent and erratic reality. The awareness serves as a mobile unit: not a counterforce of reality, but an instrument for divining reality; style as a small flexible tank. As is *newspaper*.

But beyond this, Green's booklist illustrates, I think, a weakness of perspective which sometimes manifests itself as hollow eclecticism. Green's eye sees hard but, at times, it also sees flat. Used as he is to building his own context, in *newspaper*, he sometimes demonstrates an insensitivity to other contexts: of history, of philosophy. And along with this goes a related occasional insensitivity to the softnesses of art and thought, which reside in color and form, rather than in line and diagram.

The most damaging corollary of this exaggeration of Green's essentially good conservatism, is that remarks dictated by generous emotion and frankness tend to become, in the process of Green's setting them down, snugly mechanical, glib and over-calculated. Cracks like "ive never seen a good movie" or "einstein (was) an insane killer worse than hitler" (the latter of which he later retracted) would have to bear a maximum freight of scorn and anger to make them even palatable: the kind of anger and scorn which can lend savory precision to hyperbole, which keep it solvent.

No matter; it is all-important to think of *newspaper*, and, as such, an example and rebuke to the other large newspapers of America — certainly of New York. For Green's newspaper pointed the way toward overcoming the American metropolitan newspaper's most formidable stumbling-block — the insane belief that news can be both objective *and* impersonal. Objectivity is only possible by accepting and affirming, with the most forceful, un-masochistic humility, the limitations of one's viewpoint. This truth may never have been so relevant as it is now; what with, on the one hand, newspapers disappearing ever more rapidly, and, on the other hand, books like Capote's *In Cold Blood* eroding the more conventional concepts of journalism, and, with them, the apparent boundaries between journalism and art, most of which should never have been permitted to exist. No matter how distinguished his position, the average reporter, so far as I can surmise, is still trying to play the now-irreconcilable roles of oracle and messenger: the voice of a truth removed from space and time; the deliverer of truth, that is "news," which is localized, relevant only in spatial-temporal terms. And all this he must perform on behalf of an audience as diffuse, unlocated as is the terrain from which he works.

Jack Green, as I said at the outset, built himself, defined himself through and with the armature of *newspaper*. I use armature very consideredly: Green always seemed at a remove from that freedom, sensory and intellectual, which he recognized and extolled in the works of Wilhelm Reich and William Gaddis (So he attested — both the drive toward deliverance and the sometimes-restricting consciousness — in his most moving essay, the one on *peyote*.) Green's terrain, in *newspaper*, was a small, serviceable, firmly-tooled raft: his sense of the present, of "happenings" quite different from the valuable extravaganzas of Carolee Schneeman or Allen Kaprow, since Green's are predominantly rational. And, through *newspaper*, Green has devised a kind of autobiographical writing which reveals only in terms of a stringent self-governance which makes of the autobiography a running commentary, drily attentive, on current America. Within book-covers, this would not be new, of course; in the format of a newspaper, it is remarkable, most especially for Green's avoidance of two death-traps: the mechanical self-characterization which overtakes the syndicated columnist, and the formless, characterless spewing of the less talented "underground" self-chroniclers.

Green, through the twenty issues of *newspaper*, defines and dramatizes a firmly intelligent critical integrity which is yet subject to change; and the issues of *newspaper* carry through the interplay of this *persona* with various challenges and circumstances; giving us the tough, witty clarity of Green's surveillance without the easy misimpression that Green is on top of whatever he writes about. The two best examples are the *peyote* essay, which I have mentioned (I can't recall the issue) and *metropolitan days*, which made up the whole of #18.

In looking back over this obit to Jack Green's *newspaper*, I fear that I may seem to have written an obit to Jack Green. Nothing could be less true; and the very factor that aids that false impression — the organic unity of Jack Green and his *newspaper* — assures us that *newspaper* will continue, metamorphosized — for, one hopes, many good years — in the person of its editor and author.

Essays of
a Man
Watching

On the too infrequent occasions when Robert Warshow is written about today, the tendency seems to be to
tag him as either a "sociological" or (perhaps worse, because the term is that much vaguer and seems that much
more specific) a "social" critic of films. This was the main
gambit of a *New Republic* review by Stanley Kauffmann
—an exercise in dull spite; and even John Simon's sympathetic review of the posthumously published anthology
of Warshow's essays, *The Immediate Experience,* scarcely
denied the "social" label. The gravest evil of such a
stereotype is that is sets Warshow apart from the men
who were his real colleagues—dashing, metaphor-crested
virtuosi like the New York critics, Otis Ferguson, James
Agee, Manny Farber, and William Poster. What meaningful film critic, dealing as he must with the social
peripherae of the movies, is not a social critic? Wherein
are Ferguson's review of *Gunga Din,* Farber's and Poster's
essay on Preston Sturges, not social as well as cinematic
critiques?

In an important sense, to call Warshow a social critic
of films is as little relevant to defining his criticism as to
call him a *Commentary* film critic, since for years he was
an editor of that magazine; or, for that matter, as little
relevant as to call Edmund Wilson a social critic of letters, because Wilson, like Warshow (who resembles him
more than superficially) appraises literature as it shades
off into the social flux which helped produce it. In fact,

Warshow's criticism at best (represented not only by the critiques of the film *Death of a Salesman* and Dreyer's *Day of Wrath,* but by those of Arthur Miller's play *The Crucible* and George Herriman's "Krazy Kat") manages to portray the work under surveillance as an organism, a dynamic being clambering over a web of influences: social, political, moral, and, yes, aesthetic. His essays remind me of the abstract expressionist paintings of James Brooks: glacial forms, both solid and elusively fluid, whose courtly opacity conveys glacial flickers of blue or yellow or violet.

His essay, "The Movie Camera and the American," which originally appeared in *Commentary*—it was the first of his pieces I ever read—seems to me emblematic of this solidity and this fluidity, working together to first-rate effect. In the first part, Warshow addresses himself to *Death of a Salesman*—the play and its film adaptation. The opening passage, extraordinary for its compressed density of observations and judgments ("Like many 'great' American plays, it seems to me . . . full of a self-conscious energy masquerading as profundity and a mechanical realism which hides a fundamental reluctance to give the real world its due") sums up what Warshow regards as the hollowness of Miller's play: the hollowness of a phony universality whose phoniness is demonstrated by the way in which it sells short specific reality. The second half of the article gives attention to a Goldwyn film, *I Want You,* which, Warshow demonstrates, enjoys in its commercial efficiency an alertness to the surfaces of everyday life which *Death of a Salesman* misses; therefore, a sort of honesty which the more pretentious moving picture doesn't possess. Warshow remarks of the film's peculiar grace: "It is still an untruth, but the precise area of its falsity seems no longer so easy to define: it may yet become an untruth organically assimilated, which is to say a myth."

The most notable aspect of this essay is that Warshow does *not* question the films under discussion as works of art, either good or bad; he does not even question the nature of film as an art form. He subjects film to none of those inquiries which rustle through the articles of Poster, Ferguson, Farber, or, most of all, Agee. All of these critics are themselves creative artists (William Poster, generally known as a journalist, was a sometime poet and painter). All of them, as aesthetic critics and creators, are bothered, in varying degrees, by their need to possess the nature of film, a form which resists possession as might a layer of plankton. And their work is hounded, above all, by the need to reconcile the truth of film as an art form, a re-creative medium, with the equally potent—indeed, inseparable—truth of film as a recording mechanism: as a level of response, that is, at which most art begins, but from which the most important art-works often proceed very far. They are constantly confronting, and constantly trying to surmount, the truth that film, unlike the novel, or drama, or ballet or opera, is not a metaphor for reality or a distillate of reality, but—rather like a city, or a battle operation—is an incessant barter and quarrel and romance with reality. (Manny Farber, an abstract expressionist painter, is probably less subject to these frets than any of his colleagues, since, as a painter, he can see a continuum between his art and the visual surfaces of the world; yet, he, too, is much concerned.) Often, they override these questions, in one sense at least, by creating film criticisms which are works of art in themselves, and which fill with language the gap between artist and recording device.

Warshow, in contrast with these other critics, seldom says anything directly about film as an art (although, as the foregoing quotes may have hinted, he has much to say obliquely). On the contrary, his care is for film as a life-situation, as a continuation of reality rather than an island or lacuna in the midst of reality. This may sound like a reversion to that "sociological" tag from which I have tried to separate Warshow. No; the whole point is that Warshow uses none of the analytic mechanisms, none of the defining apparatuses favored by Hortense Powdermaker and Dr. Siegfried Kracauer; nor does he ever assert that the kinds of truth in which he is interested are to be measured in graphic tables. As in "The Movie Camera and the American," as in his polemic against *The Best Years of Our Lives*, as in his essays on the gangster film and the Western, Warshow is engaged in that border country where sociological truths pass into the territory of myths, nightmares and fantasies; he is concerned with the multiplicity of truths on which these fantasies nurture, and with those truths which they poison or stifle (see "The Anatomy of Falsehood"). Some of his best essays, like the ones on *Day of Wrath* and *Paisan*, are neither fully attack nor fully praise, but fugues of approval and denigration. (The article on "Krazy Kat," in a way, is an exception to all of these remarks: a strangely shuffling performance, it seems like an admission by Warshow that he cannot summon the vocabulary or the degree of perception to deal with his antic subject.)

I think it is relevant to such criticism that Warshow was an editor, rather than a primarily creative artist, like those other critics I have mentioned. The texture of reality which one feels in his essays is a bit firmer, more jagged, less carpeted by metaphor than in the writings of his New York colleagues. His style betrays no obvious rhetorical tinting at all; its force comes from the rhythms, nervously forceful, of proposition and question and divagation; and the unobtrusive interlinking of precise scrutinies and generalizations: This scene (in *Paison*) moves so rapidly that the action is always one moment ahead of the spectator's understanding. And the camera itself remains neutral, waiting passively for the action to come toward it and simply recording as much of the action as possible, with no opportunity for the variation of tempo and the active selection of detail that might be used to "interpret" the scene; visually, the scene remains on the same level of intensity from beginning to end, except for the increasing size and clarity of the objects as they approach the camera — and thus has the effect of a "natural" rather than interpretive variation. . . .

I have deliberately selected so broad a wedge of writing to show how many angles of attack Warshow manages to concentrate in a simple-seeming description of screen naturalism; how he *questions* Rossellini's screen technique, not by imagistic whooshings, nor by projecting into the seen event all sorts of unverifiable speculations about Rosellini's artistic psychology, but rather by insisting on asking himself *how the event works.* This is, I submit, a good editor's standard of craftsmanship, on which impinges social, political, and ethical questions (when one acknowledges that the editor is no mere blue-penciling sophist). Here (and one can say this pretty generally of Warshow's essays) is none of the impressionism so often favored by Agee, Farber, and Ferguson (less often by William Poster, himself more journalistic). Their technique of rendering the critical subject through images often works powerfully in evoking a rapport among reader, critic, and subject; but the rapport it creates is frequently a kind of partnership, an instantly established equality which is based on assumption of a common vision. Warshow is much more formal and rational and authoritarian: his movements are alternately very close to his subject and away from it. As editor, he is free to regard himself not as a fellow artist, but as an appraiser, a man watching. Indeed, he could, I think, often have afforded to remain closer to his subject, particularly in his writings on Odets and Leo McCarey's *My Son John:* essays in which a constant drifting into generalization threatens to shrivel up the subject. Still, it is remarkable what a freightage of aesthetic observation he manages to suggest, without often parading his sensibilities. His remarks on acting (a litmus test for academic critics) are very sparing, yet almost invariably sensible and sharp-focused. For example, he gives very fair measure to Fredric March's unbrilliant, plain astuteness and competence, as against the kettledrum style of Lee J. Cobb. Such ample justice within so little space can serve as example to many of our phrase-makers.

The limitations of such criticism are narrowness and a rather excessive respect for power: the power of the *fait accompli,* of how something works. As I've tried to indicate, it is all credit to Warshow that he keeps judicious distance from the films he writes about, instead of trying to evoke an imaginative intimacy between reader and subject. Yet—although this distance enables him to explain and judge films or plays with unusual fullness—he finds himself, even at best, hampered by a kind of rigidity which dehumanizes his subject. By "dehumanizes" I don't mean, of course, the way in which he drains off the dropsical humors of sentimentality; but the way in which he can write about a film or other art-work as a finished job, with little betrayed awareness of the emotional and aesthetic interplay which a film can reveal: those traceries of instinct, intelligence, half-conscious extemporizing which comprise the living tissue of so many interesting pictures. In fact, Warshow stays away from such films, on the whole: his favorite subjects seem to be diesel-engine affairs like *Best Years of Our Lives* or *I Want You,* which feature an organic interworking of photography, acting, story. Even though he estimates accurately their paucity of ethics or ideas, such films evidently fascinate Warshow, and—one suspects—relieve him of the (cinematic) questions which—one suspects—less efficiently formed but more lively films might entail. As I have indicated, the "Krazy Kat" review shows him apparently baffled by the more loose-napped aspects of popular art (and surely, Krazy is far from the norm of popular art!) and fending off his subject with a brusque timidity. When he writes about gangster and Western films (the essay on Westerns seems to me much the better) he winds up inventing little fairy tales (not uninteresting) about the heroes. Although his criterion in such articles is an image of concrete reality, I feel at times that Warshow has intentionally selected films which fall safely far of that mark; in the fear that collision with such concrete reality would shake the bulkheads of his tight rationalism. All the more regrettable, since—on the evidence of his virtues—Warshow could almost certainly have profited from more, and rougher, collisions.

Of course, Warshow's selection of films enables him to tend one of his favorite motifs: the hollowness of deceptively real-seeming or artful films. Not sufficiently developed to be called a theme, it is one of those helpful obsessions which enrich a number of critics' appraisals: James Agee's reactions to "intricately bad" movies, like *Three Caballeros* and *Frenchman's Creek;* Parker Tyler's feeling for the self-perpetuating mirror-imagery of pictures like *Dead of Night* or the documentary crime-films, *House on 92nd Street* or *Boomerang.* These writers' remarks about deficient films which have moved them often seem to express the authors' most nearly inexpressible preoccupations or chimerae; often more movingly and suggestively than the writings of praise. And in Warshow's case, the obsession culminates in the fragments of what would surely have been one of his best essays: the unfinished survey of the films of Eisenstein and Dovzhenko, and the documentary, *Tsar to Lenin*. I should add that, so deeply felt and implacably even-sighted, it is also one of Warshow's narrowest essays—though the narrowness here seems to me not at all a surrender of humanity, but an assertion of it, on the only terms Warshow knew, and the best terms he could muster. And let those film lovers whom this essay brings to their feet, a-bubble with refutations, ask themselves on the way up how often within their knowledge the films of Eisenstein and Dovzhenko have been written about not merely "seriously," but with this sort of seriousness; indeed, this sort of respect.

At the center of Warshow's serious deficiencies is his deference to form. When he is good, this deference concentrates on what form should be: the way in which the writer brings his own instincts into conversation with the shape of his experience. And, to this end, Warshow's tightly caulked discipline is all to the good. But in these essays he demonstrates another sort of form as well, which is a kind of armor: a technique for consolidating his premises and theories, with massed arguments, illustrations, and syllogisms, so that not only does the theory or premise seem impeccable, but Warshow barely admits the existence of any alternative interpretation. And, unfortunately, Warshow's imagination, at best anything but visionary, almost always bends its neck to his hermetically interlocking structures of argument; so that, although he can gratify us with the evidence that a vagrant art-work may be subject to the critic's reason operating in a lofty cause, he seems incapable of liberating the imagination, of making our own imaginations bait us and challenge us. Here, he is decidedly inferior to those other critics I have mentioned.

A strange effect of this rigor is a grind of naïveté. I have in mind Warshow's essays on two films: Leo McCarey's anti-Communist *My Son John* and Chaplin's *Monsieur Verdoux*, two films which Warshow's rationalism and technical adroitness rather encourage him respectively to underrate and to overrate.

My Son John, starring Helen Hayes, the late Robert Walker, and Dean Jagger, was Leo McCarey's brochure of pious suburbia menaced by Communist doctrine. Its supposed secondary theme — actually, fundamental was that conflict of older and younger generations which McCarey had dramatized touchingly in his thirties film, *Make Way for Tomorrow*, and less effectively in *Going My Way*, where a young priest seems to threaten the security of an elderly priest, and a teenage girl clashes with her parents over her singing career. The distinction of *My Son John*, overriding many, if not all, of its ideological *bêtises*, was McCarey's sense of Communism as a sort of antichrist of the suburbs, menacing the sweet urbanity and soft gullibility of his aging couple, Hayes and Jagger, who discover that their intellectual son, Walker, is a Communist sympathizer and, indeed, agent. Nor did McCarey's sophistication, as displayed in *The Awful Truth*, abandon him. The father and mother, fondling simple-minded homilies in their reaction against Communism, are tragically silly, and McCarey — unmistakably, I believe, to anybody truly *watching* the film — fully acknowledges their silliness, with all the love he bears them. Indeed, the movie is in no wise so much an anti-Communist document as it is an affecting treatment of some middle-aged Americans' vulnerability before the cruelties of Communist thought. It is, in certain basic ways, a silly film as well, because, I think, of the distance, which neither discernment nor love can altogether bridge, between the people in the film and Leo McCarey's far more complicated — and, at times, dangerously self-deceptive — sophistication. But it is to the shame of our more Schlesingerite theater-owners that *My Son John*, since its first appearance in 1952, has not been revived.

Warshow's review of the film appeared originally in William Bradford Huie's *American Mercury*, then a bustling engine for the lively "new" conservatism of William Buckley and Ralph De Toledano and Peter Viereck. Warshow's premise was a criticism of *My Son John* for what he regarded as its crude and obscurantist anti-Communism. The morality of this stand is particularly admirable and refreshing in the context of the 1952 *Mercury*, which was preponderantly pro-McCarthy; and its acceptance by Huie seemed to augur a new Conservatism of which some of Warshow's colleagues could hardly have been aware. Yet, reading it today, I feel that in the most curious way — in a way usually associated with fanatic anti-Communism — Warshow's sense of virtue has overborne his perception. Not that this perception abandons him: he apprehends fully the conflict of parents and children (although he submerges this observation in frettings about the gauche jingoism of the father); and, in at least one respect, he not only perceived but anticipated, a strain which has become somberly meaningful in television and films alike. I mean the paternalism of institutional law, as represented in *My Son John* by the F.B.I. agent (Van Heflin). Warshow's trailing of this sinister theme is so firm and exact and attentive that I find his words rising to my mind with every fresh, dismal example that presents itself today.

Such perception, of course, serves fresh corroboration of Warshow's liberal premise for the *My Son John* essay; and only in such corroboration does his perception, in this instance, really function. Otherwise, his sense of liberal duty seems, through a kind of false emphasis, to cramp his reaction to the film as a film: meaning not something extracted from its political context, but a rather intricate work by human beings. To have accepted this would, at length, probably have reinforced Warshow's position validly; and it would have contravened the heavy blankness and sense of straining for rectitude which the article now leaves with me.

About Chaplin's *Monsieur Verdoux*, I may say that you will probably not be disappointed if you attend this film expecting a mélange of very fine, mildly funny, and strenuously mechanical *commedia dell'arte*, all by Chaplin; some virtuoso characterization (also by Chaplin) with a whirring and sputtering little voice, higher than his own, and a tirelessly skittering little animal of a mouth; a chilling performance by Margaret Hoffman and a whoopingly coloratura one by Martha Raye, both playing Verdoux wives; a conglomerate of performances by supporting actors, variously charming (the girl in the flower shop, who is wowed by Chaplin's impassioned messages to a prospective wife), funny (William Frawley as a not-to-be-shaken guest at a wedding reception), and regrettable (certain of Verdoux's relatives in the opening scenes); and some of the most beautiful photography, by Roland Totheroh, I have seen in any of Chaplin's films.

You will probably be disappointed if you attend the film believing much of the rapturous guff that has been circulated about it by critics, and which would have you expect a very devil of metaphysical wit and social satire; at worst, second-rate Shaw, or first-rate Brecht. In fact, expecting this, I found a loose-rigged and often pallid farce, superimposed upon a still looser-rigged and more pallid melodrama. I now suspect that the major influence upon its more intelligent admirers, notably Agee and Warshow (Eric Bentley's praise is more valid than either, at least to the extent that it concentrates upon Chaplin's acting), was, indeed, the *presence* of Chaplin, both in and behind the film. Not merely the ikon-like image (mainly justifiable) of heroic resilience which Chaplin must then have presented, and which was fired by the overbearingly nasty attacks of some of his opponents; but also, the charisma of Chaplin within the film; the almost tangible sense of his will and intelligence, very persuasive indeed, even when the products of that will and that intelligence are less than impressive; the sense of discipline, both exquisite and rigid, which informs his acting and pantomime (and, here, deliberately tempers that pantomime to something more within the limits of a defined character than usual with him); the audacious and sometimes crude directness; and a kind of obtuseness which can approve a variety of banalities and sentimentalities in the script surrounding him. This sense of Chaplin as several qualities and kinds of intelligence (or, sometimes, lack of it) working together within a film has informed some of his finest comedy; yet the best of these qualities — and the creative afflatus and ambition which underlie them — are, I think, obstructive if not inimical to satire. Satirists should be relatively unimaginative, or their imaginations relatively close to earth; and their ambition should be rather sour and sulky, grudging to the world what the satirist has missed. Chaplin at his best, here — courting a wealthy widow (and pretending to chase a bee for the benefit of her strait-laced companion), reacting to chloroform, trading slaps with a casual opponent in a cabaret, shuffling along the boulevard in curious approximation of his release from jail at the end of *City Lights* — is engaging in, to an extent creating anew, the pantomime of *commedia dell'arte*: pantomime which both acknowledges its dependence on the external world, and exceeds that world by evoking worlds from gestures.

Chaplin's use of it is too ebullient, as I have said, for what I think satire should generally be; and yet, it furnishes much the solidest part of *Verdoux*, along with the work of those performers I have mentioned; so that, in great part, Chaplin on screen seems to become the film, while the surrounding story and scenes seem to fade into the real world against which Chaplin counterpoises himself.

The effect of all this on Warshow was to produce the nearest thing to a purely aesthetic critique which he probably ever attempted; and, on those terms, a particularly impressive failure. His discussion of Chaplin's presence in *Verdoux*, especially the ambiguities of Chaplin's feelings toward the external world, are as acute in their way as are the comments on themes in *My Son John*. Yet, beyond a certain mark, the acuity becomes paralyzed by Warshow's apparent need to be enthusiastic about *Verdoux* and Chaplin. He is right about the questions raised by Chaplin's sense of himself, as against himself-as-Verdoux, as against his sense of himself in relation to the world. Yet he gives Chaplin credit, I feel, for the wrong sort of intelligence; for an intelligence more schematic than Chaplin's own, and distinguished by a different sort of acumen from Chaplin's. Here, Warshow's appraisal is transfixed by the single word: irony. "Taken by itself, it is a great work of irony," he concludes his essay; "and it is unique among movies, for it requires of the spectator that he should constantly reflect upon what he sees on the screen and what he discovers in his own mind." Waiving the question of whether one might not discover these unique conditions duplicated in a few other films, this whole passage strikes me as rather inflated and question-begging. The intricacies which Warshow has discovered in *Verdoux* are legitimately interesting as discoveries; and yet, scrutinizing the essay, I find that Warshow's key concept of Chaplin's irony (or "ambiguity": another critical Gladstone bag, which Warshow on occasion seems to identify with irony) seemingly empowers him to glide over various critical questions which would otherwise require some lingering. For instance, he cites Verdoux's concluding words to the court, justly recognizing that they are platitudes: "When Verdoux enunciates his ideas, they quickly become platitudes, so that in attacking capitalist society, however sharply, he simultaneously betrays the corruption of his own mind. But then, the irony takes one more turn, for, as I have said, the corruption of Verdoux's mind is precisely the corruption of the bourgeois mind, and in exposing himself he once again exposes his society." Now, in a sentence like this one, which is duplicated throughout Warshow's essay, much depends, it seems to me, on accepting irony as a positive value: a leaven which will enrich many kinds of lump. Yet has not Warshow evaded what should be the basic question in judging the effectiveness of literary irony? I mean, the sense of the author's awareness, of a controlling intention. Irony, I think, ought to appear in art as the thin edge of a thick blade. All that Warshow has pointed out here — beneath the trenchancy and even elegance of his analysis — is that Chaplin's clichés can be taken as a reflection both on Verdoux and on the society which produced him; he has not suggested the degree to which Chaplin himself may be aware of the clichés as *clichés*: a consciousness which would seem crucial to irony. He is enthralled by the concept of the Tramp-turned-bourgeois-criminal; and this leads him elsewhere to commit the gaffe of saying that in *Verdoux,* Chaplin, who supposedly kills to support his crippled wife and young son, "still feels these figures to be necessary, but he seems unable to take a direct interest in them. . . . Thus it is no longer the cripple who embodies virtue; it is only the person who loves the cripple." And yet, the wife and child in *Verdoux* embody virtue — that is to say, innocence — quite as fully as did the Flower Girl in *City Lights*. Conversely, the Flower Girl, although undoubtedly playing a more active dramatic role, often seems to me very nearly as passive and unreal — frequently hardly more than a beautiful foil to Chaplin's whimsical goodness — as the wife of Verdoux.

Through such evasions, Warshow, I feel, evades the basic problem of *Monsieur Verdoux*: the vagueness with which Chaplin handles his basic situation, the "respectable" man who turns to murder as an extension of his business practices — the seat of Chaplin's presumptive irony. It seems to me that we can recognize the unsatisfactory nature of this irony by comparing *Verdoux* with Brecht's *Galileo,* in which we are invited to speculate how far Brecht sympathizes with Galileo's final surrender to the Church, his recantation. Brecht's essential sympathy with Galileo is uncontestable, and is reinforced, rather than obfuscated, by his ambiguities. The importance of these latter is that they call on the abacus of one's own judgment: the question they pose is not a simple this-or-that, but an all-important *how much?*

Chaplin's irony, it seems to me, skirts two important conditions of irony and ambiguity in literature: his basic intention is unclear, not because it is mysterious, but because it is vaguely and platitudinously formulated; and it is never developed with very much imaginative force. I feel certain that Brecht could sympathize, up to a point, with expeditious compromise; for that matter, I feel certain that he could, from a safe remove, sympathize with violence and murder, committed in a cause which claimed his loyalties. This he at least indicates in *A Man's a Man, In the Swamp*, and *Threepenny Opera*. Chaplin, on the other hand, I feel confident from reading his published statements, from seeing him on the screen, and from reading about him, could never seriously entertain the idea of murder for profit. Yet the only intention of Chaplin which I can discover behind the ambiguities of *Verdoux* is his belief that murder is wrong, and that big business is getting away with it.

Even this seeming platitude might fool us by assuming new realistic force, if only it were leveled against a sufficiently tough and flexible sense of reality. But the only vision of the world which Chaplin offers us in *Verdoux* is a cliché. Verdoux's in-laws, viewed in the opening scenes, are a stiff-jointed ménage conscripted from fourth-rate vaudeville: the beak-nosed harridan, the brother-in-law snoozing on the couch and getting wine spilled on him, the loutish youth. The girl, a gallant prostitute supposed to offer counterweight to Verdoux's vocation of death, is a platitude who utters platitudes; nor is she made more vital by the frightened-sounding monotone of Marilyn Nash. And when Chaplin has to extend his sights further — in the Depression sequences — we get shots of executives shooting themselves and leaping from windows. Chaplin appears to assume that the truths he knows about the world are too widely recognized to necessitate very original expression: hardly a propitious attitude for a master-ironist.

Warshow acknowledges, indeed, asserts the film's "tendency to make its statements incompletely, or to take them back after they have been made, or to modify or complicate them"; yet he never attempts to evaluate aesthetically this irony, or Chaplin's purpose. He contents himself with analyzing or sometimes paraphrasing what is readily apparent. This method imparts to the subject the baroque gleam of Warshow's own intelligence, but it also, as I have tried to indicate, depersonalizes the very real intelligence of Chaplin; the way in which he often seems to be reshaping his own film, as it were, literally between his hands; and the way in which this charisma might very well persuade intelligent people to accept Chaplin's intention, in *Verdoux*, as completed act.

As I have said, this essay is the most nearly complete attempt by Warshow that I know of to wed his analytic methods to an aesthetic purpose. His respect for form did not bear him far enough in this; did not fulfill the requirements of a liberated imagination. Yet, even here, there is enough of what would have been promise to sadden us. Such fallings short of his intention in no way limit what Warshow achieved, the sheen of clarity and high seriousness; which, if they never quite achieve for us a new definition of film as art, surely put before us some essential tools for realizing such definition.

Going
for
Broke

In *Letting Go,* Philip Roth — for the first time in his career — shows an interest in evolving his art by enlarging his vision both of comedy and of society; unlike his colleagues, John O'Hara and Mary McCarthy, who have changed their original material mainly by widening and thickening it, as though the major change undergone by the world within the past two decades, had been from slender to stylish stout. Lurching and groping and grasping, as Roth does in *Letting Go,* seem to be the only valid means left to an American writer today of developing his gifts, as distinguished from merely quick-freezing the promise of first story or novel. Nor is it any very flattering reflection on some of *Letting Go's* critics (with certain important exceptions, like Irving Feldman in the September, 1962 *Commentary*) that they should have expressed confusion and even indignation at Roth's enterprise.

What is objectionable in many of these critics, is, that they overrate the presumptive virtues of *Goodbye, Columbus* and Roth's *New Yorker* stories; and that in so overrating, they fail to see in these stories the constrictions which, in *Letting Go,* Roth strives to surmount. Such fiction as *Goodbye, Columbus* and "Conversion of the Jews" is essentially unpleasant despite the enjoyability of his heavily-inlaid details, and hotel detective's ear for pretentious middle-class speech. His skill, while undeniable, seems to lie like an opulent manhole cover upon so small a story as "Goodbye, Columbus"; while the journalistic observations are often over-emphasized, with an unpleasant note of self-felicitation. Quite as unpleasant is the tone of gratuitous moralizing with which Roth dwells upon the vulgarities of his small professionals and *parvenus*. And these weaknesses, particularly in "Conversion of the Jews," are exacerbated by a superimposed hysteria, a hauled-in melodrama, which seems, in contrast with its intended effect, as chillingly pat as a TV denoucment.

Most gratifying and exciting in *Letting Go*, is the way these faults seem to have altered their perspective; like finding out, about an old and somehow unsatisfactory acquaintance, a heretofore concealed fact which makes him seem much more vital and admirable and relevant to one's own life. What Roth has done, in effect, has been to turn his abilities inside out.

Letting Go deals with four people who are, in various ways, trying to liberate themselves from their common feeling of purposelessness and discontent. The title has at least two meanings: for as these people — Paul and Libby, Herz, Gabe Wallach and Martha Reganhart — approach what promises to be release, through someone else's love or through a noble decision of their own, they see that release carries with it the threat of dissolution, of relinquishing altogether their old sense of the world. The two stories of Gabe-and-Martha, Libby-and-Paul, are told as two gigantic tracks, sometimes running parallel, more frequently intersecting. Although the general theme of the novel is the rather popular one of alienation, it is to Roth's especial credit that his mode is realistic comedy, rather than the stale quasi-surrealism of, say, Bruce Jay Friedman's *Stern*; *Letting Go* is a fugue of absurd reductions and deflations and *non sequiturs*; so that the alienation seems, for once, a genuine discovery, an experience encountered, rather than a chic intellectual property.

Roth's journalistic talents, while still evident, are now properly used, for the most part, as corroboration and counterpoint. The novel contains a couple of the most successful set-pieces he has done, each of them describing a woman's domestic morning: Martha Reganhart's Thanksgiving Day, among the importunities of children, boarder and suitor; and Libby Herz's skittish interview with a bemused visitor from a foundling home. The comedy and pain of both these lovely sequences emerge from Roth's seeming not to detach himself gloatingly (as in the domestic scenes of *Goodbye, Columbus*), nor to manipulate and point up anything; but rather to give each distraction and contretemps full weight, its own seriousness; so that the comedy seems at once nearly accidental, and perfectly right.

But the foreground of this book has been pre-empted by a talent only hinted at, and not too satisfactorily, in all Roth's previous stories that I've read (I except "Defender of the Faith"). I've spoken of the pat melodramatics which mar some of the earlier writing: the little boy, in "Conversion of the Jews," delivering his sermon on unilateral brotherhood from the synagogue roof; some of the quarrel scenes in "Goodbye, Columbus." In *Letting Go,* this vein of apparent tricky melodrama has opened into a genuine talent, and need, for dramatic largeness, which was probably embarrassed and trivialized, in the other stories, by the strictures of space, and by Roth's feeling of obligation to the form of *New Yorker* fiction. (Indeed, Roth's chief need, partly a sign of uncertainty but partly one of self-realization, is for spaciousness; for wide gait and flailing gestures.) The monologue of the uncle at the wedding-party, in "Goodbye, Columbus," contains a hint of this excellent theatrical talent, which here, in *Letting Go,* seems to enjoy longer and better stretches than ever before. At its worst, it is the mere caginess of the night-club monologist, as in some of the telephone conversation between Gabe and his dentist father, hovering so near to Shelley Berman; but at its best, it expresses humorous ebullience, compassion and exactness. At times, Roth's greatest admiration seems to be reserved for people who can use their language with fluency, eloquence and cunning.

One wonderful passage, in the book's first two hundred pages, deserves ample citation. Paul and Libby, staying at a Chicago roominghouse, become entangled with two elderly garment salesmen: sweet, sickly Mr. Korngold, who has been put aside by his son and daughter-in-law; and his legal champion, magniloquent Mr. Levy. They explain their case to Paul and Libby:

" 'He had a wife,' said Levy, 'was nobody's business.'

" 'Only half of it,' Korngold murmured. 'A son, tell him about my son.'

" 'And a son to boot.' Levy caught a glimpse of (Libby's) slip over his shoulder.

" 'And,' said Korngold, swallowing hard, 'a daughter-in-law. A bastard like that you shouldn't leave out.'

" 'Three such people picking at one man's insides,' Levy said. 'The son is on the inside with the Nike missile, coining it, we understand. Lives like a pagan, everything fancy. Korngold freezes by that Heinie son of a bitch, counting pennies, and the son has houses, we understand, all over Florida. Plus a daughter in Smith College.'

" 'Europe he's been to *twice.*'

" 'Europe twice,' Levy repeated. 'I'm coming to Europe under waste.' He opened and closed his palms. 'Korngold's life has been ruined by the serpent's tongue.

Disappreciation from all sides. Seventy years in January.' "

This shred of dialogue, of course, scarcely does justice to the essential beauty of the Levy-Korngold section: the way in which Roth sustains his characters and evolves them (see how, even in this little space, he packs in exposition, the men's interdependence and self-dramatization); with the splendid web of Jewish speech complicating, broadening, realizing; tugging into place implications and resonances. Old Mr. Korngold, palsied and put-down, might sound in description like a "natural"—or, an "artificial"—for the counter of too many contemporary modistes. In print, however—in Philip Roth's print—Korngold makes you wonder only how Roth can give to porous reality, the comedy and agonized energy of a dramatic grotesque. Unlike other set-pieces of Roth's, Levy and Korngold seem not to be bound by space, and the author's selectiveness; but, rather, to emerge from an abundant world, into which they disappear again, all too quickly.

Levy and Korngold, like Harry Bigoness, the loutish factory hand, emanate from the world impinging on the self-elected world of Gabe Wallach. Gabe, an English instructor from Chicago, wants both the insularity of his academic world, and the self-release of love and moral independence. When he finally has to confront the unsatisfactoriness of this program for living, and tries to make a noble decision which will benefit his friends, he is checked by the animal self-sufficiency of the people with whom he must deal; their imperviousness to the moral crags on which he stumbles. Henry James pokes his nose, rather clumsily and by no means coincidentally, into the novel's beginning and conclusion; as much as to say, that the world of eventualities and pratfalls, and unthinking greed for life, has so far extended itself since James's day, as to become nearly one with the universe; while the world of moral self-sufficiency, which Gabe Wallach tries to paraphrase from James, has shrunk to the dimensions of a bath-house.

The moral imagination seems almost to have become irrelevant, since morality has become so much a matter of blundering endurance and hanging onto one's possibly wrong guesses. Paul Herz demonstrates this possibility; and it is a major failing of the novel, that Herz, who is so movingly realized, and whose story embodies most of what is dynamic, should be a secondary character. (In fact, he isn't, for most of the first half, in which Gabe Wallach functions, appropriately, as a sort of master-of-ceremonies.) Paul is Roth's most successfully sustained imaginative self-release; the measure of which is, that although Paul—unlike Gabe, or Roth—is not fluently articulate, Roth is not tempted to take him on as collaborator. Rather, he is forced to let Paul run the full length of the tether which Roth's imagination can grant. He is forced to respect Paul's mysteriousness, which challenges and defines his fluency of language.

Paul has been assumed by a few critics as the antithesis, humble and visceral, of Gabe's rarified self-conceit. He *is* Gabe's antithesis; but—as my previous remarks about him may have suggested—is not thereby a virtuous, other-directed drone. Paul, in fact, demonstrates a spiritual sterility as drastic as Gabe's: the inner vacuum of a man whose will to remain intact, hardened increasingly by all kinds of economic and social pressure, has paralyzed most of his spontaneities. His single victory, a considerable one, is his decency and wish for good, which —Roth seems to say—all but compensate even the dreadful cost of spiritual petrification. In Paul, I think, the puritanism of Roth which seems so objectionable, as a kind of snobbery, in the earlier stories, justifies itself completely: through the elementary discovery that morality is infinitely exacting; and that its cruellest exactions are of the human spirit.

The limitations of *Letting Go* can be summarized as incompleteness: not of intention, which is abundantly apparent in half its length, but of imagination. Roth's writing still conveys a constraint of imagination which prevents his invention from equalling his energy and ambition. By "invention," I mean primarily the ability to render his theme complex and protean; to give it the multiplicity of forms which would confirm its reality. I mean, too, a copiousness of plot: a commodity which seems to have been snooted for too long by many contemporary writers who handcuff it to the adjective "mechanical." At best, plot is no more mechanical— or dispensable—than the skeleton to the human body. Roth demonstrates this by replacing complexity of action and event, with repetition and/or accretion; and, within the over-accommodating space of six hundred and some-odd pages these dubious resources are taxed to excess. Roth has a talent for depicting action within a circumscribed routine situation: a college staff meeting; a Thanksgiving Day party; a woman's domestic morning. His best characters are types: not stereotypes, but people whose behavior embodies a human situation, simple or relatively complex. This can carry him as far as Paul, or Levy-Korngold; but very often these characters are sustained by their articulateness, or the articulateness with which Roth describes them from a point of detachment. When he has to sustain characters at length, showing variations in their behavior, the old charley-horse frequently sets in; and the people bleach in a peculiar, tiresome way. Martha Reganhart, an essential character, Gabe's vis-a-vis, is exciting and amusing for perhaps ten pages, in which her apparent wit and humanity, and touch of ruthlessness, promise us a rich confrontation. But then, for the next several hundred pages, she is required to swing between desparate respectability and the giddy waywardness of every Ginger Rogers fan's Gay Divorcee. This willful syllogism of behavior—far more enervating and annoying than the mechanics of a worthwhile plot would be—force poor Martha to walk through her part: her wit dried up, her voice a consistent stridency, and the reader barely managing to drag his feet behind her.

In the terminal sequence of *Letting Go*, the clanking sense of obligation to the theme, of forced and grudging development, produces a near-disaster, which is retrieved almost exclusively by what has gone before. Gabe Wallach, trying to obtain a baby for adoption by Paul and Libby, enters negotiations with a Pennsylvania working-stiff named Harry Bigoness, whose wife, a moronic waitress, has had the baby by a previous lover. The deal becomes a maddening impasse for Gabe, because Harry, although a lout, has a sub-intelligent sense of responsibility to his family with which Gabe is completely unprepared to deal; and which forces Harry into all sorts of absurd demands and evasions. Harry argues and argues and argues, in perfectly-rendered Yahoo; while it gradually becomes clear to the reader, that the whole episode is supposed to be a fortissimo version of Paul Herz's catastrophic encounter with Mr. Levy. Again, the shabby blackmailer with a greed for life, triumphs over the life-fearing intellectual. But, the Paul Herz episode told us all this—besides providing the challenging Paul, in comparison with whom Gabe Wallach, unconvincingly careening from hedonism to shattered benevolence, seems twice as thin and over-stenciled. Messrs. Levy and Korngold, having made their point, like two old-world gentlemen, make their goodbyes.

"Goodbye" is obviously one of the many words never included in Harry Bigoness's vocabulary: he stands there, tugging at his crotch, wearing out his welcome and the novel, for six small eternities.

Nevertheless, even its baucheries, its vagueness about where it is going, testify to *Letting Go's* final strength, as evidence of Philip Roth straining and challenging his own abilities. This is the most encouraging sign for his future work; the next most encouraging being, that he so often succeeds.

The
Wooden
Boy

Pinocchio (Le Avventure di Pinocchio: Storia di un Burattino) first appeared in 1880, in the *Giornale dei Bambini;* and was first translated into English in 1892. Among the English translations, that of Mary Sweet (1927) is supposed to be highly regarded. The best translation I have read, and the one in which Pinocchio was introduced to me, is that of M. A. Murray: graceful and racy, and at the same time retaining many of the charming Italian locutions. Fortunately, the translation is still available, in the English edition of J. M. Dent and Sons (first published in 1951; republished in 1957); in which M. A. Murray's translation has been retained with "revisions" (not all of them happy) by Tassinari. The present edition also retains G. Folkard's delight-fully gnomish black-and-white illustrations.

There are no "levels of seriousness" among genuine works of art. A single duct of seriousness runs from tragedy to melodrama to farce; from the Tolstoyan novel to the fairy tale. Carlo Collodi's *Pinocchio* is a master-piece of children's literature, or of any literature. For in this exceptional work, Collodi not only conveyed, (with extraordinarily little "scaling down"), grown-up reality into the imagination of childhood; he unsluiced the imagination of childhood, an imagination nearly as broad and frightening as that of Dickens, into the scuffling, grasping, lowdown universe of metropolitan adult-hood.

One can say of the Disney treatment—after drying a tear for anyone who had to learn about *Pinocchio* that way!—that it does rather well, with the farce and horror sequences: rather well, that is, in a way singularly irrelevant to Collodi. Such sequences enable Disney to work something close to his best vein—the free-form hilarity of the Silly Symphonies and early Mickey Mouse things—and, in doing so, to exploit a second, or third, or tenth-hand version of American vaudeville: something a little like what Collodi does with *commedia dell'arte,* the puppet stage and burlesque. The Harpo Marx cat dunking a smoke-ring in his beer, or taking dictation at insane speed, dotting a period in mid-air; or, Stromboli the puppet-master—a richly sinister caricature of the black-bearded Wicked Father, with his unsavory overtones of white slavery; these are enough to make one, momentarily, forget Collodi; as one must, in order at all to appreciate Disney. But, Disney's art was synthetic in a competitive, gluttonous way which one never finds in Collodi (so that what begins as parody, like the Warner Bros. reform-school stuff in the "Pleasure Island" sequences, becomes an effort to out-harrow the original); his handling of the "good people" is deplorably ninnyish; and, at length, he totally belies Collodi's message, when Pinocchio instantly becomes a "real boy" after some heroic grandstanding, and a gratingly obligatory death-bed scene.

Collodi's *Pinocchio,* first of all, is violent in a crass, wrangling, casually brutal way which Disney and all the little Disneys which he leaves behind—librarians, teachers, compilers of "selected reading" lists—could scarcely ever have digested. It opens on a conversation between two old men (Gepetto, Pinocchio's "father," and the carpenter from whom he purchases the wood from which to carve Pinocchio) which, in no time at all, has both old gentlemen wrestling on the ground, clutching each others' wigs. Pinocchio makes his initial appearance, when still a piece of wood, in a barrage of Harlequinage, sassing Gepetto and cracking shins. Later along, he exchanges remarks with a talking cricket, whose censorious tone encourages Pinocchio to smash him flat with a hammer. And somewhat later still, his two supposed benefactors, hooded with charcoal sacks, try to jimmy open his mouth, to get at the gold-pieces he has secreted there; and—after Pinocchio has bitten off a hand—decide on the more sanguine course of hanging him from the nearest bough. Such violence has a kind of earthy emphasis (surely the result of *Pinocchio* originally having been serialized, whereby each incident required its own impact), a matter-of-fact bite, which are very different from, say, the ornate sadism of Hans Christian Andersen.

But *Pinocchio's* uniqueness lies somewhat deeper; for it is, in its novelistic bulk, a fairy-tale about how one confronts the real world. Pinocchio's goal is, not becoming an adult—i.e., merely subscribing to another readily provided category—but, *becoming real.* One of Collodi's modest but emphatic wonders, is the way in which he persuades us at once of Pinocchio's mischievous resourcefulness, and of his vulnerability. Pinocchio starts as a kind of elemental spirit—then, as he advances into the coils of the real world, becomes proportionately more solid, more dependent on—and easily victimized by—others; more susceptible to hunger and exhaustion and despair.

What bodies forth Pinocchio as a work of art, is Collodi's singular earnestness about telling his audience —his "little readers"—everything he feels they should know about the world. So single-minded is this pre-occupation; so thickly buttressed by Collodi's own experience, and his story-telling virtuousity—that, despite the little homilies and paradigms with which the story is polka-dotted—the result is neither thin didacticism, nor the sort of brilliantly-cabineted nastiness that one sometimes finds in Andersen. Collodi's narrative form is usually that of the fable: very close to the earth; its rhythms, those of dancing, fighting and eating. Compared with either Andersen or the Grimm brothers, his imagination often seems to lack luxuriance or inventiveness, or eccentric wit: it finds gratification most often in lists: those itemizings into which a character will plunge, at the merest provocation (when Pinocchio prepares to cook an egg, he must review whether it will be fried, boiled, made into an omelette—meanwhile, of course, the chick emerges; sends its courteous regards to all at home; and flies out the window.) But, *Pinocchio* is permeated with an excellent sense of *theatre:* the stichomythic exchanges of wisecracks ("What are you doing on the floor?" "I'm teaching the ants the alphabet"); the choruses, of puppets, donkeys, boys. The "lame" fox and "blind" cat—two walking sardonic proverbs—could be played by Eduardo di Fillipo and Toto.

And, supplanting the bareness of his imagination, Collodi deploys a wonderful sense of narrative rhythm: an essential of the fable, as I have indicated. The firecracker-strings of dialogue give way to swirls of action: chicanery, or rough-and-tumble, or simply everybody outside and onto the ever-present highway. And—not to imply that all his effects aim around the midsection—Collodi on occasion achieves the most poignant or chilling pauses: like the moment in the crowded circus-tent, when Pinocchio, as a performing donkey, thinks he sees his mother—the Fairy with Blue Hair—gazing at him from the audience; or the scene of his first meeting with the fairy—ballet-like in its eerie muted loveliness—when, fleeing the highwaymen, he drops, gasping, against the door of the little marble house; and she appears at the window, a beautiful childcorpse, with her arms crossed and eyes closed. And, by contrast, who can forget the rampaging gusto of Collodi's panoramic crowd scenes? The Breughel-like view of Boobyland, or its bleak parallel in Blockheads' Snare, with its toothless dogs and roosters who have sold their tail-feathers? Or the schoolboys' gang-fight, on the beach. And the regalia of sound-effects with which Collodi presses these theatrics upon us, is nothing short of marvellous. His orchestration ranges from the drums and brasses of Fire-Eater's puppet show, at the beginning, to the sinister little song, *During the night/all sleep,* of the Boobyland coachman.

The product of Collodi's earnestness and artfulness, is the effect of an imaginative world which can actually be shared *by children and adults,* without descent or rising from one level to another. I think, again, of Dickens. And Collodi's shrewd, benevolent determination to communicate the best of his world-knowledge to the children, produces a tone of gritty scepticism, by which *Pinocchio* says far more than Collodi can say, in his little obligatory moralizings, throughout its course. Being a real person, *Pinocchio* tells us, involves being honorable and generous and decent (and all credit to Collodi that he doesn't slight these values by mere lip-service); but it also, correlatively, involves keeping one's eyes open for con-games (because, as the astonishing chapter of Blockheads' Snare, a more harshly comic paraphrase of Jesus, reminds us: you'll not only lose your money, you'll probably wind up behind bars yourself); keeping shy of the Law (*Ibid;* also, the appearances of the *carabinieri,* who constantly show in the most terrifying aspect); and—the implication is more delicate, admittedly; but it is there—not trusting too much to respectable folk (the right-thinking fireflies, marmots, etc., who put in regular appearances); who will be all sympathy, but very little help.

As Collodi's main token of reality, eating is given an importance a bit more intense than is usual even in children's literature. The food is usually of the simplest: two pears; an egg; cauliflower and bread. The novel's feast consists of roast chicken and apricots; which, typically, turn out to be plaster-of-Paris. But the food fulfills a most versatile range of functions: not only a love-token, or its reverse (Gepetto's pears; the meal which the fairy serves Pinocchio in the peasant's hut, and the artificial meal, mentioned above, whereby she rebuffs him); it also acts as a reminder of mortality (all the scenes, either of starvation or of simple grinding hunger, which recall Pinocchio to the world he is trying to reject); and, above all, as an instrument of Collodi's morality: one of whose key axioms could be paraphrased: *You'd better be prepared to eat anything; you'll be hungry enough, sooner or later.* I can remember three scenes pointing to this axiom: the scene in which Pinocchio, after rejecting the rinds and cores of the pears, eats them afterward; on the Island of Busy Bees, when he eats vetch, which has always nauseated him; and the scene when, transformed into a circus-donkey, he is forced to eat hay and straw.

Counterpart to the theme of eating, is the recurrence of the sea; into whose all-ingesting, all containing belly, Pinocchio disappears four times. The sea first appears as the boundless turbulence which separates Pinocchio definitely from his childhood: i.e., his father, whom Pinocchio sees borne away in a little boat after Pinocchio's first serious break with home. Pinocchio's frantic efforts to reclaim his babyhood, bring him, instead, to the workaday bustle of Busy Bee Island, where he must earn his own livelihood. Nor can he reclaim his past, until he pursues it into the innermost darkness of the sea. The second time is immediately after the disastrous gangfight on the beach; when, in flight from the carabinieri, he dives into the ocean; only to find himself in a school of fish—counterpart to the "school' of maddened boys—which is swept into the nets of a demon fisherman with green whiskers: Satan-Proteus. Here, the sea is the hellishly predatory aspect of reality; where, attempting to lose yourself, you lose only what small identity you possess, and, very nearly your life. Pinocchio is rescued by a grateful police dog whom he saved from drowning; and his next encounter with the sea is considerably happier; when, metamorphosed into a donkey by the vices of Boobyland, he is thrown into the sea by the circus-owner, in whose service Pinocchio has broken his leg. The circus-owner hopes to make a drum from his hide; but it is Pinocchio in the wood who next appears to the astonished man, describing how the little fishes obligingly nibbled away his assinine exterior. The belly of the sea is the source of renewal, conversion and resurrection.

Pinocchio's last descent is the deepest of all; into the belly of the sea's belly; into the monster dog-fish which has swallowed his father, Gepetto: the father who has disappeared since the opening chapters of the novel; the past which Pinocchio had thought to abandon, and which —having now comically shed the vices of childhood—he must seek out, willingly, one last time. I shall return to this episode.

I have scanted, so far, Collodi's most striking success: the love-story of Pinocchio and his Mama, the fairy with blue hair. The romantic portrayal of young boys' love for their mothers, was rather a staple of 19th-century children's writers like Frances Hodgson Burnett and J. M. Barrie; and its freshness, as used by Collodi, must be explained partly by our having banished it almost totally from current children's fiction (although Edwin O'Conner gives it a good, nasty trimming in *Benjy*) in probably excessive counter-reaction against occasional sentimental unpleasantnesses. But by no means does that entirely explain the startling beauty, amid its rough-and-tumble surroundings, of Collodi's love story. The fairy embodies all womanly attributes, and by no means only the virtues: she flies into rages; she can be remote and, at times, enigmatically cruel. Writing with his peculiar buoyant economy—writing, too, in the serial form, with its special obligations to time—Collodi is able to show the fairy, in a series of re-appearances, as personifying womanly growth and change: the growth and change of life, much as the sea—that formidable Mother—personifies the demands of life for self-immolation and conversion. The fairy—the only outright supernatural being in this fable—is the one who shows most graphically the effects of time. Throughout the story, she becomes more earthy, more mature, and (by inference) more vulnerable herself to mortality. When she first appears, it is as a beautiful and ethereal child, whom Pinocchio decides to adapt as his "little sister." They are separated; and, after a long interval, she reappears on the Island of Busy Bees, as a young peasant woman, who offers Pinocchio work. There follows that lovely and rueful moment when Pinocchio asks her if he can still be her litle brother; whereupon the fairy tells him that she is too old for that, now—although he has, of course, not changed. However, she will consent to be his mother. So she does; and gradually, almost imperceptibly, her supernatural power becomes more remote and dreamlike when her personal maid, the little snail, informs Pinocchio that "after a thousand misfortunes, she fell ill, and had to be taken to the hospital."

The fairy-mother is most impressive, perhaps, in contrast with Pinocchio's father. Not only does Gepetto fade in the course of the story (from the irascible old gentleman of the first chapter, whom the neighborhood boys tormented about his yellow wig) into something all too much like the insipid old dear of Disney; but Gepetto, the father, embodies that domesticity and security which we often associate with wives and mothers: hearth and home and all the little attendant maxims—constantly on his lips—enjoining patience, thrift, cleanliness. When Pinocchio first leaves Gepetto's fireside, he has—for every practical purpose—left Gepetto for good. Thereafter, Gepetto becomes Pinocchio's infancy, the fantasy of home, which he must at last rediscover, in its feebleness, in the ocean's bowels.

The fairy, on the other hand, wields an authority far less equivocal than Gepetto's: she has the power to punish, and not merely by lengthening Pinocchio's nose when he lies. For around the fairy hovers the threat of death: not merely Pinocchio's death (which she nearly precipitates at their first meeting, when she turns him away from her door to face the highwaymen); but her own death. One might say that she dies successively, throughout the story; nor can it be otherwise. When Pinocchio first sees her, she pretends to be dead; later, after their first separation, he returns, only to find the house gone, a marble tablet in its place, telling him that the "beautiful child" died of grief for him. Indeed, she is dead: we never see the beautiful child again: the fairy next appears as a young woman.

Throughout the story, the goddess, with hair of sky and sea, embodies both romance and its opposite; the ideal, and the unceasing reminder that the ideal must perish. Pinocchio's courtship of her is a gently comic parody of the chivalric romances. Small wonder, then, that she and his father never meet! Even when the little snail tells Pinocchio that the fairy is ill and impoverished, he does not ask the hospital's whereabouts, does not insist on going there; he must accompany his father: his "real" father, in the sense that the bewitching, protean woman can never be his "real" mother. So, reconciled with life, Pinocchio gives up something of mystery and wildness and plasticity, which he and we must regret. *Pinocchio* is no simple moral tale.

Ignorant
Armies

I don't believe that William March's reputation ever actually re-emerged with *The Bad Seed:* a book which I never read (and a play, by Maxwell Anderson, which I never saw); but which sounds, in all I have heard and read about it, like the kind of glib monogram which a writer may produce from his younger obsessions and meditations, after half their power is gone, or half his power or will to deal with them. For only one example, reviewers have generally discussed the book as though original sin and inherited evil were fixations of March's; whereas the unique early novel, *Company K,* makes patent that March never, at least when he wrote the latter book in the late twenties, believed in such concepts: rather, he was able to perceive and render their power, as popular myths, to dominate and force the lives of certain people. At best—and even if it were far better than second-hand evidence makes it out to be —*The Bad Seed* could have been scarcely more than that pallid false moon which one sees in a late-afternoon winter sky. The main reason for this is *Company K* itself, which, again, I call a unique work: unique in the dry, small way of Chekhov's stories and William Carlos Williams's finest poems. Small and dry, but—like tumble-weed—persistently and erratically seed-scattering: for, although I have no proof that Hemingway or Dos Passos or E. E. Cummings read this book—a novel of America in World War One, contemporary with many of their own writings—I can readily believe that its dry singularity infiltrated and loosened their writing, and writing about war by Americans for years to come. Such a book impounds whatever we may call a writer's "reputation": after reading it, we must start William March's career all over again, with the novels (*The Tallons, Come in at the Door, The Bad Seed*); the multitudinous stories and the fables.

I read *Company K,* for some little time, in the expectation, mixed with cowardly hope, that it would turn into something other than what, from its opening pages, it plainly was. There is a short coda, in which March himself appears. The remainder of the book comprises the lives of the men who made up K Company in World War I France: from just before their embarkation, until immediately after the armistice. The book is not these men's lives, but rather their presences: a sifting, sometimes whirling horde of monologues, gripes, anecdotes, orations. Some men are glimpsed rough–housing in the snow; a sergeant complains about the degenerate calibre of his men, still another sergeant describes the childhood incident which, he thinks, accounts for his toughness. A sniper boasts of how he bedevilled his German opponent by shifting his position. The orderly describes his frightened, detested captain. A soldier develops hysterical blindness and is mustered out; another soldier is blinded, and is clubbed to death by Germans.

For a time, as I say, I read along half awaiting some reassuring contour of plot to persuade me that March was in control of his book, that I was in control of March; I kept one Creative Writing course-indoctrinated eye open for "significant details." Of course, there are none, in the formal sense, the mechanized sense of "significant." Like portions of glaciers, certain incidents recur, and are further amplified: a group of soldiers is detailed by the captain to execute the German prisoners who are incommoding them in their course; and that shape of horror bobs into view, again and again, through the glimpsed lives of the executioners, in battle and in peace. Yet, this atrocity is not so terrible as some of those—the killing of the blind man, hungry men foraging blood-soaked crusts from a dying German—which are shown only dartingly. The story told by the Unknown Soldier —ripped open, slung across barbed wire, trying with despairing hatred to tear his ring from his finger, so that no particle of his identity will be left the army— this is another such incident; crucial, yet not bestowing conventional form upon the maze of human flak.

Here, I think, lies the filament of the book's immutable, dry eloquence, its greyish-tan passion. Although Company K *is* the book, seeming to direct its shape and movement and peculiarity, March never deludes himself or tries to delude his readers that Company K is a community of any kind save of the most gaunt and brutal exigency. At best, unities form *within* the company, usually as the result of such brutal exigency; this, I think, is the most terrible importance of the execution sequence, of the Unknown Soldier episode, of the young messenger's agony at killing the enemy soldier. Although the autonomy of war is not to be denied, March, I feel, never credits war with form, either esthetic or social. Nor, I think, does he share the fallacy of Edgar Lee Masters; whose sometimes eloquent "Spoon River Anthology"—hauntingly recalled, here and there, by March's novel—seems to me based on the sentimental premise that death imposes a kind of wholeness even on the tormented or jejune lives of Masters' characters. Of the men in Company K, some are living, some are dead, but—with the possible exception of the Unknown Soldier—the dead seem to have no more sense of their lives' entirety than the living. It is often hard, indeed, to tell from what distance of time they are recounting their stories. Most of them seem to be talking (at least in the battle section) from a shelf of the recent past, the almost-present. And in the common voice, which is neither precisely that of a distinct character, nor yet that of the author: a voice low and, even in anguish, somehow constrained; and, often, anything but serene.

There emerges from the throng of partially—seen lives, the impact of a way of life which, however many human existences it ingests, is not centered at all in human beings as those outside of war recognize them. The collective horror of these shard-like vignettes is their very flatness and incompleteness: our inability to lay hold of them. Their very accumulation, which, in a more conventional novel of war, might give rise to insights, discernments, veins of revelation—all add up to the centrifugal force which draws them near each other only to flick them apart. That almost-even, pseudo-serene voice is, of course, not March's voice at all, but the voice of war: of war as a human vacuum. And the viewpoint of war is the consistent, the controlling viewpoint of the novel.

Yet, I describe *Company K* wretchedly, if I imply that its achievement is simply one of authenticity; not that such authenticity, in describing war, would be very simple, or negligible, accomplishment; but March's novel is about March at least as much again as it is about World War I. It is written from a single-prismed —the words "limited" and "prejudiced" are available to whoever thinks they have meaning—vision, which, as I get it, devolves in great part on March's skepticism of human society: his suspicion that the bonds which people impose on one another may too often debilitate or warp or flatten; may compress people into roles, or stereotypes, which, in time, kill them as efficaciously as tanks and shells.

This is what, in no pejorative sense, I call the small-ness of *Company K*, the smallness of its uniqueness. The only other novel of March's I have read, *The Tallons* (republished in paperback, recently, under the throat-constricting title, *My Brother's Bride*) is a larger book structurally, and amplifies the theme I have just stated, encapsulated in *Company K*. In this other, strangely Hardy-like novel, two brothers in a Southern lumber town flounder into marriage and romantic love: both of which relationships have been more imposed on them —by muddled feelings of obligation, by jealousy, by loneliness—than elected by them. The resulting spiritual dry rot gives rise to mutual torment and, finally, murder. The novel is more bulky than *Company K,* and on its own terms, in many ways, a very good book. But it is not the organism which is *Company K* I am inclined to suspect, from the as-yet-tiny sample of March's other work that I have read, that he was one of those writers who, in a most important sense, cannot benefit by "giving full expression" to their most private involvements, the obsessions and apprehensions which they can never truly let loose. They must, in some way, divert these obsessions into forms, or conventions, or camouflaged visions like *Company K.* March, I feel, was working from an attitude watchful, self-defensive and bleakly fundamental to him, that even to attempt giving it full and direct voice must almost certainly have resulted, perversely, in cinching more tightly than before his creative daring, the ex-pansiveness of his imagination. I don't wish to press the speculation more than it is worth, but that may be why he wrote so many short stories and so few novels. As wonderful as it is, *Company K* now and then suggests a prolonged exercise in weaving and feinting, a virtuoso piece of self-dissolution.

Yet, it is far more—as any work of art, or any man of

individual substance is far more—than a summary of personal hang-ups. It is a novel of the war, a superb one, because March submitted himself to his own experience of the war; not because he tried to imprint himself on the experience. In spending so much time on what I would call, not so much its limitations as its demarcations, I have failed to mention, for example, the powerful, never-overstated and, indeed, poetic importance which March gives to the fantasy life, the necessary delusions and the microcosmic folklore of the men: read the sergeant's vision of Christ on the battlefield, or the story of the unseen "litle old German man" and his wife, or the dog-face's explanation of how a fortune teller helped him get through the war unmarked. Nor can I leave the impression that all, or the most important part, of the novel takes place on the fields of France. Some thirty per cent of the book—as the statements become gradually longer, the pace, attached now to a historic past, becomes more narrative—concerns the trickling home of the cripples, the make-outs, the ordinary men and the eternally hag-ridden.

I have little expectation—little desire, I suppose—that either *Company K* or its author will see any resurgence of popularity. I have Jack Green's excellent newspaper, *newspaper,* to thank for reminding me of March and of this work. I think, however, that anyone, reading, at any time, this 1920's novel of the first World War, will find it most expressive—in its hard, pure, non-topical way—of certain not-quite-formed perceptions left us when hope has been whittled to its thinnest durable edge. This is really all the fame that this novel—the strongest freshet of its author's talent—will require.

Reprise:
"Love
and
Death"

George Alexander (Gershon) Legman's *Love and Death* is a thunderous, overloaded, angry juggernaut, surmounted by a loudspeaker system which continuously blares Legman's message: American censorship thwarts the imagery of normal sex, and encourages images of brutality, perverted violence and blood-letting. Legman published the book himself, late in 1949, after submitting it with methodical pessimism, to an alphabet of publishers, from A for Aberdeen Press, through X, for Xavier Publishers for the Blind. The critics were hardly more receptive: Malcolm Cowley, in the *New Republic*, contributed a mildly sympathetic review, bristling with reservations; Robert Warshow, in the *Partisan Review*, was angrily contemptuous.

The edgy reception given *Love and Death* can probably be partly explained by Legman's affiliation with Jay Landesmann's now-defunct magazine, *Neurotica*, in which sections of *Love and Death* had appeared during the writing. Despite its hospitality toward vigorous or even brilliant writers, like Legman and Jack Jones, *Neurotica* was inflected with the same defiant comedy which permeated *Love and Death,* and which defines a great deal of beatnik writing today. This reckless self-parody, so often close to self-contempt, could hardly invite party manners from Warshow or Cowley.

Beyond this, however, the aversion to *Love and*

Death — Warshow's, especially — reflects the difference of two critical worlds. Warshow's partiality, as critic and editor, was toward hermetically solid essay-writing, in which every idea and attitude was buttressed by an opposition-proof wall of logic, illustration, paradox and, occasionally, sophistry. At its worst, this approach tended to neutralize the original idea, and the emotion it contained, into near-emptiness, and to reduce all argument to the issue of plausibility. On the other hand, it disabled Warshow entirely for dealing with the virtues of Legman's book: whose crude moral urgency and angry excitement propelled it beyond any question of technique or self-justification.

But time is the polemicist's chief witness, and time has certified *Love and Death*. The extent of violence within the mass entertainment industry — both as substitute for emotion and insulation against emotion — has almost corroborated Legman's jocular, ruthless hyperbole, and makes us forget, momentarily, the absence of discrimination, of critical finesse or of deep-reaching sensitivity in *Love and Death*. For this, undoubtedly, Legman must share credit with Time, which has its obliging way of confirming rhetoric.

His favorite technique, like that of the 19th-century French authors, Balzac or Mirabeau (*Love and Death* suggests occasionally the declamatory passages of Mirabeau's *Torture Garden*), starts with a large, free-floating generalization which he then bombards, like a scientist assaulting a raincloud with sand, with a volley of concrete examples. He exploits his basic irony — the togetherness of sexual repression and untethered violence — as a furnace-heated metaphor, rather than an occasion for fine-spun critical analysis. His material consists primarily of comic-strips, movies, and paperback novels; although — in one of the most effective chapters of this book — he has not neglected to anatomize at least one hard-covered breast-seller, and, later on — more regrettably — turns his rather frantic attention to Hemingway. Legman's impatient questing and hoarse-throated rhetoric make you, every so often, miss the number of ripe and exact insights he can achieve when he slows down a little. In the rather sketchy and secondary section on detective stories, he gets precisely the spinsterishness of Raymond Chandler's private eye heroes, the covert woman-baiting of Richard Powell's Mr. and Mrs. mysteries, and the way in which Hammett, in *The Maltese Falcon* and *The Thin Man,* presents sex as an atmospheric vapor, as indefinite and nearly as phoney as the opium in Chinese melodramas of the twenties.

The theme that Mr. Legman extracts from such material is a growing hostility toward women which is both reflected in, and exploited by, popular art. He might as easily have discovered that the hostility is toward all pliability, tenderness and generosity of emotion. The virtue of good polemic like *Love and Death* is the way it occasionally, by its perception and vehemence, extends itself to allegory and symbolism. The theme which nudges us throughout Legman's essay, is the threat to our culture of a violence which underlies even the violence of bludgeonings, murders and mutilations which Legman itemizes. This primary violence is the violence of bad art; the violence of unremitting contempt. This contempt is evident in the later movies of Elia Kazan, with their wracking, mechanical abuse of the emotions, no less than in TV shows like "Rifleman," or "Surfside 6." And this contempt is a hundred times more potent today than twenty years ago, because it is bolstered with the apparatus of pseudointelligence, which offers the toys of complexity without the responsibilities. Such violence is no less virulent, because it is dedicated to self-preservation: see Harold Rosenberg's comments on the middlebrow in *Noble Savage* #1.

The most important disclosure Legman makes is that our popular literature at present is deficient in an imagery, a vocabulary, of normal heterosexual love. Even the "four letter words," which cop most of the blame for sexual excitement, are not the descriptive images which one finds in the Oriental languages, or in the Song of Songs. They are grunts and gutturals, the pure extract of aversion and contempt. They suggest the warning sounds you might hear from a lookout "laying chickie" at the doorway of a poolroom or cathouse. The real attraction of beatings, bindings and kidnappings in the movies, is that these events offer *specific images* of sex, which give the frustrated viewer a sense of palpable rapport with what he is looking at.

I wish that Legman had taken a bit of time to make these points more explicit; for *Love and Death* shares with so much other polemic a basic conventionality of moral and artistic attitudes. The function of the polemicist, of course, is to tell the public what it is supposed to know. The forcefulness of his argument always depends heavily on the impress of personality which he gives it, far more than on the cogency or originality of his reasoning. Mr. Legman sees the contrast between "normal love" and sadistic violence; but he chooses not to see the extent to which normal love and violence, in life as in art, may fortify each other. Instead — like the sadists whom he seems to be attacking — he tries to *isolate* sexual pleasure and pain. His attitude toward any psychology much beyond a Psych. 1 course occasionally suggests a man embarrassedly paying off his poor relation. His points about anti-feminism, and the exaltation of the cutie-bitch, Dotty Dripple type in popular art, seem to be shrewdly taken; but he doesn't make sufficiently clear whether he is offering these observations as explanation of the violence kick, or merely as corroboration of it.

Legman's most serious weakness, though, is a deficiency of taste: what should have been his heaviest gun. By "taste," I mean the ability to notice the identity of a creative work, and to relate that identity to the world outside. Legman, I feel, has deliberately withheld this sort of taste from his investigations; and the result is, occasionally, to reduce the decent outrage of his writing to the self-satisfied peeping of a village gossip. A humorous remark by Stephen Leacock about his passion for murder mysteries is "worthy of any compleat lyncher's consideration"; and, so we'll know he isn't kidding, Legman, a little later, snaps that: "Make no mistake about it: the murder mystery reader is a lyncher." His comment on Hemingway resounds like a pennywhistle in Lewisohn Stadium, besides which he misses the most interesting characteristic of Hemingway's writing: the essential *feminism* of the esthetic taste, graceful reticence, reliance on forms and modes of behavior.

Despite its occasionally faulty brakes and erratic steering, however, the Legman cannonball heads a forceful and often exhilarating course. The deficiency of clean, abandoned anger in our recent criticism should make *Love and Death* a preferred item today.

A
Second Look
at
Pornography

Recently, while glancing through Norman Mailer's *Advertisements for Myself,* I turned with definite expectations to the chapter titled "A Note on Comparative Pornography." Alas for my expectation, the note was more of Mr. Mailer's alarmed hallooes over the advance of Mass Culture on America; so I felt reinforced in my long-held notion that even genuine liberals in America still require Tums in order to swallow the idea of pornography as a valid art form. I should like in the space available to me, to define pornography as art; to suggest some of the reasons why it hasn't received intelligent recognition in America; and to present my impressions of the directions good and bad pornography have been taking in this country.

It's necessary to recognize that every generation of criticism entertains its shibboleths: ideas of territory which is off-limits to critical attention. For a good while — until the friendly offices of Gilbert Seldes, and, much later, Jim Agee and Parker Tyler — the movies were the chief victims of the Blue Book attitude among critics. It took abstract expressionist painting some fifteen years to accrete a body of serious criticism. Pornography, however has carried its poison sac for at least double this total of years in America. Even though it has been for centuries a recognized cultural staple in India and Japan; and continues to receive cordial treatment in Paris and

Berlin; pornography in America has helped maintain an often ridiculous *entente cordial* between some intellectuals and a good many philistines. Jim Agee, one of the most receptive and knowing of critics, once wrote that "Pornography is invariably degrading to anyone who looks at or reads it"; not specifying, to my recollection, whether he meant the pornography of Gee Whiz Funnies or the pornography of the Song of Songs. I don't care to sneer lengthily at a man whom I so admire; but Agee's remark only suggests how difficult it is, for even very worthy people, to sense the existence of an art behind the word which they have learned to identify with a lifeless and gutter-squashed version of that art.

Even though literary modes and insights have evolved immeasurably within the last ten years, pornography — like the pea in any shell-game — has always managed to turn up in the wrong location. Sex — its images and the attitudes they embody — has certainly changed at least as radically as "style," within the past American decade; but it is still a grade-A bargaining point when at odds with Post-Master Sodbottom, or Senator Stuckwhistle, to argue that the art work you're trying to get past their censorship mechanism is not on friendly terms with that ghastly thing, pornography. This, in great part, was the operating point in clearing *Lady Chatterly's Lover* with the fretful Mr. Summerfield; although proof that the book was, indeed, sexually stimulating (I'm far from convinced, myself) would have been its strongest endorsement as a work of art. As in every war of expediency, however, the more intelligent side had to make the biggest concessions. The nonsense and cowardice of the situation were, that people like Alfred Kazin and Malcolm Cowley based their appeal on the contention that the novel was not pornography at all, but Art (by their definition of the moment, not pornographic); whereas

Summerfield and Company obviously could not care less that it might be Art, and, to their infinite credit, could not see why Art shouldn't be stimulating to anyone whose pancreas wasn't stuffed with mattress lint. By this route, sex was converted into something exquisitely unreal: not even D. H. Lawrence's sex-in-the head, but sex-in-the-air; and the word "pornography" overhung the gathering like a fragment of gossip which everyone had heard, and half-believed. Had Messrs. Kazin and Cowley's skirmish been directed against censorship, rather then against unseemly art, they would have honestly and properly retorted to Mr. Summerfield, that of course the work under discussion was more potentially horny than say, *The Caine Mutiny,* or *The Forty Days of Musa Dagh*; that this was nothing to Lady Chatterly's detriment, that it did well what the "art studies" of some mail-order houses do so badly; that its sexual pleasure was only a single band within a spectrum of imaginative experiences; that instead of atrophying the emotions, it exhilirated and glorified them.

Probably the history of American jazz demonstrates best how sexual and artistic conservatism promote each other. On its first appearance, encrusted with the spilled booze, sawdust and congealed snot of how many saloons and cabarets, jazz was under universal attack as an aphrodisiac, and low-grade art. At this time, the nobler defenders of jazz music held that, contrary to the slanderous nonsense circulated by its vicious detractors, the music of Armstrong, Waller and Dodds was less phallically inspiring than the Art Songs of Robert Schumann. As decades passed, it became obvious that jazz had no intention of surrendering to its accusers; although with the increasing popularity of the music, everyone was perfectly aware that it was more randy than ever. However, artistic conventionalism had scored a hands-down

win over sex morality; the detractors contented themselves with saying that jazz was low-class, and likely to
inflame the proletariat with false ideas of art; and the
flood of jazz and jizzum continued unstemmed, and, if
anything, greatly amplified.

For much of its existence in America, pornography has
been the fulcrum not only of objections by critics to
popular art, but of objections by philistines to art in
general. The converging point of such objections, is
usually the word, "waste," or more specifically, 'masturbation." The subject of attack is accused of being an un-
profitable expenditure of energy; of being self-centered;
of being anti-social; of being reactionary; of ruining the
mind. Most of these protests can be discerned as clearly
in a New York Times advertisement by Huntington
Hartford—outraged at DeKooning's "Woman" paintings
— as in Edmund Wilson's writings on detective stories, or
Irving Howe's articles on movies and television.

Nevertheless, an art form can frequently be defined
best in terms of the intelligent objections which it
garners. In the case of pornography, especially, such
objections are almost inseparable from the definitions
which they evoke, or the replies which those definitions
embody.

The basic difference between pornography and erotic
naturalism like that of Zola, or more conventional romanticism, is the way in which pornography isolates a
single prism of experience — sex — from the context of
sweat, fret, psychological tensions, and infinite finagling,
with which — certainly, in America — this experience is
usually interwoven. The genuine voice of pornography
is the voice of fantasy; its favorite mode is the fugitive
glimpse: limericks, *contes*, movie stills, jazz numbers.
Boccacio's *Decameron*, which seems to answer in every
respect the Drs. Kronhausen's definition of "erotic real-

ism" in *Pornography and the Law,* in fact exhales an atmosphere of fantasy, in which sex is always exhilaratingly present, and far more available than it could have been even in Renaissance Italy. The reckless acceleration of mischances, pranks and intrigues, lends the stories a dreamlike briskness and vagrant suggestiveness, as unrealistic and persuasive as the stories of Kafka.

Until recently in America, a key criterion of serious art, among conservative critics, was that it should incorporate slatherings of Experience: the smorgasbords of John Dos Passos and Thomas Wolfe; or, for those who looked down at the "naiveté" of these writers, the cold buffets of Faulkner, Flannery O'Connor, or William Styron. Art was not certified art unless it emanated a sense of depth: a term which had become increasingly complicated throughout the years, but no less persuasive to its adherents. Among even critics like Edmund Wilson or Lionel Trilling, art which tried to be too elliptical, or vagrant, or momentary, ran the risk of being charged, at worst, with decadence, and at best, with gold-bricking.

Only within the last five years, the arrival in this country of Samuel Beckett's novels and plays; of Jack Gelber's *The Connection*; of Paul Goodman's allegorical monologues, has brought to the intelligentsia's notice an elliptical, community-minded, essentially *sidelong* art, whose chief effect is to relay to its audience the fretfulness and speed of present-tense existence. At least one example of this trend — Jack Gelber's *The Connection*—suggests pornography at a careless reading: not for the "dirty words" but for its scrappy, makeshift informality and rhythm of anticipation. Even comic strips, like "B.C.", and entertainers like Bob and Ray, have moved into a scanty, elliptical style which might be a miniature refraction of contemporary art.

Such writing, instead of trying to gorge itself with

experience — which has become a crawful within the last decade — hangs onto experience as if it were a porch-post in a hurricane. I don't mean to suggest that any of this work is seriously related to pornography; but the response it has aroused, suggests a change in the critical attitude which has often regarded short-hand, allusive writing as self-indulgent, or cheaty; and to this extent, we may eventually look for pornography to acquire a change of status.

The objections to pornography I've mentioned are connected, in a spiralling curve, to a more basic objection. Pornography features the consumer, rather than the creator: instead of illuminating or recreating the sex drive, pornography banks and stokes it, as in those Oriental drawings where the sex act is the invisible apex of the intricate, converging lines. At its basic level, pornography doesn't awaken the artist in the consumer, but engages both consumer and artist in a sort of collaboration.

In my opinion, this criticism of the spectator-as-consumer is probably the most valuable single objection to pornography; not only because it makes the most sense, but because it comes closest to the center of most such objections: not that pornography might encourage sexual promiscuity, or rape, or V.D., or birth control; but that it probably encourages masturbation: one of the last vestiges of private enterprise in the United States (One might expect this fact to engender a certain sympathy among more conservative thinkers; but it doesn't seem to work out this way.) Most pornography, I think, depends on the *ejection* of emotion through an image, or group of images, which intensifies that emotion for a fleeting instant, then dispels it.

Any argument by me either for or against masturbation would — self-evidently, I trust — be ridiculous. It is worth noting, though, that the prejudice against the consumer I mention has probably never existed in Paris or Stockholm, or other European cities which enjoy flourishing markets in pornography; and where the consumer is generally regarded, when intelligent, as a valuable fellow-citizen of the artist, and, in his own way, a creator. The prevalent notion in America that the consumer — like the creator, in the eyes of art-haters — ought to pay his own way, seems to be slowly evaporating in America, also, with the appearance of the Beats. Despite their frequent resemblance to the more informal fraternity houses, the Beats at their most intelligent— as represented by Jack Green, or Diane Di Prima, for instance — seen like our closest equivalent in decades to the microculture of the Paris bohemians. Semi-documentaries like "The Savage Eye," and fiction films like "The Subterraneans," where the spectator is stationed in every frame as a passive supporting player — suggest that the consumer is gradually attaining respectable citizenship over here.

The best medium of pornography is probably the hard, metallic daylight of satire, allegory, the lyric poem or the critical essay. Before American criticism began to take on the aspect of an extended slumber-party, writers like George Jean Nathan, H. L. Mencken and Joe Gould availed themselves of pornography's intensity, raffishness and, occasionally, sexuality; and, very recently, Jim Agee and Manny Farber have confiscated the methods of pornography for their angry, jocular criticisms. Agee's comments on *Princess O'Rourke* or *Tender Comrade*; Farber on *Hard Sell Cinema,* would surrender half their brine in any milieu west of Hot Book Row on Times Square. Like the pyrotechnic blasts of these critics, the pornography of Balzac's *Contes Drôlatiques*, or the *Decameron* specializes in flare-lighting the incongruities of any and all pretensions, or relationships. The methods of such pornography are the methods of comedy: undercutting relationships with the common denominator of sexual desire; and deploying the chief weapons of comedy, action and time, to show absurdity in motion.

The worst of American pornography — like most bad popular art — reflects the backside of democracy. To corroborate this, I think, George Legman's pamphlet *Love and Death* (which I'll discuss further) is unimprovable in its depiction of American mass culture's pact with violence. I wouldn't try to amend Legman's Sears-Roebuck catalogue of atrocities; but I would suggest that because of Legman's moral conservatism, his work misses the most depressing thing about American pornography. I mean, the fat-hammed power-morality which has underlain so much TV and movie entertainment within the last five years; and which makes the outcries about "sex and violence" which are so popular at present, seem childish. This attitude uses Boccacio's comic technique of *reductio ad absurdum,* as though it were a ruthless steam-roller. To me, the most disconcerting thing about the carefully-swaddled pamphlets that are still obtainable from hot-book crannies, is the *dullness* of the pamphlets' contents. Not their sadism (hippo-like scuffling by unwieldy-looking females); and not their technique (the fashion-ad line of "Dick Tracy," combined with the claustrophobic, gadget-crazed decor of "Buck Rogers"); but their dullness, which does not modify their violence, but is inseparable from it. Cruelty can both be esthetic and reflect sensitivity. Brutality — the kind you encounter here, and run into from every other "hot joke" in circulation — never refers to art or to artistic taste. Cruelty, I think, is the violence of intelligence; brutality is the violence of mindless power. Combined with pornography, this brutishness is a perfect instrument for expressing the worst in democracy: a hostility toward, and determination to punish, anything sensitive, self-sufficient and reserved. Forgive me for sounding like Dwight MacDonald — but whenever I visit Times Square, I can't help wondering whether rape isn't less a sexual, than a political crime: a crime against the last suggestions of aristocracy we have.

However, let's withdraw from Times Square, and examine a choice selection of bad native pornography: an opulent opus by one of our most noisily-touted free-speakers.

Widely touted as Captain Billy Wilder's Whizbang, the movie *Some Like It Hot* was probably one of the least sexual films Hollywood has produced since *The Lost Patrol*. The film dealt with the excruciations of two 1920's jazz musicians — Jack Lemmon and Tony Curtis—who, disguised as a lady bass-fiddle player and saxophonist, enlist in an all-girl orchestra whose *artistes* include Marilyn Monroe. The movie's outstanding achievement was the way in which potent pornography was shaded off into burlesque. Wilder's dubious route to this effect consisted of focussing on abnormality (the impotence of Curtis and Lemmon, in their female guise; Curtis, impersonating a frigid yachtsman; the carefully suspended imputation of Lesbianism between the pretended and *bona fide* girls); so that, like a fast ping-pong game, the grotesqueness of each situation deflected the scene's amorous overtones. Wilder had done this before, in *Miss Tatlock's Millions,* with its *pianissimo* suggestions of incest between sister and (pretended) brother. Billy Wilder's affection for blood-bucket Gothicisms (the gang-massacre which opens this comedy is a five-minute horror-movie) and for using innuendos as though they were ball-peen hammers, makes him, as in previous films, resemble a far less intricate and talented Ernst Lubitsch. Probably his greatest deficiency is the absence of Lubitsch's timing and restraint: the resourceful mime, Joe E. Brown, is forced to repeat the same unfunny mugging about six times; the word "bull *fiddle!*" is reiterated until a beginner at normal school couldn't miss the point. Billy Wilder's hard, blatant vaudeville, although occasionally refreshing in its audacity, hammars what might have been an erotic romp into an endurance contest between audience and cast.

I can't feel much more peppy about the so-called men's magazines. Since *Playboy* became stud-whale of American periodicals, a score of replicas have turned up in its grenadine-tinted wake: Jem, Tiger, Satan, Dude, Rogue, etc. Each of these publications is dedicated to presenting its audience with a full-scale ovarama: sex, humor, velvet-drape culture (reprints from Boccacio, Aretino) and stylish masculinity, with infrequent time out for serious thinking like *Playboy's* famous editorial on fallout, which none of the imitators has shown excessive haste to duplicate.

My objections to the sallies of these pulse-racers, is that I can't help sharing their authors' obvious embarrassment at having to ladle out this *bon vivant* sex to a twentieth-century American audience. The whole trouble is, that every suggestion of sex excitement is so shlubbed up with slipper-handed archness, toe-scuffing coyness, and the magazines' notion of high living, that the whole performance generally suggests a fancy bordello, whose proprietors insist on preceding the main event with a performing seal playing fourteen choruses of "My Country, 'Tis of Thee," on the xylophone. Another objection is, that these people's idea of what makes a woman attractive, is indistinguishable from the Powers Agency's idea of what makes a woman attractive, so that, to my own eccentric gaze, their females have the allure of three-day-old clam fritters. A third objection is, that making any of these creatures involves somewhat less exertion, on the average, than going down to corner store for a package of chewing-gum. *The Affairs of Casanova,* a generally unlikable film, demonstrated its superior know-how in this respect by giving each of Casanova's lady conquests a jigger of personality; so that his one-man-army-game seemed a little less monotonous than usual.

As a respite from such deluxe-processed porno, let me cite some different illustrations, as follows;

Very recently, I had the privilege of viewing some classical Japanese pornographic prints owned by a friend. They embody so beautifully every quality of which fine pornography is capable; and they are so different from anything of the kind that you can usually see in the states; that — even for someone who feels as sympathetically as I do — to see them is like being enlightened about a hitherto unknown neighborhood of art. The motif of these pictures, at first glance, seems almost to be, not the sex act at all, but the characters' billowy, encompassing clothing — gowns, sashes, robes — which both conceals the participants, and decorates their love-play; which appears, from picture to picture, as an ocean, in which the lovers charge each other like passionate sharks; as a curtain, from which vagrant faces peer at the spectator; or as an abstract pattern, against which the action, by turns, seems to be asexual as a Mondrian painting, or as bright and exact as an acid-burn on a sheet of tin. Their effects range from the ornate and dense, to the oblique and illusory. In one such picture, the man and woman are inseparable from the tumbling swells of clothing, sculpted buttocks and thighs. She grasps his penis, as delicately ugly as a Japanese dwarf-tree; he sucks her nipple with a goldfish-mouth; and — in a visual metaphor which recalls the Song of Songs — both are girdled by a charging current of sperm. In another print, woman and man are serenely poised against a winter field. She is clothed, with her buttocks exposed, as he sedately prepares to enter her from the rear; her only gesture of reaction is to nip the corner of her veil with dainty intensity. In still another print, two female lovers are enfolded so closely within a cataract of gown, that they seem like mirror images of each other. Here, the sexual inflection is as reticent yet as definite as a razor-edge barely protruding from a velvet cushion.

Like most of the best pornography that I can remember, these prints convey the impact of line, rhythm and composition meeting together in an irreducible whole. The sex act draws together the converging elements of the pictures, like the point of horizon in a traditional landscape painting. Luxuriance and austerity set off and intensify each other: the glossy shadings and the shimmering-wire lines; the molten churning of draperies and the clean, nipping movements of hands and mouths. Everything in these drawings honors the complexity of experience: there is no suggestion of the tendency to deprecate and over-simplify reality, which we must expect from cheap pornography; rather, the warmth of sex permeates different levels of existence, like seminal fluid. Different kinds of experience, different prisms of meaning, concentrate into a unit of multi-fluent intensity, like the silver bullet of water at the center of a park fountain.

The only western duplicate of this quality that I have recently seen, takes place in Ingmar Bergman's *Smiles of a Summer Night*. The scene — a girlish exchange of sex lore between a young mistress and her personal maid — veers into a kittenish scuffle, with both girls enveloping themselves in the bedcurtain, as in an amorous cocoon.

The scene's delectable fragrance of both homosexuality and "normal" sex; and its cat's-cradle of emotional and physical tensions; also, the visual rhetoric of struggling entanglement, whiteness and sharp daylight; make this scene the only serious western contender with oriental pornography that I can remember in some little while. (Addendum: Stanley Kauffman, film appraiser for the *New Republic,* regretted that the picture didn't measure up to the wit and lightness of French films — Maurice Chevalier's, he must have meant.)

The virtues of these gems entitle them to inclusion in my own Informal Treasury of Pornography, which includes also the following:

1) *The Scandals of Clochemerle* (Novel) by Gabriel de Chevalier.

2) *The Affairs of Casanova* (Film) Chiefly for some of the best erotic photography in years.

3) *Los Olvidados* (Film) The scene in which Jaibo, juvenile criminal, encounters the mother of his friend, Pedrito, to the accompaniment of fiesta drums and trumpets. (I still do not know whether I prefer this to the exquisitely done puberty-nightmare of Pedrito).

4) *Have You Anything to Declare?* (Film) starring Raimu.

4) *Fish Flying Through the Air* Roswell G. Ham's scabrous, amusing novella.

6) *The Long Hot Summer* (Film) A few scenes: The symposium of late-twentyish Vassar types, supervised by Lee Remick's frontage; the buttock-happy views of Joanne Woodward, in her boudoir interview with Paul Newman.

It is no coincidence that half the partial list noted above consists of scenes from moving-pictures. The comic-strip, the movie scene, the movie still, are possibly the only creative modes available in America, which are volatile and evasive enough to contain pornography as a more than incidental quality (For more perception than I could hope to supply on this subject, I commend Manny Farber's article, "Hollywood's Peepshow Naturalism," in the *New Leader*, February 16, 1959). Like dreams, remembered comic strips or movies can become inextricable from the shape and coloring of stores, or streets, or faces, which memory has processed from life. I note without comment, Lenny Bruce's assertion, in a recent interview in "The Realist," that as a boy he masturbated to "Popeye."

The most widely known and least reputable examples of pornography's debt to popular culture, are those pocket-sized comic books which, for more years than anyone can remember, have rivalled box-ball as a feature of American high-school playgrounds. The regular subject of these comics, is the sex world of Moon Mullins, Pete the Tramp, or Professor Wottasnozzle and Sappo; all of whom are shown at recreation that Coulton Waugh, author of *The Comics*, would tremble to recognize. The outstanding characteristic of these fuckies, outside of the ten-inch phalluses on Popeye and Lord Plushbottom, is the way they carry on the echoes of rowdiness, smuttiness and disreputability, which rebounded about their originals, in earlier years. The fuckies, in their crumby way, seem like continuations of the comic strips as they once existed, rather than the milk-chocolate hand-grenades which so many of them have become. On the same *sub rosa* level, these extra-licit comic strips are a seedily authentic record of an American adolescent's sex myth: hyperbolic, vulgar, disrespectful, hysterically aggressive.

For anybody much over fourteen and in good possession of his faculties, the fuckies are less obscene — and much less stimulating — than, say, the lipstick mouth

which was recently given Mrs. Mutt, of "Mutt and Jeff."
Ironically, within the past few years, pornography has
been making faster headway in the popular arts through
the untoward route of "family" comics like "Hi and
Lois," "Beetle Bailey" or "Mr. Abernathy." The rhythm,
tempo and ingenuity of these strips give them considerable edge over professional glamor strips like "Prince
Valiant" and "Juliet Jones," in which the women's deter-
minedly worked-over faces have as much zing as an exhibit by the J. P. Morgan Library. It is difficult to
overlook these strips' cute-folksy situations and gags,
until you ask yourself whether they could have gotten
away with so much delicately siphoned sex ten years
ago. In "Beetle Bailey" or "Mr. Abernathy," the girls'
flip bosoms and behinds — they seem to be drawn with a
single pen-twist — are as unequivocal, and as suggestive, as
the infinity sign in an algebraic formula. When Beetle —
the lecherous private — or Mr. Abernathy — the lecherous
multi-millionaire — demurely patterned after the Esquire
roué — make their Wagnerian overtures, the ladies turn
aside faces as serene as those of the Japanese pornog-
raphy-heroines. Until recently, Milton Caniff exhibited
the same dexterity with his piquant shadow-lines; but
within the last year or so, Caniff's penchant for cuteness
has prevailed over his tough discernment. I doubt
whether his recent deluge of adolescent-heroines would
prove worth the effort to anyone but Franz Wedekind.

Sex and sadism are fairly often united in these and
other modes of pornography. Sadism distils many of pornography's basic elements: fantasy, intensity, anticipation, the comic vulgarity which spares no participants. I
hope I won't be misunderstood, and fully expect to be,
when I say that sadism within careful limits is as worthwhile and possibly as necessary, to pornography as are
many other facets of emotional experience. Unfortu-

nately, too many of the television and movie critics who couple "sex and sadism" (or, more often, "sex and violence"), apart from their overwillingness to exert their own sort of violence against such horrors, have shown themselves all too ready to overlook the worst sort of violence: that of bad art. They usually resemble, in boiled-off form, the kind of liberals who carefully evaded the most important moral issues of World War Two, and, since then, have tried to evade the consequences of their evasions, by declaring themselves all-out against violence "in any form." For these reasons, sadism in pornography deserves a couple of hundred words.

Sadism consists essentially, not of violence, but of an attempt to control violence, to keep it in suspension. As Havelock Ellis and other psychologists have pointed out, the sadist derives gratification not from inflicting pain *per se,* but from its association with sexual experience. In fact, I'd suggest, the sadist is haunted and repelled by the relationship between sexual ecstasy and pain even in the context of "mature" sex adventure. He directs most of his passion and ingenuity toward isolating pain and sexual pleasure, and keeping them as predictable as he can. The sadist is usually something of an artist: in that he concentrates such effort on conserving, hoarding and retaining experience, instead of squandering his emotions unthinkingly and freely. Sentimentalist that he is, he spends all his sexual career — usually, with not-quite-complete success — in consecrating some memorable humiliation of his childhood: usually from the toilet-training period, and very frequently, I believe, from receiving the enema. The sadist is fascinated by this apparent interdependence of pleasurable relief, and enforced indignity and fear; as well as by the differing sensations which this combination represents: on the one hand, constriction, hardness, tightness and humiliation; on the other hand, relief, softness, relaxation and unexpected pleasure. A metaphor of orgasm, ready-made. The sadist's big concern, ever after, is to keep sexual experience as pleasurably mysterious and contradictory, (yet predictable, and with the pain kept under conscious control) as on this celebrated occasion.

I've deliberately given short shrift to the Marquis so far; because, aside from lending his name to this *esthetique,* he seems as little relevant to a description of average sadism, as Karl Marx would be to a description of average Marxism, or Sigmund Freud to a description of average Freudianism. De Sade occupied himself with translating sadism into an elaborate, self-conscious and intensely romantic philosophy. The chainings, poisonings and decapitations of DeSade's fiction are irrelevant to usual sadism, I think, except as they reflect the dilemma of a violent and, essentially, pathological mentality in trying to *perpetuate* the gratification of sadism. De Sade, I think — with only second-hand knowledge of his work — was habitually violent, rather than, like most sadistic people, intermittently violent. In order to find genuine escape through sadistic practises, he had to exaggerate bizarreness and ferocity of his fantasies far beyond the necessities of ordinary sadism. Those other heir presumptives to the word "sadistic" — the Nazis — bear, I think, as much and as little relationship to the word as do violent criminals of any level; although the Nazi government *in toto* — based on an esthetic, rather than a political, philosophy — is much more germane to the escape-fantasy of the sadist.

In plain English, I believe that what I have called sadism is, within civilized limits, probably desirable and possibly necessary to a mature sexual life. The hair-tugging irregularities of American life, the distressing imminence of either injury or sexual pleasure at every daily encounter probably accounts in part for the recurrence of sadism even in better American pornography, as well as in the most innocuous settings. The abduction sequence in *The Sea Devil* (Rock Hudson and Yvonne DeCarlo), with its effortless rhythm, its sexual fragrance, and its teasing sense of both inevitability and myteriousness, left most art-photo specialists in sadism at the post. In its way, sadism is as much a pure distillate of pornography, as pornography is a pure distillate of popular art. The comic element of sadism — the sadist, always trying to recast his experiences, in terms of his private order, is a natural comic hero — makes its recurrence in pornographic art entirely natural. More specifically, the typical situations of movies — women being bound, abducted, spanked, etc. — concentrates the main effects of pornography in a special way: by refracting the conditions of masturbation: stealth, anticipation, solitariness; the contrasted tensions of flesh and clothing, of softness and stiffness. The mysterious and unexpected outrage being depicted on the screen is a miniature mirror of masturbation, just as the darkness and isolation of the theater itself duplicate the ideal conditions of masturbation. The violence in these fantasies never exhausts itself as violence; nor does it end in the broken spirits, shattered kidneys, mashed faces, lifeless bodies of real-life violence. Violence is magically transmuted into a kind of electrical energy, pleasurably unnerving, and suspended in the imagination for all time.

The most reliable evidence of the developing change in attitude toward pornography, is probably the increasing emergence of books on the subject by psychiatrists and social scientists. Norman Mailer, in the essay I mentioned at the opening of this treatise, observed that most critical attention in America is at present devoted to sex in mass culture; which, to my thinking, leaves us in a pleasurable calm between the universal indifference of a few years ago, and the Niagara of hooey which we can almost surely expect a few years hence.

The most fruitily publicized of the recent books was *An Unhurried View of Erotica* (Helmsman Press; 1958); whose mode of presentation might have seemed over-enthusiastic for Shakespeare's letters to Anne Hathaway. Compiled and written by sociologist Ralph Ginzburg, the book was attended by an introductory note from George Jean Nathan, a preface by Theodore Reik, and a luxurious boxed edition which sold for a pre-publication of — if I remember — sixteen dollars. Unfortunately, *An Unhurried View* gives the reader very much the sensation of being imprisoned in a lavatory booth while, say, a Mardi Gras takes place directly outside. "An Unhurried View" gives the effect of the scuffling feet, and muddled voices, but very little else. The best thing in it are some amusing observations by Mr. Ginzburg on the impedimenta offered by many public libraries to the disinterested researcher trying to gain access to the "forbidden books" divisions: the atmosphere Mr. Ginzburg portrays is as suspicious as, and, if anything, more antisocial than, the old-time speakeasies. For the rest, I'm afraid that the word "unhurried," in the title, is the book's biggest inaccuracy (the second biggest: the unmodified word, "erotica," which is represented almost entirely by Anglo-Saxon selections.) The volume skips like a brake-clogged subway train from one selection to another: some octogenarian's scatology by Ben Franklin; a selection from Frank Harris's autobiography; some dribbings from 18th century English flagellation literature, and so on. The worst impression all this gives, is that the book's sketchiness was arbitrarily determined by Mr. Ginzburg's suspicion that more exhaustive detail would commit him to a more demanding system of scholarship, and/or original point of view.

Drs. Eberhard and Phyllis Kronhausen, authors of *Pornography and the Law* (Ballantine Books, Inc., 1959) are trying to define pornography, largely in terms of what it isn't. To this effect, they have evolved a genuinely enlightening and suggestive category: that of "erotic realism," which might be defined as sex presented within a matrix of realistic experience. This, as might be inferred, corresponds pretty closely with my own idea of pornography as a type of fantasy. My main reservation about the category is, that the authors don't resist the temptation to use it for a platform of respectability-in-literature. It is good to suggest that erotic realism "is part of a basic rebellion against the social supression of elemental drives and needs common to all mankind"; but this notion occasionally, in the course of the book, gets too close to the art-should-be-good-for-something-moral attitude which seems to move Eric Bentley when he suggests that all comedy writers ought to be (my definition) burlesque anarchists with satchels full of celluloid bombs. This attitude not only restricts pornography, but more important, realism as well, by trying to thrust an ever-evolving form back into a 19th century mold. The ubiquitous Dr. Theodore Reik, on hand with some more introductory notes, helps matters very little by referring to "high quality works of erotic realism" and "obscenity." The authors' literary naiveté (although their history of erotica is infinitely more rewarding than Ginzburg's) shows up in their chariness about comedy in sex literature and art. They fall over themselves (in more ways than one) denying that *Lolita* is comic. I don't know how to answer the remark that "If laughter can kill anything, it can certainly make short shrift of sexual excitement" except to recommend that the authors await the next television showing of any old Mae West or Clark and McCullough movie; or buy themselves the recent album of recordings by Negro comedian Red Foxx.

Laughter may alternate with sexual desire, or provide desired relief from it; so does orgasm. Nevertheless, *Pornography and the Law* is the most sensible, and — within a perhaps too narrow limit — most promising American work that I have recently seen.

One closing thought: I should be foolish attempting to predict the form that pornography will presently evolve in American culture. I think that, at present, pornography in its broadest interpretation — which I've tried to suggest here — is probably better equipped to help the conscious and sub-conscious liberate and cross-pollinate each other, than any other creative expression except religion, which is almost as remote from its ancestral meaning. The prospect of a religious pornography seems much more welcome right now, and much less a scabrous joke, than at any time, possibly, since the Renaissance. I can't think of anything more potentially effective to clean away the smegum of bad art and smelly morality which we have accreted in recent years.

And — lest the professional censors, whom I have mentioned before, gleefully infer that I am trying to make up: I could understand, and probably subscribe to, any decently exasperated campaign against lousy art and its depridations of feeling and imagination. The trouble is, that official campaigns like Mr. Summerfield's seldom embody any genuine passion at all. The strongest feeling one can locate behind their ruthless, lumbrous movements, is the hangdog resentfulness of a distempered idiot boy. They always shy away from the accusation that they are trying to arbitrate art, whereas they ought to rush this charge with belligerent glee, if they were decent crusaders at all. But they lack all the creativity, all the good-seeking, of a Savanarola or a St. Ignatius. I stay away from defacing posters, usually, for the same reasons that, on occasion, I have stayed away from blowing my brains out; it seems rather futile, and I'm not 100% positive I'd be around to see the fun. But when I walked into the post office at Lexington Avenue and 44th Street last week, and saw the huge rattlesnake glowering at the little boy and girl who, I infer, get art photos through the mail, I couldn't resist the feeling that the spirit of the appeal would have been clarified immeasurably, if the snake had been drawn so as to resemble an erect and menacing penis.

Footnote

I have decided to reserve this rather extended footnote for recommending Paul Goodman's impressive article, "Art, Pornography and Censorship," appearing in the March, 1961 issue of *Commentary*. I knew nothing of Mr. Goodman's ideas on this subject until the publication of his article; I think, however, that the several parallels I find, between his ideas and my own, offer valuable comment on the situation we are discussing. As usual, I admire Mr. Goodman's bustling incisiveness, his sincerity, and his deploying of a rhetoric which thrusts and cauterizes, rather than plopping and polluting like so much critical oratory. Mr. Goodman feels, with my general agreement, that the punitive and repressive atmosphere toward sexual art in America today, itself encourages the "bad" sado-masochistic pornography which is the supposed target of censorship. He feels, too, that the situation of pornography presents, in relief, the muteness and impotence of much American art today.

As usual, Mr. Goodman implements his sociological discernments with the straightness and fervor of a poet. I object, however — again, as usual in his writing — to a glibness which, I feel, over-varnishes many of the specifics, intricacies, jaggednesses which are part of the problem he is discussing. His solution to the situation — which he apparently feels is rather bold — is to legalize pornography generally. Now, I think that three intelligent people in every ten, harbor no doubt that pornography eventually (that is, probably in very short order) *will* be legalized. But Mr. Goodman, it seems to me, never altogether faces the issues (a) of defining pornography so as to reform the *attitudes* which would remain untouched by any legalization; and (b) of attacking the *taste* for bad pornography, which certainly is not solely the product of repressive, puritanical censorship. Almost as deep-laid as the instinct for pornography, is human laziness, seeking a cheap, simple and easy substitute for something which, in any worthwhile form, is demanding, complex and hard. But despite my reservations about Mr. Goodman's solution, I urge his article on anyone who reads this essay.

Bite
Size

Just recently, I severed relations with six of my teeth: six little hangers-on, become as viciously parasitic as courtiers in 18th century France, and at least as obstreperous when faced with any responsibility. They had formed their own little cadres, either by coaxing or coercion, with the honest teeth of my parish. Neither them, *nor the teeth flanking them* (honest teeth, as I say, which I know would have done their jobs, had their consciences, as well as good, been free); none could be approached for even token work, save with a delicacy verging on sycophancy.

I acknowledge my guilt, through too-sanguine indulgence, by which I brought those teeth to their state of worse-than-rebels: theirs was the fitful rebelliousness of the dissolute, of victims: no Castroes, no Mao's, even! I own my guilty part in over-estimating their freedom of will, until it became the boundless bondage of delirium. But responsibility, unfortunately, is a narrow trail, along which we must single-file: we, our dependents, and our victims. And when at last, along that trail, we face our dependents, and our victims —

Yet, however, meanly they filled their status, a tooth is a tooth; and losing them was a shock, with just a bit of outrage about it: indeed, the outrage of some indecent, yet half-consciously expected, revelation about one's self. Our relationship with our teeth, is our relationship with children, with employees, with partners, with our own remote past: a past in which every part of ourselves which we could observe by using, was a possession; and every possession a talisman of unfingerable intimacy.

The death of teeth is like the birth of children: blood and anguish, writhing, the intrusion of intrusions.

Yet, we can always be Christians to our wicked teeth (as we cannot always be to our children, or our underlings, or partners) even as we supervise their extinction. Actually, is not their vulnerability (I speak of *all* teeth, here) the basis of their charm? Far more, I think, than their purposefulness. H. L. Mencken and George Jean Nathan, in *The American Mercury,* once cited teeth as an outstanding (no pun) refutation of Nature's alleged efficiency. I should prefer to salute them as epitome of Nature's (or God's) sense of esthetic gratuity. (Mencken and Nathan, even in their literary criticism, showed a slight puritanical bent toward the strenuous, the self-sufficient.) The most rudimentary intelligence, it seems to me could have produced teeth (made of rock, perhaps, or cement; segmented as chopping wedges?) capable of Doing the Job Right. How much more endearing, these little white-collar workers with which we have been staffed! Like little Jewish poets working in a 1910 sweat-shop on the East Side; plugging at work which is always at least a little bit ahead of their capacity and their temperament. How Homerically cunning, to delegate *teams of* teeth for each job; making the fulcrum of their technique, not the strength of the individual tooth, but its weakness!

Even their pain is, at last, endearing; for teeth, almost alone among our organs, have preserved their maladies against the gross superstitions which have enfolded the illnesses of our other organs. Medical science, inundating us with cures and palliatives, has stolen the familiarity from our pains. They are no longer our property: every microscope-watcher in every laboratory owns a share in our back-ache. That decent old nuisance-peddler, the common cold, has become a Henry Ford-like dynast, over an empire of viruses.

What can we do, we old-time colonials of our bodies? The teeth are the last loyal colonies we can claim: the faithful, threshing hold-outs, reassuring us that our sicknesses, at least, are still our own.

Freud's apostrophe of teeth as little phalluses was surely one of his wittiest metaphors; for teeth represent not merely the crude power-politic of sex, but the whole range of esthetic contradiction, of dialectic. They deliver both coup-de-grace, and slow fondling, kneading. They can hold intact (the sensation of a paper-shell almond between the canines!) and they destroy, as the fulfillment of holding-intact. In their way, they are more sexual than the organs of sex: they are like the secondary sexual characteristics of the so-called lower animals, the rooster's plumage, the carp's gilded scales. When Freud saw them as sexual symbols, he saw them as symbolic in their own reality. Their illusory hardness safeguards the softnesses of the mouth. The mouth is a secret grotto when they are intact, these wondrous pretenders; a haggard, Lear-like — but adventurous — continent, when they begin to fail. Teeth, more than any of our limbs, are the instruments of rhythm, sexual and — but what other kind? —

Like those stalwart valets and waiters of the czarist novelists, the teeth are at once gallantly inadequate to their task, and decorous. Thus they become our most familiar emblems of our health and our decay. Much more than hair; because our hairs have not the familial intimacy of our teeth. Gray hair, suddenly encountered in the mirror, seems a non sequitur, like hearing of some distant relative's death. The failing of our teeth, even without the attendant pain (although the pain, of course, is an almost indispensable orchestration) is the tragedy of a house, like the terrible crumbling of the Golovlovs, in Saltykov-Shchedrin's mighty novel.

The teeth, then, are precious to us as tools and partners, just inadequate enough also to serve as emblems and ornaments. The very imminence of decay furnishes, strangely, both the proof of their power, and the assurance of their safety, their amiability toward the beholder. A smile is like an exhibit of slightly rusty weapons. At least, we hope that they may be rusty; and so, I think, we find more welcome, in our contemporaries, the slightly yellowed teeth (while gapped teeth look outward friendly, as an old musket hanging over a mantle-piece may look friendly). Only in young girls or small children, I suspect, are white teeth really tolerable; for in young girls, their ornamental unreality makes them part of the girlish syndrome, which challenges all the rest of us (men included); while in young children, the weapon-like peril of too-healthy-looking teeth is neutralized; so that they become cute, like the insane violence of babies.

False teeth are no longer, I think, the potential burlesque-images that they once were. The basic reason would seem to be, that increased opulence and intricacy of dental techniques, have dissolved the paradox which our teeth once enjoyed: the state of being both our tools and extensions of our flesh. Our *own* teeth always seemed a little false; and this lent a more fine-honed edge to the humor of so many false teeth jokes (surely, too, the sound, aww-ee, had *something* to do with the laughter?) many of which concerned false teeth which bit their owners, or total strangers; false teeth which jumped with excitement (one of the lines I recall from Jack Garfein's stage adaptation of Calder Willingham's *End As A Man,* had to do with an elderly major becoming so excited during marital felicities, that his false teeth jumped out of the glass!) A great many concerned the energumen of teeth being transferred to their simulacrae; often with that musky sexual overtone. The last such joke that I recall hearing, rather a scandal in its own right, was told by Jean Carroll, on the Ed Sullivan Show; about how her husband threw his false teeth in the fountain at Lourdes. "Scandalous," I might add, only in the sense of being somewhat indiscreet: the sort of joke, surely, not derisive of religion but merely informally familiar toward it, which many adult Catholics must tell each other privately; although on this occasion, a few very public Catholics, in the daily press, chose to take very public umbrage at its "bad taste" (demonstrating again perhaps, the insurmountably Pan-like associations of false teeth).

Because of their half-mechanical relationship to us, teeth, I should guess, tend to impose, at times, a mechanical overlay upon our lives. Their gradual decay, their falling-out, is rather a slur on our status; much as we would feel mortified by having to ride around in an overage automobile, or use hand-me-down chairs and bureaus in our homes. Because their repair does not entail quite the drama of a kidney or stomach operation, the teeth in their deterioration subject us to a more subtle reproach. That is why, I presume, the bewitchingly intricate armory of modern dental work has achieved such distinction: the dual distinction of medicine and cosmetics; oh, yes, and mechanics, too. Its array of caps and bridges, root canals and inlays, exercises an essentially *military* glamour. And why not? Our present standards of behavior have all but abandoned the idea that heroism is directly measurable by the degree of physical suffering involved. Everyone knows that a file clerk may be suffering just as much as, and very probably on a more refined and complex scale, than a G. I. stuffed into a Vietnamese dugout. The principles of higher mathematics prevail over those of mere romantic instinct. So, the painfulness of teeth is interesting, is impressive, even; rather than simply laughable or demeaning, as once it was. Teeth have lost much of their prestige as biting-weapons; but, in relinquishing this charisma, they have gained the increased dignity which, in this clear-eyed age, attends semi-obsolescence. They have, in fact, attained a state somewhat like that of the walking-stick, as Thorstein Veblen characterized it in his "Theory of the Leisure Class." The walking-stick, Veblen pointed out, was plainly derived from the club carried by primitive man. As the circumstances which required such weaponry altered, the walking-stick evolved into an object of decoration, then — as its elegant associations mellowed and eroded — into a token of muted gallantry. Glimpsing those patches of silver and gold, those bands and squares, we say: Oh, gallant teeth! So inseparable from your work of biting and rending, that even the loss of your fleshly casing cannot deter you! For, unlike, say, an artificial arm, an artificial tooth is no mere substitute; but rather, a fulfillment, something like a higher reincarnation. The tooth transfigured. And — glimpsing such patches — we may reserve a separate salute, at lower pitch, for the man wearing them; who so willingly acknowledges to us *his* capacity for decay — indeed, for glorifying decay! — that, in transcending it piecemeal, he seems to be offering us an earnest that he can transcend it altogether.

But as much as they have recouped in dignity, the rebuilt teeth may have jeopardized nearly as much of the tooth's primal activity: the magical exercise of chewing. An activity? Rather, a nimbus of activity: feeding; consolation for the nerves and spirit; meditation (indeed, from where else does "rumination" derive? Or, "chewing it over?") Masturbation in the highest; and, last but in no wise least, *dance*. The teeth, rather the legs, are the basic limbs of dance; the rhythms of chewing are more original with the spirit, more innate than, I believe, the dances of Bali. It destroys as it converts; prolongs as it terminates.

I can't help feeling as though, over recent years, I have seen this repertoire of values being reduced to, finally, the mechanical two-step of gum-chewing, or seed-munching. These activities are too ingrained in habit, now sustained by the expediencies of a nervous life, entirely to disappear. But the other graces of chewing — more contemplative or more erotic — these, I suspect, are on the way out. The exquisite pleasures of lip-chewing (not only the eminence, of course, but the moist and pliant inner lip) barely survive, I fear; how could they? All I notice are the impatient nibbles elicited by crisis.

The dissolution of chewing results in great part, I think, as I've already suggested, from the improvement of dentistry. They can dispatch, those capped and spacesuited teeth, and they can mash; but they have, I cannot resist feeling, killed the *vocabulary* of mastication. Their performance is the equivalent of journalese. One may try chewing esthetically, with them; but, I find, the metal taste keeps getting in the way.

I should like to propose for the redemption of chewing as genuine ritual, a measure which could produce an important corollary result. Many Americans, I should imagine, are familiar with the wafers issued in lieu of bread during the sacrament of Communion. To me, these are as conducive to spiritual nourishment as to corporeal: about as much, that is to say, as a digestion tablet. I should acknowledge that, for reasons largely following from my own repeated readings of the New Testament, I do not believe in the doctrine of transubstantiation. Nevertheless, I suggest that my words may be both esthetically and religiously worth considering. Where symbolism is concerned, in any capacity whatsoever, I believe in the gold standard: that is, I believe that the symbolic object should itself be as concrete, as verifiable, as possible, in order to focus as intensely as possible its symbolic meanings. The bread which was served at the Last Supper was very tangible, very chewable Jewish bread, I take it; no contrary evidence exists within the text. Not to be superfluously vulgar: why replace the image of this very tangible and masticable bread with the digestive equivalent of a subway token? As to the wine — but let me not overstrain my, I suspect, slightly raveling welcome.

Church ceremony, at present, is sustaining all manner of buffets on behalf of modernity; the Roman Catholic church in particular. I would propose, that the introduction of *real* bread (in the sense of recognizable; not in the sense of any loss in its transubstantiative meaning for those people who believe in it) would provide two valuable benisons: first, a profoundly human and humanly elevating ritual would be incorporated quite validly into the very heart of the service; second, this not-so-much-innovation-as-amplication, would dispatch as at a single stroke, much that strikes me as reaching and pseudo-genteel and second-or-third hand, imaginatively and spiritually, in the service of the American Christian church; while guiding the minds and souls of even the most conservative (sincere) church-goers, toward a fuller and warmer and — in every sense! — more loving cognition of the sacrament. Jews and many Central European Christians, have long recognized the dignified relevance of *real* gnawing, *real* munching, *real* consumption of food, to the corpus of their faith. Let us, then, put teeth where they are most needed — including back in religion!

About the Author

Donald Phelps was born December 13, 1929, in Brooklyn, where he has lived since. He attended Brooklyn College, where he first encountered contemporary literature (in a Modern Poetry course) and did his first writing of any importance, a term paper on Dylan Thomas. At one time he considered teaching, only to decide later that whatever he might have to teach could be better incorporated into writing.

Book design by Connie Avon. Typesetting by H. Sweet-
man Typesetting Corp., South Hackensack, N. J.
Printed by The Colonial Press, Clinton, Mass. Croton
Books are edited by M. Perkins and published by
H. Wit.